Additional Praise for *Hope in Action*

"Edward Schillebeeckx and Johann Baptist Metz were the leading Catholic figures engaging themes of hope and the future during the huge revival of interest in eschatology in the latter half of the twentieth century. In examining the work of each of them and then bringing them into critical conversation, Steven Rodenborn has done the theological community an immense service, illuminating their work and casting important light upon how Catholic theology turned 'toward the world' in the post-Vatican Council era."

Robert Schreiter
Catholic Theological Union

"*Hope in Action* systematically traces the development of Schillebeeckx's and Metz's mature theologies as distinct responses to the surd of human suffering amidst a social and technological frenzy of evolutionary progress. Incisive and engaging, Rodenborn's analysis comes at a time when the victims of history are not only multiplying exponentially but are also perhaps more than ever in danger of being absorbed into an evolutionary consciousness that is theological as well as cultural. As Schillebeeckx and Metz issued disruptive warnings via their respective eschatologies, Rodenborn's critical retrieval summons theologians of the twenty-first century to attend carefully to the cries of suffering victims even as they continue to construct a necessarily evolutionary theology."

Kathleen McManus
University of Portland

Hope in Action

Hope in Action

Subversive Eschatology in the Theology of Edward Schillebeeckx
and Johann Baptist Metz

Steven M. Rodenborn

Fortress Press
Minneapolis

HOPE IN ACTION
Subversive Eschatology in the Theology of Edward Schillebeeckx and Johann
Baptist Metz

Cover Image: "Balla, Giacomo (1871-1958) © ARS, NY, Mercury passes the sun,
seen through a telescope. Tempera on canvas, 1914. Location: Museum Moderner
Kunst, Vienna, Austria, Photo Credit: Erich Lessing / Art Resource, NY"
Cover design: Tory Herman

Library of Congress Cataloging-in-Publication Data
Print ISBN: 978-1-4514-6928-8
eBook ISBN: 978-1-4514-8763-3

The paper used in this publication meets the minimum requirements of
American National Standard for Information Sciences — Permanence of Paper
for Printed Library Materials, ANSI Z329.48-1984.

Manufactured in the U.S.A.

This book was produced using PressBooks.com, and PDF rendering was done by
PrinceXML.

Contents

Introduction

"Always be ready . . ."

"Always be ready to make your defense to anyone who demands from you an accounting for the hope that is in you" (1 Pet. 3:15). Within this biblical charge, addressed to early Christian communities suffering religious persecution at the turn of the second century, we find a concentrated expression of a task that has persistently pressed itself upon Christian theology. What is that hope which would sustain Christian communities down through the centuries? How might theologians offer an account of that hope responsive to the distinct demands of their time? Although the history of Christian theology might be read profitably as an effort to respond to these questions through the range of traditional theological topoi, beginning in the 1960s a number of prominent theologians in Europe would move these questions to the center of their theological projects as they attempted to renew the Christian tradition's reading and appropriation of the doctrine of eschatology. Examined from a new historical vantage point, they identified in this doctrine a potent and compelling resource for offering a defense of the Christian's hope under the conditions of the modern world.

Two Catholic theologians who contributed to this turn to eschatology in the mid–1960s and for whom eschatology has been a

1

crucial concern ever since are Edward Schillebeeckx (1914–2009) and Johann Baptist Metz (b. 1928).[1] In their early writings, each of these theologians worked to uncover the manner in which the Christian's eschatological expectations for the future radically impinge on the present. Seeking to respond to what they described as the secularization of European society and its accompanying crisis of faith, they positioned eschatology as a passionate hope in action committed to the innovating and changing of the world toward the kingdom of God. As Schillebeeckx's and Metz's worksteadily matured, however, both theologians came to argue that the central problem pressing upon the Christian's hope was not primarily this modern crisis of faith but the unrelenting crisis of history's suffering people. Still seeking to respond to the biblical charge with which we began, and now more attentive to experiences of suffering such as those from which that charge initially emerged, they recognized the need to offer a defense of the Christian's hope in the midst of a world marked by so much injustice and tragedy. Coupled with the insights developed in their earlier work, each of these theologians committed himself to fashioning a subversive account of eschatological hope that might animate and sustain a life of practical resistance in the face of history's unmitigated suffering.

A number of articles, dissertations, and books have been written on the eschatological visions of Metz and Schillebeeckx.[2] Despite the

---

1. Other prominent representatives of this turn to eschatology in European theology, at the time frequently associated with "the theology of hope," include Jürgen Moltmann, *A Theology of Hope: On the Ground and the Implication of a Christian Eschatology*, trans. James W. Leitch (New York: Harper & Row, 1967); and Wolfhart Pannenberg, *Jesus: God and Man*, trans. Lewis Wilkens and Duane Priebe (Philadelphia: Westminster, 1968). We will take up Moltmann's project in the postscript of this study.

2. For Metz, see J. Matthew Ashley, *Interruptions: Mysticism, Politics, and Theology in the Work of Johann Baptist Metz* (Notre Dame, IN: University of Notre Dame Press, 1998), and "Apocalypticism in Political and Liberation Theology: Toward an Historical *Docta Ignorantia*," *Horizons* 27 (2000): 22–43; Rebecca S. Chopp, *The Praxis of Suffering: An Interpretation of Liberation and Political Theologies* (Maryknoll, NY: Orbis, 1986); Alan John Revering, "Social Criticism and Eschatology in M. Walzer and J. B. Metz" (PhD diss., Harvard University,

unmistakable similarities in their projects, however, few scholars have attempted to place the two theologians in dialogue with regard to this issue.[3] In part, this can be explained by the different ways in which each theologian retrieved the doctrine of eschatology in his later writings.[4] As Metz's position toward prevailing interpretations of history became even more critical in his mature theology, he argued that contemporary eschatology has been compromised by the myth of evolutionary progress and suggested an apocalyptic eschatology as

2001); Gaspar Martinez, *Confronting the Mystery of God: Political, Liberation, and Public Theologies* (New York: Continuum, 2001); Cynthia Rigby, "Is There Joy before Morning? 'Dangerous Memory' in the Work of Sharon Welch and Johann Baptist Metz," *Koinonia* 5 (1993): 1–30. For Schillebeeckx, see Brian David Berry, "Fundamental Liberationist Ethics: The Contribution of the Later Theology of Edward Schillebeeckx" (PhD diss., Boston College, 1995); Bradford Hinze, "Eschatology and Ethics," in *The Praxis of the Reign of God: An Introduction to the Theology of Edward Schillebeeckx*, ed. Mary Catherine Hilkert and Robert J. Schreiter (New York: Fordham University Press, 2002), 167–83; Tadahiko Iwashima, *Menschheitsgeschichte und Heilserfahrung* (Düsseldorf, Ger.: Patmos, 1982); Derek J. Simon, "Provisional Liberations, Fragments of Salvation: The Practical-Critical Soteriology of Edward Schillebeeckx" (PhD diss., University of Ottawa, 2001), and "Salvation and Liberation in the Practical-Critical Soteriology of Schillebeeckx," *Theological Studies* 63 (2002): 494–520; Elizabeth Tillar, "Critical Remembrance and Eschatological Hope in Edward Schillebeeckx's Theology of Suffering for Others," *Heythrop Journal* 44 (2003): 15–42.

3. See Tillar, "Critical Remembrance and Eschatological Hope." Lieven Boeve's *God Interrupts History: Theology in a Time of Upheaval* (New York: Continuum, 2007) should also be noted. It is a more constructive than descriptive theological work, but he explicitly employs the eschatological thought of both Schillebeeckx and Metz in developing his project.

4. Another factor may be the manner in which contemporary scholars frequently categorize modern theologians according to broadly defined methodological schematics. Though Metz and Schillebeeckx trained and worked within twentieth-century expressions of the Thomistic tradition early in their careers, as their work matured both theologians sought to develop projects with a greater attention to the historical and interpretive dimensions of theology than they believed their earlier methodological commitments allowed. However, because of the distinctive ways in which each of them performed this task, as well as future developments in Catholic theology, particularly in Latin America, Schillebeeckx's work is frequently presented as an example of twentieth-century phenomenological Thomism, whereas Metz's project is categorized with political and liberationist theologies. See, for example, James Livingston and Francis Schüssler Fiorenza, eds., *Modern Christian Thought*, vol. 2, *The Twentieth Century* (Upper Saddle River, NJ: Prentice Hall, 2000). As we will see, this distinction is not without merit. Nonetheless, it need not obfuscate their profound similarities and the value of comparative study. For his part, Schillebeeckx has suggested that he understands his own project as a "liberation theology" and is hesitant to embrace the language of "political theology" because of potential confusion with classical expressions of political theology. See Schillebeeckx, ed., *Mystik und Politik: Theologie im Ringen um Geschichte und Gessschaft; Johann Baptist Metz zu Ehren* (Mainz, Ger.: Matthias-Grünewald, 1988), 56.

the most effective way to maintain sensitivity to history's suffering persons in a culture marked by apathy. The temporal framework of evolutionary time makes it impossible to remember suffering. Only hope in a God who will interrupt history soon, he believed, can secure a future for the suffering and even the dead. Imminent expectation of the second coming, time framed apocalyptically, allows for dangerous memories that bespeak a future freedom and that stimulate action now. By proposing an apocalyptic narration of time, Metz sought to rescue the subversive power of Christian eschatology as a protest unto the end.

Schillebeeckx, by contrast, consistently argued for a decidedly nonapocalyptic eschatology as he looked to ground his notion of negative contrast experiences in the very protology he initially put forth in his earliest effort to respond to the challenges he believed had accompanied the unfolding secularization of Europe and North America. Grounding his mature eschatology upon this position, he argued that the experience of innocent suffering is a worldwide phenomenon confronting all men and women, one that calls for an ethic of worldwide responsibility. Moreover, the prereligious experience of indignation and protest to this suffering is equally universal. Consequently, for Schillebeeckx, modernity's distorted and rigidly defined expectations for the future, rather than the onset of apathy, were the focus of his mature prophetic eschatology. By offering an eschatological narration of history from the side of history's victims, when protestation against suffering is located at the heart of history rather than when suffering is legitimated as a necessary, if unfortunate, consequence of history's progress, Schillebeeckx believed a limitless hope is found for all people. In his hands, a prophetic eschatology articulates an inexhaustible horizon of hope that he grounds in the absolute saving presence of the Creator God and that receives its concrete contours and is definitively inaugurated and confirmed in the life, death, and resurrection of Jesus. Here, Schillebeeckx intimately connected his eschatology to a theology of creation and Christology. Hope in a future beyond our expectations, an eschatological surplus, is supported by an inexhaustible surplus of creation and concentrated in the eschatological prophet, providing a limitless source of strength and encouragement to protest against all injustice unto the kingdom.

In this study, I argue that by our attending to these distinctive modes of speaking of eschatology while at the same time remembering their shared starting point and concerns, a fuller appreciation of the unique resources as well as the insights and limitations of each theologian's project can be realized. In turn, by our placing these two projects in dialogue, it will be possible to evaluate the relative capacity of Metz's apocalyptic eschatology and Schillebeeckx's prophetic eschatology to articulate an account of hope capable of responding to the particular cultural and historical contexts that consistently remained the horizon from which they theologized.

A "Zero-Sum" Theory of Secularization and the Idea of Progress

Because eschatology came to the fore in the work of each of these theologians in the 1960s amid debates surrounding the future of religion in modern societies, some initial comments about those debates are in order before we turn to the early writings of Metz and Schillebeeckx. Often under the rather unwieldy appellation of "secularization," during the 1960s a surprisingly consistent interpretation of twentieth-century European and North American societies emerged through the social sciences. Influenced in part by Max Weber's earlier interpretation of the "disenchantment" of the modern world, a number of sociologists began arguing that as men and women decreasingly experienced the world as mysterious and uncontrollable and gradually seized responsibility for fashioning their future, religion no longer would be needed to make sense of human existence and the unknown.[5] Dramatic advances in technology and the ability to understand and even manipulate nature and society offered an increasingly efficient and productive future. In the wake of these modern advancements, the embracing social character of religious belief and practice was widely believed to be in decline. In the nations of the West, those nations deemed sufficiently "developed," it was alleged that as the processes of modernization assumed a more prominent role in society, less and less would the images and priorities of the Christian tradition inform public life. Charles Taylor has referred to this interpretation of secularization as the subtraction theory, whereas Lieven Boeve has described it as the zero-sum theory of secularization.[6] Modernity's advances could come only at the price of religion's retreat. "In short, the sum of modernization and religion is always zero," Boeve writes. "[T]he more religion, the less modernization, and especially the reverse: the more modernization, the less religion."[7]

Though allied, this often-rehearsed twentieth-century theory of secularization was not immediately related to the grandiose theories of historical progress that emerged out of the Enlightenment in the

5. For a prominent account of this interpretation of modern society from the context of Northern Europe, see Bryan R. Wilson, *Religion in Secular Society: A Sociological Comment* (London: Watts, 1966). For equally well-known accounts by American sociologists, see Peter Berger, *The Sacred Canopy: Elements of a Sociological Theory of Religion* (New York: Doubleday, 1967); and Talcott Parsons, *Structure and Process in Modern Societies* (Glencoe, IL: Free Press, 1960). A helpful historical and conceptual overview of these and similar interpretations of secularization can be found in Daniel Olson, ed., *The Secularization Debate* (Lanham, MD: Rowman & Littlefield, 2000).

6. Charles Taylor, *A Secular Age* (Cambridge: Harvard University Press / Belknap, 2007); Lieven Boeve, "Religion after Detraditionalization: Christian Faith in a Post-Secular Europe," *Irish Theological Quarterly* 70 (2005): 99–122. See also, Boeve, *God Interrupts History: Theology in a Time of Upheaval* (New York: Continuum, 2007).

7. Boeve, "Religion after Detraditionalization," 100.

eighteenth and nineteenth centuries. In his study *History of the Idea of Progress*, Robert Nisbet argues that although the idea of progress can be traced back to classical Greece and the philosopher's pursuit of knowledge, it was only in the eighteenth century that the view arose that "all history could be seen as a slow, gradual, but continuous and necessary ascent to some given end."[8] In the writings of prominent thinkers such as Immanuel Kant, G. W. F. Hegel, and Karl Marx, philosophies of history emerged in which world history no longer provided merely the possibility of advancing human knowledge but was itself inscribed with a unified pattern of inevitable progress directed toward a more ideal human condition. These influential interpretations of history's progress would not guarantee the full realization of an individual life, or even of a particular historical epoch, but humankind was believed to be caught up in the unbroken march of a history ultimately moving toward its proper telos. The rapid development of science and technology during this period, the advent and growth of modern industrialization, and the rise of an educated and self-governing middle class only seemed to confirm such an understanding of history. A future of remarkable promise appeared to be just over the horizon, a future presumably within human reach.

The eventual disruption of the enthusiastic optimism that accompanied this modern "belief" in the evolutionary progress of history, particularly in its European context, was aggressively diagnosed almost as soon as it occurred.[9] As the nineteenth century came to an end and the twentieth century began, the idea of progress

8. Robert Nisbet, *History of the Idea of Progress* (New York: Basic Books, 1980), 171.
9. See, for example, Oswald Spengler, *The Decline of the West*, 2 vols. (New York: Knopf, 1926–28). T. S. Eliot's *The Waste Land* (New York: Boni & Liveright), published in 1922, also illustrates well the philosophical and cultural transition under way in Europe. For a contemporary defense of progress as an appropriate category for understanding history, see Charles Murray, "The Idea of Progress: Once Again, with Feeling," *Hoover Digest* 3 (2001).

would confront a series of crushing historical challenges. "The nineteenth century ended on August 1, 1914," Paul Tillich is said to have announced at the beginning of each year to his students at the University of Chicago.[10] The failure of modern rationality to prevent the commencement of World War I (1914–1918), as well as the ruinous price of modern technological advancements put toward the service of that war, would bring to a halt the "carousel" of progress and expose such belief as both naive and indefensible. As the Great War then reemerged as World War II (1939–1945), with the exacting efficiency of Nazi Germany's Final Solution and the scientific competence of the Manhattan Project in the United States, a decisive turn in the philosophical milieu unsurprisingly surfaced. Prominent voices among the European intelligentsia began tearing away at what remained of the idea of progress. With his "The Question concerning Technology," from 1949, Martin Heidegger was one of the most prominent among them.[11] Also important were the social theorists associated with the Institut für Sozialforschung in Frankfurt, Germany. The "dialectic of Enlightenment" investigated by Max Horkheimer and Theodor Adorno, which will be considered later in this study, exposed the idea of progress as a dangerous ideological illusion and attempted to articulate a philosophy of history doggedly committed to unearthing the ambiguous effects of instrumental rationality and technological advancement.

The "zero-sum" theory of secularization emerged amid these critical reevaluations of the idea of progress and, thus, did not depend immediately upon the hubristic philosophies of history of the preceding centuries. No longer was historical advancement presumed inevitable. Nevertheless, with the unprecedented prosperity of the

10. Paul Tillich, quoted in Douglas John Hall, "'The Great War' and the Theologians," in *The Twentieth Century: A Theological Overview*, ed. Gregory Baum (Maryknoll, NY: Orbis, 1999), 3.
11. Martin Heidegger, "The Question concerning Technology," in *Basic Writings*, ed. David Farrell Krell, rev. ed. (San Francisco: HarperSanFrancisco, 1993).

1950s and 1960s in Northern Europe and the United States, the question of social and historical progress once more would return to the public discourse. A renewed enthusiasm determined by the ongoing economic and material productivity of the sciences, as well as a progressive optimism in the possibility of sociopolitical transformation illustrated by the well-known student movements of 1968, reinvigorated confidence in the possibility of historical progress and a better future. Although this theory of secularization did not necessitate continuous progress into the future, once again historical advancement was envisioned as attainable. What now was predicted by its proponents, though, was the dissolution of religion. As the prosperity and technological prowess accompanying modernization emerged, religious faith would subsequently surrender its influence on public life and increasingly fade in importance.

Beginning in the late 1960s, this theory of secularization gradually encountered greater resistance and, like the idea of progress itself, in the end has failed to withstand serious scrutiny.[12] Tested against the ongoing viability of traditional religions in many highly modernized nations, particularly the United States, as well as the rapid development of alternative or "new-age" spiritual movements, its inability to account for the socioreligious dynamics of contemporary culture has become evident. History did not unfold to the exclusion of religion. Indeed, as José Casanova and others have pointed out, religion survived and continues to occupy a privileged, if at times ambiguous, place in the lives of many men and women and in

12. For an early reevaluation of the secularization theory, see Andrew Greeley, "The Secularization Myth," in *The Denominational Society: A Sociological Approach to Religion in America* (Glenview, IL: Scott Foresman, 1972), 127–55. For contemporary reevaluations of the secularization narrative by two of its most important proponents during the 1960s, see Peter Berger, ed., *The Desecularization of the World* (Grand Rapids, MI: Eerdmans, 1999); and Harvey Cox, "The Myth of the Twentieth Century," in Baum, *Twentieth Century*, 135–44. A contemporary defense of the thesis can be found in Steve Bruce, *God Is Dead: Secularization in the West* (Oxford: Blackwell, 2002).

the ordering of modern cultures.[13] This is not to suggest that the historical processes that this theory sought to describe were of no consequence. Instead, subsequent efforts to interpret the phenomenon of secularization have had to become both historically and philosophically more rigorous.[14] Undoubtedly, wide disagreement still exists among these more recent interpreters of the process of secularization. Common to many of these projects, however, is the recognition that the zero-sum theory of secularization inadvertently functioned as an unmarked carrier of the idea of progress. As we have seen, there are significant differences between this idea of secularization and the idea of progress prominent in the eighteenth and nineteenth centuries. Nonetheless, both prescribed an understanding of history itself, even if one did so under the auspices of the social sciences.

13. José Casanova assesses this "deprivatization" of religion through a number of helpful case studies in *Public Religions in the Modern World* (Chicago: University of Chicago Press, 1994).

14. Along with the writings of Taylor, Boeve, and Casanova referenced above, see also John Caputo, "How the Secular World Became Post-Secular," in *On Religion* (New York: Routledge, 2001), 37–66; Mark Lilla, *The Stillborn God: Religion, Politics, and the Modern West* (New York: Knopf, 2007); and David Martin, *On Secularization: Towards a Revised General Theory* (Burlington, VT: Ashgate, 2005). Although in this study our interest in interpretations of secularization will be limited to Metz's and Schillebeeckx's theological responses to this phenomenon in the 1960s, and more specifically the manner in which their responses relate to the development of their early eschatologies, these recent and more critical analyses of the issue offer helpful insights into the limitations of what I have referred to as the "zero-sum" theory. Interestingly, Metz also has returned to the debate surrounding the meaning of secularization in his more recent writings, though, again, the interests of this study will be limited to his earlier work as it pertains to the development of his eschatology in the 1960s. See, Metz, *Memoria passionis: Ein provozierendes Gedächtnis in pluralistischer Gessellschaft* (Freiburg, Ger.: Herder, 2006), and "Under the Spell of Cultural Amnesia?," in *Missing God? Cultural Amnesia and Political Theology*, ed. John K. Downey, Jürgen Manemann, and Steven T. Ostovich (Münster, Ger.: LIT, 2006).

Theology in the Wake of Secularization:
Developments in the Eschatologies of Metz and Schillebeeckx

Further sustaining the zero-sum theory of secularization was a theological judgment regarding the inherent opposition between Christianity and modernity, a judgment often shared by those with and without Christian commitments.[15] Theologians and advocates of the process of secularization did not need to agree upon which side of the equation they advantaged in order to agree that the sum of modernization and religion was necessarily zero. Of course, this theological presumption for the essential incompatibility of Christianity and the modern world was not without its prominent critics. Within Catholic circles, the stage had been set for a more critical engagement with the phenomenon of secularization by philosophers such as Dominicus De Petter and Joseph Maréchal, whose own projects had sought to retrieve and appropriate the Catholic theological tradition precisely by way of a critical conversation with the epistemological developments of modern philosophy. With the completion of initial reconstruction in Europe in the late 1950s, the productive dialogue with the modern world exhibited in the thought of these thinkers would find powerful and original expression in postwar attempts to engage what now appeared to many to be an increasingly secularized European society. Metz's and Schillebeeckx's early theological projects offer an entrance into this work.

Independent of one another initially, Metz and Schillebeeckx each sought to respond to the interpretation of history underlying this idea

---

15. The rejection of religion in the name of historical progress found a theological counterpart, for example, in the antimodernist movement of the Catholic Church during the mid-nineteenth and early twentieth centuries. For a helpful introduction to this period, see Darrell Jodock, ed., *Catholicism Contending with Modernity: Roman Catholic Modernism and Anti-Modernism in Historical Context* (Cambridge: Cambridge University Press, 2000).

of secularization by challenging the perceived opposition between Christianity and the modern world that each theologian believed was provoking a crisis of faith. Ascribing wider meaning to the term *secularization* than that suggested by social scientists, they rejected the theological presumption of the essential incompatibility of Christianity and the modern world yet critically affirmed the modern world's self-assured hope for the future. As we will see, the factors in their decisions for such a response were theologically and culturally manifold. Though highly suspicious of naively construed theories of historical progress, these two young theologians also shared in the renewed cultural confidence and the tempering of postwar skepticism characteristic of the period. Although Metz, a Catholic priest from Bavaria, would explicitly and powerfully confront his own memories of World War II later in his career, and even more significantly the horrific events of the Shoah, the completion of his philosophical and theological studies under Emerich Coreth and Karl Rahner in the 1950s coincided with the zenith of the *Wirtschaftswunder*.[16] By the end of that decade, a West Germany left in ruins at the conclusion of World War II had emerged as one of the strongest economies in the world. On the strength of modern technology and aggressive socioeconomic-policy engineering, the German people had achieved a level of prosperity far surpassing that of prewar Germany.[17] Though surely not willing to concede that the gains of modernization

16. For Metz's reflections on his draft and military service during the war, see "In Place of a Foreword: On the Biographical Itinerary of My Theology," in *A Passion for God: The Mystical-Political Dimension of Christianity*, ed. and trans. J. Matthew Ashley (New York: Paulist, 1998), 1–5. Beginning in the 1970s, Metz increasingly scrutinized contemporary Christian theology's alarming negligence of the Shoah, which he spoke of under the historically concrete name Auschwitz, and frequently lamented that the memory of these events appeared "slowly, much too slowly" in his own theological reflections. See, for example, "Theology as Theodicy?" in *Passion for God*, 54–71, first published as "Theologie als Theodizee," in *Theodizee: Gott vor Gericht?*, ed. Willi Oelmüller (Munich: Wilhelm Fink, 1990), 103–18. Though we will not take up this powerful theme in Metz's writings in this study, we can note that the positions and categories examined in chapters 5 and 6 find concentrated expression in his efforts to do theology "after Auschwitz."

required the ruin of religion in general or Christianity in particular, Metz had witnessed firsthand the potential of technical rationality and the power of the modern person to determine one's own history.[18]

Writing from the Netherlands some thirty years later, Schillebeeckx would look back on this same period and write, "At that time we were still living in a world which had emerged from the chaos of the Second World War and which had become over-bold as a result of economic progress and an international perspective on peace."[19] Certainly, this boldness characterized the experience of the Dutch Catholic Church during the 1950s and early 1960s. Though a native Belgian born into a Flemish family, the Dominican priest was appointed chair of the Department of Dogmatics and the History of Theology at the Catholic University of Nijmegen and relocated to the Netherlands in 1957.[20] He assumed that position just as the Dutch social system of *verzuiling*, or columnization, began to break down, a social and theological process that would shape

17. For an introduction to the postwar economic transformation of West Germany, see Armin Grünbacher, *Reconstruction and Cold War in Germany* (Burlington, VT: Ashgate, 2004).
18. Johann Baptist Metz was born on August 5, 1928, in Auerbach, a small town in Bavaria. After the war and a brief period in an internment camp in the United States, Metz returned to his studies and earned doctorates in philosophy with a thesis on Heidegger and a dissertation on Thomas Aquinas. Ordained in 1953, he was assigned to a small parish near Bamberg from 1958 to 1963 before accepting a chair in fundamental theology on the Catholic faculty at the University of Münster. He was a cofounder of the journal *Concilium* in 1965, where in the early 1980s he served with Schillebeeckx as the director of the section for dogmatics, a collaboration that he would later recall "with great gratitude." Currently, Metz is the Ordinary Professor of Fundamental Theology, Emeritus, at Westphalian Wilhelms University in Münster.
19. Edward Schillebeeckx, *Church: The Human Story of God*, trans. John Bowden (New York: Crossroad, 1994), 235; originally published as *Mensen als Verhaal van God* (Bloemendaal, Neth.: Nelissen, 1989). The English version of this book will be referenced in this study.
20. Edward Cornelius Florentius Alfons Schillebeeckx was born November 12, 1914, in Antwerp. He entered the Flemish province of the Dominican order at Ghent in 1934 and was ordained a priest in 1941. He studied in Louvain and at Le Saulchoir in Paris before completing his doctoral studies in 1951 under the direction of M. D. Chenu. He taught dogmatic theology at the Dominican House of Studies in Louvain before accepting the position in Nijmegen, the academic post he held until retirement, in 1983. Schillebeeckx was a cofounder of the journal *Concilium* and in 1982 became the first theologian to win the Erasmus Prize from the Dutch government for his contributions to European culture.

Schillebeeckx's thinking profoundly. Under that system, Catholics, socialists, and the Dutch Reformed Church had managed to coexist within a single political community by establishing three distinct "columns," or social structures, that supported and mediated civic life. Social and ecclesial stability were determined through this system of volunteer separation. In *The Evolution of Dutch Catholicism, 1958–1974*, sociologist John A. Coleman offered a valuable analysis of the Catholic response to the midcentury breakdown of this system.[21] After a brief period of hesitation, he demonstrated, the church responded with a robust sociological confidence that it could overcome the refuge of self-segregation and successfully engage in cultural and ethical leadership, occupying a position of "integrated autonomy" within the wider society. Although they were not altogether neglected, less attention was given to the possibility of lost ecclesial identity, doctrinal cohesion, and critical independence. A progressive hopefulness, what Coleman even described as an experience of "collective effervescence," marked a church reenvisioning its relationship with the broader world. It was from this context that Schillebeeckx would engage the theological and pastoral challenge of secularization. As we will see, the self-assurance of the Dutch church, its ambitious transition from volunteer separation to "integrated autonomy," came to mark his own mode of engaging the modern world.[22]

21. John A. Coleman, *The Evolution of Dutch Catholicism, 1958–1974* (Berkeley: University of California Press, 1978).
22. The Second Vatican Council's pastoral constitution *Gaudium et Spes,* a conciliar document to which Schillebeeckx directly contributed, further suggests that the effort to reinterpret the role of the Catholic Church in the modern world extended beyond the unique context of Dutch Catholicism. Indeed, although John XXIII's opening speech to the council carefully warned against "excessive confidence in technical progress," he preceded these comments by chastising those "prophets of gloom" within the church who saw in modern times "nothing but prevarication and ruin."

Sympathetic to this collective enthusiasm, though never uncritically committed, Metz and Schillebeeckx looked to develop a response to the secularization narrative that would secure the legitimacy of the modern project while refuting its predictive conclusions regarding Christianity. In formulating this response, both theologians first sought to establish a theological foundation for the modern process of secularization through Christian protology and Christology, affirming the autonomy and freedom of the world by way of standard theological topoi in the Catholic tradition.[23] Having offered this systematic foundation, they then turned to the category of eschatology to make theological sense of the future-oriented dynamic that came to the fore in modernity. In doing this, they were then well positioned to look anew at uniquely Christian notions of history and hope. Eschatology would quickly move from the periphery to the heart of their theological projects.

Metz and Schillebeeckx located within modernity's privileging of the future an important impulse derived from the Christian eschatological vision.[24] They argued that eschatological hope no

---

23. The attention given to the doctrine of creation in particular can be linked to the antimodernist interests prevalent in the Catholic Church leading up to the Second Vatican Council, precisely the period within which both theologians had begun responding to the issue of secularization. Following the promulgation of Leo XIII's *Aeterni Patris,* in 1879, Catholic theologians had been largely limited to working within the Thomistic tradition in an effort to curtail the influence of modern philosophical thought upon theology. Though shaped in distinct expressions, Metz and Schillebeeckx were subsequently trained within the Thomistic theological tradition, including Aquinas's metaphysics of creation. As we will see in chapters 1 and 2, this training plainly influenced their earliest writings, and it was from this vantage that both theologians located in the doctrine of creation a permissible yet effective resource for their initial responses to the situation of Europe in the early 1960s. Along with Jodock's *Catholicism Contending with Modernity,* Erik Borgman offers a helpful discussion of the historical context of the church's antimodernist agenda and the privileging of the Thomistic tradition, with particular attention given to the early work of Schillebeeckx, in *Edward Schillebeeckx: A Theologian in His History,* trans. John Bowden, vol. 1, *A Catholic Theology of Culture (1914–1965)* (London: Continuum, 2003), 191–99.

24. It is important to note that the coupling of eschatology and secularization was novel to neither Schillebeeckx nor Metz. In 1949, Karl Löwith published *Meaning in History* (Chicago: University of Chicago Press), a study in which he argued that modern understandings of history, diverse expressions of the idea of progress, are "secularized" derivations of Jewish and

longer could leave the Christian aloof and indifferent to the dynamics of history, choosing to direct hope toward an eschaton located outside of the world and its history. Rather, they insisted that eschatological hope in a God who is the future of all people energizes Christian efforts to participate in the historical inbreaking of God's reign. Yet, Metz and Schillebeeckx also recognized dangerous limitations in the secularization narrative beyond its hubristic predictions of religion's demise, and they located within the eschatological hope of Christianity a resource for confronting those limitations. In response to the narrative's rigid segregation of faith and public life, both theologians argued that if the hope of the Christian, grounded in the promise of a peaceable kingdom, is not to be envisioned as a private affair indifferent to a future in the making, then the religious commitments of the modern person cannot be hermetically located within the private sphere. Moreover, if there is to be an authentic hope for the future, that hope must not be exhausted by the limits of what the human person can envisage as progress. In that case, nothing genuinely new can be hoped for the future, because the human alone has become its sole author.

By retrieving the doctrine of eschatology within the context of mid-twentieth-century Western European culture, both Metz and Schillebeeckx came to speak of eschatological hope as a practical and active hope that cannot be accounted for adequately through a

Christian concepts of eschatology. In the mid-1960s, Metz and Schillebeeckx would offer related arguments as their eschatological projects developed. In 1966, Hans Blumenberg, a professor of philosophy at the University of Münster, responded to Löwith with a rigorous philosophical and historical critique of his position. In *The Legitimacy of the Modern Age* (repr., trans. Robert Wallace, Cambridge, MA: MIT Press, 1983), Blumenberg argued that modern understandings of history are not dependent upon the eschatological structure of Christianity but offer fundamentally distinctive accounts of a future that is the creation of an immanent process of development rather than a transcendent subject. As we will see, although Metz and Schillebeeckx continued to advocate the Christian provenance of the modern interest in freedom, their positions found new expression in their later writings. For a helpful introduction to this debate, see Robert M. Wallace, "Progress, Secularization, and Modernity: The Löwith–Blumenberg Debate," *New German Critique* 22 (Winter 1981): 63–79.

detemporalized and theoretical reflection on the eschaton. Only the praxis of Christian hope can make an eschatological faith meaningful in a culture oriented toward a future in the making. Yet, at the same time, both theologians insisted that Christian praxis could never be identified unambiguously with a particular human project or endeavor. No political or even religious program can claim a singular identity with God's plan for the future. The excess of definitive eschatological salvation places a proviso on or makes conditional all particular and therefore fragmented acts or movements of emancipation. God's promised kingdom cannot be conceived adequately under the conditions of the present.

Thus, by the mid-1960s, both Metz and Schillebeeckx had identified and started to exercise the critical function that eschatology could play in a culture presumably operating under the secularization narrative. Soon, however, both theologians would begin to ask new and more fundamental questions of this culture. Can and should modern history be narrated as one of advancement and success? Whose future does this account of history address? Is modern society constructed such that the futures of all people possess significance? Reflecting on those questions, Metz and Schillebeeckx arrived at similar conclusions. It is not only inaccurate but dangerous to frame history as a continuous advance toward an ever-greater future. That narrative is told from the side of history's victors alone and is ultimately incapable of securing genuine human freedom. The processes of modernity self-destruct and undermine the very hope animating the historical interest in freedom. It is only when history is told as the story of those who suffer, from the perspective of the victims rather than the victors, that a stimulus is located in which the hope and freedom sought after and promised in the life, cross, and resurrection of Jesus Christ are made available.

It was in response to these concerns that Metz began to speak of dangerous memories in the late 1960s. In the memory of suffering, *memoria passionis*, a negative consciousness of future freedom is revealed and a stimulus to overcome injustice is found through the narration of past sufferings. During this same period, Schillebeeckx in turn began to speak of negative contrast experiences. The fundamental human protest and rejection of evil and suffering discloses an unfulfilled yet powerful hope that is the basis on which such protestation is made possible. Negative contrast experiences are eschatological experiences of a limitless hope that energize efforts to overcome suffering in the present.

Moving beyond the challenges presented by the secularization narrative, though not abandoning the claim to freedom that the modern subject seeks to achieve in history, Metz and Schillebeeckx located human suffering at the center of an ambiguous history. By doing this, they would each witness to a uniquely Christian eschatological narrative of history. In their ongoing work over the next three decades, both Metz and Schillebeeckx developed an account of eschatological hope that avoids offering a blueprint for history that either empties history of significance or locates the totality of history within the human project. Rather, eschatology stimulates a practical or productive resistance unto the eschaton that is motivated or catalyzed by taking the history of human suffering seriously. We have not yet experienced the full flourishing of the free human. A just and peaceable kingdom is yet a vague ideal. Nonetheless, past and present suffering remains all too real, and through solidarity such suffering must be remembered, experienced, and challenged. Significant differences in their projects notwithstanding, in the hands of Metz and Schillebeeckx, the Christian eschatological vision provides the stimulus by which a life of subversive resistance and rebellion against injustice can be realized and sustained in history.

Outlining the Analysis and Argument

The goal of this study is twofold: to analyze the development in the eschatological thought of both Metz and Schillebeeckx while at the same time highlighting the relative strengths in each project for offering a contemporary account of the Christian's hope that might animate and sustain a life of practical resistance in the face of history's unmitigated suffering. For that reason, the chapters of this study are structured as a chronological analysis of the shifts in each theologian's work and proceed toward the goal of bringing these projects into explicit dialogue in the concluding chapter of the book. In this introduction, however, it is important to underscore that there is a similarity in the development of the two projects that can be seen in three identifiable, if inexact, stages of their respective works. We will see that, during the earliest period under consideration, it was in fact by first taking up the concept of secularization that eschatology then moved from the margins to the center of Metz's and Schillebeeckx's theologies. Thus, the first stage begins with their efforts to interpret theological categories in light of their social analyses. We will see that it was precisely this manner of engagement that allowed both Metz and Schillebeeckx to develop and advance the practical character of eschatology. The distinctly modern route by which they retrieved the doctrine of eschatology allowed them to critically affirm the enthusiasm and ambition of modern European society while repositioning the hope of the Christian tradition as a hope in action. The emergence of a "political" eschatology in Metz's writings is examined in chapter 1 and the emergence of an "active hope" in Schillebeeckx's writings is considered in chapter 2.

In the second stage, as Metz and Schillebeeckx began to encounter the voices of those twentieth-century thinkers who had problematized the overly ambitious philosophies of history of the preceding period, as well as the violent sociopolitical consequences of a cold war then spreading throughout Europe, Southeast Asia, and Latin America, we will see that by the mid-1960s Metz and Schillebeeckx began distancing themselves more acutely from the enthusiastic understanding of history that marked their still-emerging practical eschatologies. Although eschatology had moved from the margins to the center of their thought through their engagement with the concept of secularization, as this engagement matured and became even more critical, eschatology transitioned to the privileged vantage point from which to resist and subvert unexamined assumptions about the modern world. The autonomy of Christian eschatological hope, it might be said, was being reclaimed. This gradual process began in the mid-1960s and unfolded throughout the course of Metz's and Schillebeeckx's careers. Consequently, evidence of this modification will surface throughout each of the chapters that follow.

Corresponding to Metz and Schillebeeckx's heightened awareness of the ambiguous relationship between eschatology and the process of secularization, in a third stage of their work we will examine the intensification of their concern with prevailing interpretations of history that arose in the wake of the Enlightenment. Relying in part on insights culled from Frankfurt theorists, both theologians came to acknowledge internal inconsistencies within the processes of modernity that inadvertently corrupted the very hope animating the historical interest in freedom. Though never dismissing the validity or even the implicitly Christian character of the modern claim to freedom in constructing the future, Metz and Schillebeeckx both seek to offer their own narrations of modernity that highlight the oppressive and dangerous implications of a history framed in light of the idea of progress. A theologically adequate understanding of history recognizes history as inescapably marked by suffering. Consequently, both Metz and Schillebeeckx heighten the attention paid to the history of human suffering and insist that the practical eschatological hope of the Christian must be realized as a subversive protest to that suffering. The Christian's hope in action becomes a life of practical resistance in history. Chapters 3 and 4 will trace these developments in Schillebeeckx's writings, and chapters 5 and 6 will take us through Metz's work.

By providing the reader with both thematic and chronological heuristic resources, I hope to attend more deliberately to the rich and even prophetically subversive contributions made by both Metz and Schillebeeckx without hazarding superficial harmonization. Despite the profound similarities in these two theologians' writings, similarities that I hope will allow us to underscore the particular pressures confronting a practical eschatology, the concerns and interlocutors peculiar to each of these men acutely orient their projects in original and creative directions. By our tracing the development of each project in the chapters that follow, these distinctive features can also come to the fore, which in a complementary fashion also will allow us to draw out the challenges facing a practical eschatology as well as to measure the relative strengths of their divergent responses. The conclusion of the book, then, will initiate this productive dialogue between the two theologians' mature eschatologies. At this point, our task will be twofold. First, we will consider the challenges confronting contemporary eschatology jointly underscored by Metz and Schillebeeckx. Then, by means of comparative analysis, we will identify distinctive characteristics, contributions, and limitations of each project. In particular, attention will be given to Metz's sensitivity to the apathy of modern culture and the enduring significance of protology in his Belgian colleague's thought. In doing this, we will seek to draw out and place in greater relief the potent resources introduced by both theologians as they struggled over the course of four decades to offer an account of hope responsive to the demands of the world.

1

Metz's Response to Secularization

From a Transcendental-Linear to a Utopic Theology of History

This chapter begins by examining Johann Baptist Metz's early understanding of the modern process of secularization and his effort to present a positive interpretation of this process in light of Catholic theology. By tracing the manner in which Metz approached this task in his writing through 1966, we will see that it was through engaging the process of secularization that a distinctive eschatology emerged in his theological program. His transcendental-linear theology of history presented a productive apologetic resource, allowing him to affirm the ongoing validity of Christianity for those who experienced the process of secularization as a threat to their faith. The advantages of this tack, the legitimization of both Christianity and the secularization process, complement his early apologetic interests. As we will see, though, encounters with new interlocutors, particularly Ernst Bloch, repositioned his evaluation of the cultural situation and the appropriate theological response. The importance of the practical character of Christian hope, as well as a utopic understanding of history that could allow for the possibility of the genuinely new, came to characterize Metz's thought by the mid-1960s. While continuing to address an increasingly secularized society, the manner in which he approached this task was in flux. It was here that his promotion of an eschatologically framed "political theology" surfaced.

The emergence of a creative and practical eschatology, however, would not signal a departure from Metz's concern with the process of secularization. He continued to argue that this process need not be experienced as contrary to a Christian understanding of the world and history. Indeed, he repeatedly championed the Christian provenance of modernity, though we will see that this now was affirmed by a hope mediated within history rather than the transcendental structure of history itself. It was not without reason, then, that by his first taking up the concept of secularization, eschatology moved to the center of his thought. The very renewal of eschatology that Metz called for was engendered by the future-consciousness characteristic of the modern world; his eschatology emerged out of his apologetic engagement with secularization. Moreover, he insisted that eschatology underwrites secularization; eschatological hope determines the future-oriented dynamic of modern culture.

Yet, having now reconsidered the manner in which he understood history theologically, Metz was better positioned to locate within the Christian's eschatological hope an inherent resource that radically resists the identification of eschatology with the future-oriented dynamic that came to the fore with modernity. Thus, by the mid-1960s, eschatology would begin to emerge as a potent source of cultural criticism. Read alongside chapter 2, on Schillebeeckx's early eschatological writings, this chapter will reveal the important relationship between the theological engagement with mid-twentieth-century interpretations of secularization and developments in the doctrine of eschatology, the emergence of practical eschatology in Catholic theology, and, ultimately, the beginnings of an even more critical employment of Christian eschatological hope as it meets the challenges of a modern world. This study of Metz's early writings will proceed in three steps: an investigation of his initial theology of history, in which Metz employs a transcendental-linear framework; Metz's political turn to a utopic understanding of history and the practical character of hope; and the consequences of Metz's political turn for a critical reading of secularization and his articulation of the Christian's eschatological hope.

A Transcendental-Linear Theology of History

Secularization as the Advent of History

In even his earliest writings, it was apparent that Metz believed that by the middle of the twentieth century, Western European society had entered into a process of secularization and would only continue along that course. Though little agreement existed regarding the theological validity and consequence of that process, there was general consensus among sociologists and theologians alike that a new historical reality was emerging across the Continent. In engaging the issue, then, Metz's primary interest was not with whether the widespread secularization of European culture in fact was in progress but with the significance of that process for modern Christianity. What challenges does the secularization of society present the believer, he asked, and what does the believer have to say in response?

As secularization is a notoriously difficult concept to define, it is important that we begin by looking at the particular way in which Metz understood the secularization process. Although he made it clear that he was aware of a range of both theological and nontheological interpretations of secularization, it is his own use of the term that interests us here.[1] The earliest appearance of what would become his "secularization thesis" (*Säkularisierungsthese*) can be found in a 1957 article entitled "Die 'Stunde' Christi."[2] Though the secularization of European society was not yet a central issue in this article, it was here that he made an early attempt to speak of the "historical power" of Jesus Christ (*Geschichtsmächtigkeit*), an important theme that would reappear in other early writings and will be examined in the first part of this chapter. His dissertation, written under Karl Rahner and published in 1962, *Christliche Anthropozentrik*, in which he attempted to correlate the formal structure of Thomas Aquinas's theology with the anthropocentric shift characteristic of modern epistemology, also provided Metz the opportunity to reflect on the rise of secularization in modernity, though, again, only briefly and by way of footnote.[3] It would be with the publication of his first major collection of essays, in 1968, under the title *Zur Theologie der Welt* that Metz directly turned his attention to the theological significance of secularization as a sociohistorical phenomenon and placed it at the center of a programmatic agenda. Containing essays

1. Along with the work of Talcott Parsons, Karl Löwith, and Hans Blumenberg cited in the introduction of this study, throughout *Zur Theologie der Welt* (Mainz, Ger.: Matthias-Grünewald, 1968) Metz references the work of a number of Protestant theologians, including the influential writings of Friedrich Gogarten and the American Harvey Cox. Schillebeeckx is among the numerous Catholic theologians cited. This text was published in English as *Theology of the World*, trans. William Glen-Doepel(New York: Herder & Herder, 1969), and subsequently will be abbreviated in citations as *TW*.

2. Metz, "Die 'Stunde' Christi: Eine geschichtstheologische Erwägung," *Wort und Wahrheit* 12 (1957): 5–18; see 16–17.

3. Metz, *Christliche Anthropozentrik: Über die Denkform des Thomas von Aquin* (Munich: Kosel, 1962), see 132n22.

written between 1962 and 1967, the first two parts of this collection, which include essays written through 1966, provide our point of entry in this chapter into his efforts to engage modern European society. Read alongside a number of other uncollected articles published during this period, these writings reveal a theologian searching for an adequate response to the challenges of his time and, consequently, a theological project in transition.

The most developed account of what Metz understood by the historical process of secularization appears in an essay delivered at an academic conference in 1963 and later published in *Theology of the World* as "The Future of Faith in a Hominized World."[4] Here, we find the social analysis of modern culture that would orient his theological project throughout much of the 1960s. In this essay, Metz characterized secularization as the transition from a divinized to a hominized world, a process he claimed parallels modern epistemological developments, in which there is a reorientation of thought from the known object to the knowing subject.[5] In the divinized world of the past, men and women encountered the world as sheer "nature" (*Umwelt*). It was the pregiven default context of human existence and, as such, was experienced as mysterious and beyond human control. The world as nature provided the nourishment and resources needed to sustain life but also bestowed inexplicable catastrophe and death. The precariousness of human existence was beyond address, with protection and danger coming

---

4. This essay was first published as "Die Zukunft des Glaubens in hominisierten Welt," *Hochland* 56 (1964): 377–91, and was edited for compilation in *Zur Theologie der Welt*. For Metz's brief reflections on the conference in a later interview, see Ekkehard Schuster and Reinhold Boschert-Kimmig, *Hope against Hope: Johann Baptist Metz and Elie Wiesel Speak Out on the Holocaust,* trans. J. Matthew Ashley (New York: Paulist, 1999), 21. First published as *Trotzdem Hoffen: Mit Johann Baptist Metz und Elie Wiesel in Gespräch* (Mainz, Ger.: Matthias-Grünewald, 1993).

5. For Metz's understanding of the relationship between hominization and modern epistemology, particularly as this relates to the influence of Aquinas, see *Christliche Anthropozentrik*, 41–95.

from the same incomprehensible source. Nature, and not humankind, reigned sovereign in such a world. Metz argued that it was by approaching the world from this cosmocentric perspective that nature itself predictably functioned as the primary locus of religious life. Men and women bestowed nature with divine qualities, finding in it the power of God directly revealed. In a divinized world, the flux of an immediately numinized nature reflected the outworking of divine providence.

The process of secularization initiated a shift from this cosmocentric perspective to an anthropocentric view in which the world now could be appropriated as "history" (*Mitwelt*). The emergence within modernity of a secularized worldview exposed the historicity of human existence and, thus, marked the advent of history itself. In the wake of this process, Metz argued, humans experience the world no longer as mysterious and uncontrollable nature but as a history in the making in which men and women are the "masters" of creation. The human person discovers "that he is more and more removed from the enfolding unity of a pre-given nature and experiences himself as the active subjectivity of nature which stands over against it and interferes with it, planning and transforming, in order to construct a world out of it."[6] Humans themselves are now the demiurge responsible for the world. A hominized world no longer relies on the logic of myth and magic found in the religious imagination of a divinized world. The nature that had embraced or attacked the human seemingly on divine whim now was seen as ordered according to natural laws accessible to human understanding and control. The world became material for manipulation and could be subdued and managed by human hands. An explosion of scientific and technological advancements in the

6. *TW*, 60.

modern era followed, fostering a new confidence and progressive optimism regarding what humans themselves could accomplish in the world. Secularization, therefore, inaugurated history; it dedivinized a world experienced as nature and transformed it into a world experienced as history, fostering the historical consciousness of freedom.

Metz's Secularization Thesis as Apologetics

Metz took up the question of secularization because he was concerned that many Christians were experiencing this process of hominization, in which the human person comes to reign as sovereign over nature, as a frightening crisis or shattering of faith.[7] What once seemed to proclaim the work of God now was seen to be the work of humans alone. "What shines out of the world today, primarily and directly, are not the *vestigia Dei*," he wrote, "but the *vestigia hominis*."[8] A hominized world was without magic and mystery. Seemingly affirming the zero-sum theory, the process of secularization had removed God from the world, leaving the divine nowhere to be found and the believer distraught and unsure of where to turn. Metz insisted that theology could not ignore the pastoral consequences of this phenomenon. If theology was to avoid descending into an ahistorical "mythology" unable to address the lived experience of Christians, it must take up its responsibility to

---

7. See ibid., 60 and 14. The latter citation appears in the first chapter of the text, "How Faith Sees the World: The Christian Orientation in the Secularity of the Contemporary World," an edited translation of "Weltverständis im Glauben: Christliche Orientierung in der Weltlichkeit der Welt heute," *Geist und Leben* 35 (1962): 165–84. Though this particular understanding of a crisis of faith was not yet present, Metz's earlier effort to respond to what he described as men and women's "deliberate effort to forget the coming of God" is notable in a small meditation he published for the Advent season in 1959. See *The Advent of God*, trans. John Drury (Paramus, NJ: Newman, 1970), n.p.; originally published as *Advent Gottes* (Munich: Ars Sacra, 1959).
8. *TW*, 61.

accompany the modern person for whom the dedivinization of the world had made God invisible.[9] Secularization demanded of the theologian a new apologetic tack.

In his treatment of the subject written in 1962 and later published in *Theology of the World* as "How Faith Sees the World: The Christian Orientation in the Secularity of the Contemporary World," we find the clearest and most complete expression of Metz's secularization thesis. At the center of his apologetic response stands the belief that the modern crisis of faith betrays an insufficient appreciation of the Christian theological tradition. The process of secularization need not be experienced as contrary to a Christian understanding of the world, nor should Christians resist its realization in world history. In his own words, he sought to construct "a positive interpretation of this permanent and growing secularity of the world in the light of Catholic theology."[10] Supporting this positive interpretation would be the bold claim that, rather than having arisen against Christianity, the modern process of secularization was fundamentally Christian in character and provenance. Indeed, it is through this process that the world ultimately fulfills its created purpose. Secularization represents the growing awareness within history that God has given the world to humans with the authority to govern and cultivate.

According to Metz, it is the protological and christological structure of human existence that determined the modern transition from an experience of the world as the reign of numinous nature

9. Ibid., 14.
10. Ibid., 13n1. As is mentioned earlier, Metz was well aware that other theologians had engaged in similar projects, but what he found lacking in these efforts was this genuinely positive interpretation of the growing secularity of the world. He acknowledged that in many cases theologians had advocated "a less inhibited openness to the world," but he equally criticized them for maintaining the "obvious assumption that the secularity of the world as such is something that is actually contrary to the Christian understanding of the world and must therefore be totally overcome by Christian means." Prominent among those Metz criticized in 1962 was Yves Congar (*TW*, 14–15). We will have an opportunity to return to these remarks in chapter 2.

to that of transformable history. More specifically, he argued that a hominized worldview is made possible because of the way in which creation and the incarnation transcendentally orient the human person toward the world. Consequently, Christian understandings of protology and Christology uniquely clarify the historicity of the world that only through the course of secularization was now experienced as constituting human existence.

Beginning with the significance of Christian creation faith, and revealing the influence of Aquinas's theology of creation that he examined in *Christliche Anthropozentrik*,[11] Metz grounded the modern subject's experience of autonomy and freedom upon the protological distinction between the Creator and the created. The God of creation, he argued, does not usurp human autonomy and freedom but, rather, grants and secures it: "The majesty of the freedom he bestows is that he is the one who truly lets things be what they are. He is not in competition with, but the 'guarantor' of the world."[12] God's existence is the sustaining source of created existence and, thus, the transcendental ground of human freedom. In creating, God does not seek to divinize that which is created but establishes and accepts humanity precisely as that which is different from God's self. As transcendent Creator, God lets the world be the world. Needless to say, Metz was not seeking to describe the transcendent God of the deist here. The radical transcendence of the Creator does not alienate God from creation but denotes a distinction that allows for intimacy without confusion, freedom and autonomy without estrangement.

While grounding the experience of autonomy and freedom in a secularized world upon the nondualistic divine–human relationship established in creation, Metz argued that only through the

---

11. We will briefly examine Aquinas's theology of creation in chapter 2, where Schillebeeckx more explicitly appropriates Aquinas's writings with regard to the process of secularization.
12. *TW*, 27.

incarnation was the definitive and eschatological acceptance of the "worldliness of the world" realized and made manifest in history: "In Jesus Christ, man and his world were accepted by the eternal Word, finally and irrevocably. . . . [W]hat is true of this nature that Christ accepted is also fundamentally true of the acceptance of man and his world by God."[13] Complementing his understanding of creation, Metz believed that the incarnation should be construed not as the divinization of the world but rather as God's historical acceptance of the world as that which is not divine. From the perspective of Christology, the autonomy and freedom of the world are compromised only if a christological monophytism is presumed in which that which is human is collapsed into the divine. Properly understood, it is precisely in the person of Jesus Christ that the world is set free to be the world.

Again, then, the radically transcendent God "does not remove the difference between himself and what is other, but rather accepts the other precisely as different from himself."[14] It is in the incarnation that God's acceptance of the world as nondivine, as worldly, is made historically manifest. In Jesus Christ, for the first time, the world is recognized as truly world, and at the same time God is revealed to be wholly divine. It is in and through the incarnation that the process of secularization is let loose in history, revealing both the sovereignty of God and the freedom of humanity. The modern process of secularization should be understood, consequently, as the historical continuation of the incarnation. The apologetic value of Metz's position is clear. There is no need for a crisis of faith surrounding this process; indeed, secularization is the historical extension of that which was accomplished in Christ. Rather than envisioning them as inherently incompatible, Metz believed there is

13. Ibid., 26.
14. Ibid.

an intrinsic connection between the Christian faith and the modern world.

Metz's Secularization Thesis as a Theology of History

If creation and the incarnation reveal the historicity of the world at this early stage in Metz's writing, it is important that we also consider how he conceptualized the theological character of history during this period. Although he first considered this question in 1957 with the writing of "Die 'Stunde' Christi," it is in the essay from 1962 presently under consideration that Metz directly located this question within the context of secularization. The theological foundation he developed for secularization, in which the process is approached from the perspective of protology and Christology, here can be seen to inform his theological understanding of history in three significant ways. First, it allowed him to reposition divine transcendence temporally; second, it made it possible for Metz to speak of the incarnation as the condition for the possibility of authentic history; and finally, he could contend that history is eschatologically determined by the historical power of the incarnation.

To the first point, Metz noted that it was through the incarnation that God appeared in history as the God of history. Again, divine transcendence must not be seen to engender estrangement. Through Jesus Christ, transcendence becomes a historical reality: "God is no longer merely 'above' history, he is himself 'in' it, in that he is also constantly 'in front of it' as its free, uncontrolled future."[15] In the incarnation, God was revealed as the ground of history as well as the ground of being. In turn, divine transcendence becomes a temporal

---

15. Ibid., 22–23.

category as well as an ontological category. From the perspective of a hominized world, then, God's radical transcendence no longer should be approached as an exclusively static claim about ontological otherness. Such a claim would fail to account for the ramifications of secularization: "God for us is not merely a God who is always the same, colorlessly and facelessly present as the numinously shimmering horizon of our being. . . . Transcendence itself has become an event. It does not simply stand above and beyond history, but is still to come in history."[16] In the wake of secularization, Metz believed, to speak of divine transcendence is to make a temporal claim concerning the inexhaustible meaning of history.

Second, Metz warned that the "historical power" (*Geschichtsmächtigkeit*) of Christ is not like that of any other single historical factor, nor is Christ to be understood as simply the greatest or most significant factor within history. The Word of creation and salvation is not one among many finite beings in the world, acting in history as creatures act in history. The Word "does not merely reign *over* history, by appearing in it (beside other historical phenomena) and setting up a universal kingdom in it (*beside* other 'kingdoms'), but he reigns within it by historically giving it its basis."[17] The historical power of Jesus Christ is that which founds the possibility of history. Christ, it can be said, is the very beginning of history. It is the incarnation that sets the world free to be the world as history rather than nature. The incarnation is not merely a "'principle' that is *applied* subsequently *within* history (to particular phenomena), but the inner principle of history itself; its coordinating point, its final ground . . . its 'fulfillment,' its absolute concretion, in which alone what is earlier and what is later in time become genuine history."[18] Undoubtedly, the incarnation is a historical event. But

16. Ibid., 22.
17. Ibid., 23. See also "Die 'Stunde' Christi," 5.

theologically construed, and more germane to Metz's early position, the incarnation constitutes the transcendental structure of history itself; Jesus Christ is the condition for the possibility of authentic history and human freedom.

Finally, it is important to emphasize for our purposes, and to understand properly what Metz was seeking to accomplish at this early stage in his writing, that the emergence of the modern hominized understanding of the world was not dependent upon the *idea* of the incarnation. Metz's secularization thesis is not his attempt at a history of ideas, nor is secularization merely the result of church teachings. Rather, Metz was searching for a way to speak of history as having been eschatologically determined by the power of the incarnate Son of God.[19] History in the perspective of the incarnation has a unique christological dynamic and inner teleology in which a Christic transcendental subject is persistently coming to be in history through the very process of secularization: "The 'spirit' of Christianity is permanently embedded in the 'flesh' of world history and must maintain and prove itself in the irreversible course of the latter."[20] Secularization, as we have seen, is the process by which the incarnation continues to be made historically effective. Secularization is historical progress theologically understood; it is a "historically irreversible process" transcendentally determined by the Christ.[21] The incarnation "reveals the world not only in its general historicity, but above all in its *eschatological character*. In an historical movement forward that [the world] cannot itself know[,]it has to attain an end that has already been promised to it. It must itself become what it already is through the deed of Jesus Christ."[22] Secularization, it can

18. *TW,* 23n13.
19. See, for example, "Die 'Stunde' Christi," 10, and *TW,* 23n13.
20. *TW,* 16.
21. Ibid.
22. Ibid., 25.

therefore be said, is an eschatological event in that through it, history progressively becomes what it already is in the incarnation.

Thus, by Metz's engaging secularization from the perspective of creation and the incarnation, his earliest theological understanding of history came to support what may be described as a transcendental-linear metaphysics of history, in which the future is determined by and deducible from the beginning.[23] This understanding of history in turn established an eschatological vision of history in which what is hoped for stands in direct continuity with that which has already been realized.[24] Continuity is the mark of an eschatologically charged history. The future is transcendentally determined by the past. Nothing "wholly new" is revealed in history, according to Metz, for everything is drawn from the incarnation of Christ: "As it moves forward, the world passes ever more deeply into its historical origin and places itself more and more seriously beneath the star and the law of its beginning, which is: acceptance by God in Jesus Christ."[25] The process of secularization, then, is the gradual realization in history of that which has been realized already in Christ. It was for this reason that when Metz wrote of the historically *neues* during this early period of his career, he often found it necessary to put quotation marks around the word in order to restrict what was meant by the term.[26] And when that was not the case, he was sure to qualify the term carefully. World history, he averred, "no longer reveals anything of a radically new nature, but draws everything from what

---

23. See Francis Fiorenza, "The Thought of J. B. Metz," *Philosophy Today* 10, no. 4 (1966): 250.
24. Though Metz's understanding of the eschatological structure of history would soon evolve, we should note that his position during this period largely paralleled the position being developed by his mentor, Karl Rahner, during this period. See, for example, Rahner, "The Hermeneutics of Eschatological Assertions," in *Theological Investigations* (London: Darton, Longman & Todd, 1966), 4:326–46. For a helpful study of Rahner's eschatology, see Peter Phan, *Eternity in Time: A Study of Karl Rahner's Eschatology* (Selinsgrove, PA: Susquehanna University Press, 1988).
25. *TW*, 33.
26. See, for example, *Zur Theologie der Welt*, 14.

is of Christ."[27] The modern process of secularization is a historically "new" happening, but its historical realization is made possible and determined by the *Geschichtsmächtigkeit* of the incarnation.

In light of this way in which Metz accounted for the eschatological character of history during this early stage in his career, he was careful to denounce a theological understanding of history that betrayed an unfettered world-optimism or an uncritical belief in inevitable progress. World history is intrinsically coextensive with the history of salvation, but the two cannot be identified: "We cannot and must not simply *identify* the actual modern process of secularization with the secularity of the world that Christ made possible and intended."[28] Metz engaged and affirmed secularization as a theologically positive process fundamentally Christian in character. But it was precisely in light of its Christian character that he simultaneously attended to the persistent ambiguity of secularization, an ambiguity he found christologically signified in the cross. The cross uniquely reveals both God's definitive acceptance of the world and the world's ongoing rejection of that acceptance mistakenly received as an attack on human autonomy and freedom. The cross reminds the Christian that the course of secularization within history must be approached judiciously, for God's acceptance of the world provokes the world's free protestation even as that acceptance establishes the condition for the possibility of the world's autonomy.

The historical freedom established in the incarnation, then, can be set against God's gift of freedom. In the essay from 1962 already considered, Metz warned, "The secular world of modern times will always appear also as contradicting, protesting, shutting itself off secularistically from its origins."[29] In the essay published in 1964,

27. *TW*, 33.
28. Ibid., 40–41.
29. Ibid., 40.

he developed this warning even further. The hominization of the modern world, he insisted, offers no guarantee of genuine humanization, the historical flourishing of human freedom. In fact, this modern process introduces a unique danger into human history: "[N]ot only the world as nature but also man himself threatens more and more to become 'manipulatable.' Not only is he, as subject, in charge of the hominization process, but he is more and more in danger of himself being degraded to the object of all this planning."[30] At great human cost, the very freedom gained with the rise of secularization can break down in its aftermath. Significantly, at the time, Metz resisted attributing this danger to the structure of the modern world as such. Indeed, he insisted that only by accepting this historical development can men and women overcome this danger and realize genuine humanization.[31] We will look closely at Metz's reevaluation of this position in chapter 5 of this study. Nonetheless, his resistance to an uncritical belief in historical progress, and his recognition of the dangers that accompany construing history accordingly, was already clearly evident.

It has been noted elsewhere, however, that even having attended to the ambiguous and even dangerous character of secularization, Metz's presentation of this process as an ongoing advent of the incarnation left Christianity poorly positioned to address the failings and limitations of the modern world.[32] By offering a transcendental analysis of history, he attempted to identify the theological origins that determine the historical realization of secularization. As a result, the progressive optimism of modern society was theologically

---

30. Ibid., 74. It is likely that here Metz is drawing on Max Weber's influential concept of instrumental rationality (*Zweckrationalität*), though Weber is not cited and Metz does not use the term. As we will see in chapters 5 and 6, this concept will receive an increasingly central role in his evolving analysis of the modern situation.
31. Ibid., 76.
32. See Rebecca S. Chopp, *The Praxis of Suffering: An Interpretation of Liberation and Political Theologies* (Maryknoll, NY: Orbis, 1986), 67.

legitimated in advance and, thus, only subsequently could be evaluated and called into question. Metz's apologetic affirmation of the inner connection between secularization and the Christian faith came at a high price. Within his transcendental-linear theology of history, the transhistorical identification of the incarnation and secularization presumed an essential continuity that, though ambiguous, risked compromising the Christian voice as it engages secular culture. Christianity, inadvertently for sure, had taken its place among the rear guard. Whatever the consequences of modern mores, Metz's position made it difficult to direct any structural or systemic criticism against the ongoing historical process itself, leaving Christianity to identify mere abuses and misapplications.

As his project continued to develop, Metz would reevaluate the manner in which he linked Christianity and modernity with precisely this concern in view. This will be clear in what follows. It is important to remember, however, that during this period (1962–64) Metz was concerned primarily with reestablishing the viability of Christianity in a new historical context. He wanted to locate a vantage point from which to affirm the ongoing significance and validity of Christianity for those who experienced the process of secularization as a threat to their faith, not a vantage point from which to criticize that process. As we have just seen, Metz surely recognized the dangers that accompanied the historical developments of the modern world.[33] Nonetheless, secularization had unleashed in world history the very essence of Christianity, and the prospects of modernity certainly appeared promising. To that point, Metz argued

---

33. Though his concerns remained largely underdeveloped, in *Christliche Anthropozentrik* Metz also had warned that care must be given not to detach the process of hominization from its Christian origins lest the freedom achieved with the rise of modernity slip away (128). As we will see in chapter 5, these concerns will take center stage in his later work. At this time, however, his primary interest was with antimodern "Christian philosophies" that set the Christian tradition over against modern philosophical thought construed as alien and incompatible with the faith, precisely the theological presumption underwriting a zero-sum theory of secularization.

that in "terms of the theology of history," the power of evil in the world was "already on the decline." The "'prince of this world' is already 'cast out,'" because of God's definitive acceptance of the world in Jesus Christ.[34] It is just such a claim, coming less than twenty years after the atrocities of World War II, that may reveal most clearly Metz's understanding of the eschatological character of history at this early stage in his career. He approached history from the perspective of the incarnation and explicitly warned against an uncritical and simply optimistic view of historical progress by attending to the distortion of freedom signified by the cross. Nonetheless, within his transcendental-linear theology of history, secularization was positioned as a "historically irreversible process"; historical progress is transcendentally determined as the "spirit" of Christianity irreversibly proves itself in the "flesh" of world history.

The Political Turn to a Utopic Understanding of History and the Practical Character of Hope

The Provocation of Ernst Bloch: The Possibility of the New in History

In 1963, the same year he received an appointment to the University of Münster as professor of fundamental theology, Metz participated in the conference at which he delivered "The Future of Faith in a Hominized World." Notably, the organizing theme for this conference, held in Weingarten, West Germany, was "The Future of Man." It was there that Metz met for the first time Ernst Bloch, a left-wing revisionary Marxist whose unique and revolutionary work on the philosophy of hope Metz admittedly knew very little about.[35]

---

34. *TW*, 25n21.
35. See Schuster and Boschert-Kimmig, *Hope against Hope*, 21–22.

This initial meeting would evolve into an important and lasting relationship between the atheist and the Catholic priest that, along with other Christian–Marxist dialogues sponsored by the Paulusgesellschaft in the mid-1960s, influenced and reoriented Metz's thought in a number of important ways.[36] As we will see, the exchange of ideas that followed presented Metz with an opportunity to reposition the category of the "future," to move practical reason to the fore of his work, to reexamine his theological engagement and affirmation of secularization, and, ultimately, to transform the way he envisioned the eschatological character of history.[37] These developments would leave an indelible stamp on Metz's future writings.

Like many leftist intellectuals of the time, Bloch looked with regret upon a century of Marxist theory and practice that had failed to transform the repressive social structures that once were presumed to be on the brink of inevitable collapse. Furthermore, he feared that the very hope for such a revolutionary transformation, the will to bring about a better and more just world, had disappeared from the men and women of late modernity because of the sedation of an entrenched cultural hegemony and the corresponding inability to imagine even the possibility of an alternative future. In response,

---

36. Responding to the mounting pressures of the Cold War in Europe, the Internationale Paulusgesellschaft sponsored a series of discussions during the 1960s aimed toward fostering a more critical dialogue between theologians and Marxist intellectuals. In a later essay, Metz observed that it would be these dialogues and his encounter with Bloch, along with his encounters with members of the Frankfurt school (discussed in chapter 5), that "politicized" him "out of the existential and transcendental enchantment of theology." Metz, "In Place of a Foreword," in *A Passion for God: The Mystical-Political Dimension of Christianity,* ed. and trans. J. Matthew Ashley (New York: Paulist), 2–3. The significance of this transition in Metz's thought will be explored in the following sections as well as in chapters 5 and 6.

37. For Metz's account of his relationship with Bloch, see especially "Ernst Bloch: Im Spiegel eines theologishch-politisches Tagebuchs," in *Unterbrechungen: Theologische-politische Perspektiven und Profile* (Gütersloh, Ger.: Gütersloher, 1981), 58–69.[37] For a fine summary of Bloch's influence on Christian theology, written by one of Metz's former students, see Francis P. Fiorenza, "Dialectical Theology and Hope," *Heythrop Journal* 9–10, nos. 2, 4, 1 (1968–69).

Bloch departed from the economic analysis of "orthodox" Marxism and took up a wide range of intellectual and cultural sources, including religious sources, in search of a "philosophy of hope" (*docta spes*) that could hold open the possibility of a truly indeterminate future and, subsequently, reawaken the possibility of an insurgent hope.[38] In particular, his extensive writings repositioned the historical materialism of Marx and the psychoanalytical work of Freud in an attempt to locate a hope-filled orientation embedded within reality by which both the human person and the cosmos itself dynamically transcend the present and move toward an open and undetermined future. Upon this work, Bloch constructed a decidedly antimetaphysical ontology of history in which the future cannot be tied to that which is made possible by the past but remains open for the genuinely new. The future is not determined by what comes before it, he argued, but is truly free, creative, and original. Such a future is the novel (*novum*) not yet of history; it has never occurred before and, in turn, can sustain an ever-greater hope for human freedom and flourishing. According to Bloch, retrieving what he believed was this repressed understanding of the future was an indispensable measure in reclaiming the revolutionary hope absent from the modern imagination.

Of particular importance for our understanding of Metz's evolving thought was Bloch's criticism of metaphysics. Bloch warned that rescuing the category of the future from circumscribed accounts of history requires abandoning the metaphysical categories of traditional philosophy. By its very nature, he argued, metaphysical reflection can consider only that which already existed in the past or that

---

38. Bloch's three-volume *The Principle of Hope*, trans. Stephen Plaice and Paul Knight (Oxford: Blackwell, 1986), lies at the center of his philosophical project. For an introduction to his thought, see Richard H. Roberts, *Hope and Its Hieroglyph: A Critical Decipherment of Ernst Bloch's "Principle of Hope"* (Atlanta: Scholars Press, 1990).

which exists in the present. An authentic future is inaccessible to such contemplative and conceptual consideration, for it is precisely that which does not yet exist. Metz's encounter with Bloch's impassioned defense of a truly novel future, a philosophy of hope, drew his attention in a rather short period of time to what he referred to as the "hiddenness" of the future in Christian theology. He was persuaded by Bloch's critical analysis of the limitations of metaphysical speculation and began arguing that modern theologies, whether conservatively neoscholastic or progressively transcendental in character, inadvertently contribute to the veiling or hiddenness of the future.[39] Dependent upon metaphysical reflection, these theologies unavoidably distort the category of the future. If the future is made available at all, it is at the expense of being truly novel. The future is made accessible for consideration only in that it is deemed wholly determined by the past or present; it is available, therefore, only in that it is presumed to already "exist." Metaphysical analysis distorts historical consciousness, then, compromising the consciousness of freedom advanced through secularization: "So long as history is considered in terms of the primacy of the origin and present, it can be conceived as a reality that has come about, that already exists, and hence again seen as nature."[40] The future so construed, Metz now feared, allowed for nothing genuinely new and merely confirmed convention.

In the short essay published in 1966 in which he first engaged these ideas, "On the Hiddenness of the Problem of the Future in Metaphysics," Metz argued that if theology was to overcome the veiling of the future inevitably inscribed through contemplative-metaphysical reflection, theologians would need to cultivate an active

---

39. *TW*, 98. Entitled "On the Hiddenness of the Problem of the Future in Metaphysics" in *TW*, this essay was first published as "Verantwortung der Hoffnung," *Stimmen der Zeit* 177 (1966): 451–62.
40. Ibid., 99.

and practical awareness of the future. Betraying the unmistakable influence of Bloch and the Marxist focus on practical reason, Metz called for "a new and authentic combination of theory and practice, as it were of reflection and revolution, which lies wholly outside metaphysical thinking."[41] A purely speculative theology of history, he warned, cannot escape the inherent restrictions of metaphysical thought. Theological reflection can engage the category of the future only when approached practically. As a wholly new and discontinuous reality, it is unavailable for theoretical knowledge. The future, qua future, cannot be interpreted; it must be made, and therefore must be known practically.[42] In taking this position, there could be little doubt that the practical character of theology had received a privileged place in Metz's agenda. As we will see, this move decisively reoriented his theological project.

Though somewhat surprising, given Bloch's Marxist commitments, Bloch's influence upon Metz also extended to his reading of Scripture. In his effort to draw attention to the dynamic, hope-filled orientation of reality, Bloch saw in the Judeo-Christian tradition an invaluable resource for awakening human hope.[43] The biblical narratives were not to be discarded or even demythologized but to be read in such a way as to locate the human longing for a new and free future embedded in the text.[44] He identified in a wide-ranging selection of scriptural stories, as well as later Christian and

41. Ibid.
42. We can recognize in the background of this position Marx's eleventh thesis against Ludwig Feuerbach. Metz would make frequent use of this important statement throughout his writings in the 1960s.
43. Bloch's reinterpretations of religious motifs and biblical stories can be found in *Thomas Münzer as Theologian of the Revolution* (Munich: Wolff, 1921), as well as *Atheism in Christianity: The Religion of the Exodus and the Kingdom*, trans. J. T. Swann (New York: Herder & Herder, 1972). John Marsden offers a helpful introduction to Bloch's appropriation of Jewish and Christian texts in "Bloch's Messianic Marxism," *New BlackFriars* 70 (1989): 32–44.
44. Bloch, *Atheism in Christianity*, 82. Francis Fiorenza recounts a 1966 lecture at the University of Münster in which Bloch criticized Bultmann's work in demythologization; see "Dialectical Theology and Hope," 388.

Jewish textual traditions, a revolutionary people directed toward a future kingdom. In Bloch's telling, these narratives bear the marks of human hope. The messianic and prophetic voices of the Bible take center stage as they are allowed to proclaim the hope that resides in and looks toward a transcendent and better future. It needs to be remembered, however, that this is the "theology" of an atheist. It is the human who is the subject of history, and the hope grounded in the novelty of the future is to be the work of humans alone: a transcending without transcendence. To posit a transcendent subject of history, Bloch feared, would risk the very circumscription of history and subsequent oppressive hegemony that a revolutionary hope looks to overcome. Nonetheless, in the hands of Bloch, religious faith, properly qualified, need not be the opiate of the people. The stories remembered within religious traditions have the power to confront the repressed expectations of the present with a radical and subversive hope capable of inspiring revolutionary action.

Bloch's reading of the Bible as a resource of hope oriented toward the future seized Metz's imagination, and his writings soon began to depend more explicitly on rich biblical imagery and categories. In particular, he came to locate at the heart of the biblical message the proclamation of God's "promise." The Scriptures, as he anticipated in his earlier reflections on history, herald the relationship between the transcendence of God and the future. "I will be who I will be," he frequently translated Exod. 3:14.[45] Such a translation speaks of a

---

45. See the largely similar essays published as "The Responsibility of Hope," *Philosophy Today* 10, no. 4 (1966): 280–88, and "The Church and the World," in *The Word in History*, ed. Patrick Burke (New York: Sheed & Ward, 1966), 69–85. The latter text was delivered at the St. Xavier Symposium in Chicago in 1966, a conference also attended by Schillebeeckx. A revised version of this essay appeared as "Kirche und Welt im eschatologischen Horizont," in *Zur Theologie der Welt*. See also "The Controversy about the Future of Man: An Answer to Roger Garaudy," a translation of a lecture from a 1965 meeting of the Paulusgesellschaft held in Salzburg and published in the *Journal of Ecumenical Studies* 4, no. 2 (1967): 223–34. An expanded version of this essay was published in a Festschrift for Ernst Bloch as "Gott vor

God who is the source of temporality as well as existence. God is revealed in the Old Testament as the "God-before-us," the power of a boundless future and, in turn, a boundless hope. Indeed, Metz argued, the experience of the world as history preceded the modern rise of secularization: "In the Bible the world is a world of history, existing for the divine promise, and those who hope are responsible for moving it forward."[46] Having entered into a historical covenant that promised the passing of what is and the coming of something new, the Israelites also experienced the world as history. Returning to an argument he first developed in *Christliche Anthropozentrik*,[47] Metz contrasted the Israelites' experience of history with a Hellenistic cyclical view of history in which the "never-yet is the impossible, since there is 'nothing new under the sun.' All that happens is only a variation on what has already happened, the actualization and confirmation of anamnesis. For the Greeks history is the indifferent repetition of the same things with the rigid cosmos. . . . Nothing really new ever happens."[48] The biblical view of history, by contrast, reveals a people urgently longing for the genuinely new and trusting that something not yet realized can come to fruition. God's promise to Abraham and those who came after him was made within the horizon of the future, making both hope and historical consciousness possible.

Turning to the New Testament, Metz again discovered the trace of a radical orientation toward the future. He warned, "It would be a mistake to suppose that the Christ-event puts the future behind us, as if after the birth of Christ the future were no longer being realized but only unfolded. On the contrary, His coming sharpens the focus

---

uns: Statt eines theologischen Arguments," in *Ernst Bloch zu ehren: Beiträge zu seinem Werk*, ed. Siegfried Unself (Frankfurt am Main, Ger.: Suhrkamp, 1965).

46. "Responsibility of Hope," 284.
47. *Christliche Anthropozentrik*, 97–115.
48. "Responsibility of Hope," 284.

on a future not yet realized."[49] In the span of just a few short years, he had begun revising his understanding of the "historical power" of Christ. Here, the coming of Christ intensified hope-filled expectation rather than determined it, heightening anticipation among his followers for a future soon to come. As the historically definitive promise of a new future, the promise of God shone forth in Christ, redirecting the early church toward the future in fervent expectation: "The New Testament community was characterized by its immediate expectation of the end of the world and by its universal missionary task; it was a community of expectation and of mission, even of expectation in mission."[50] Faith in this promise today, Metz further insisted, continues to possess the power to call humans beyond themselves and the possibilities of the present. It need not lull men and women into a passive state of waiting for another day, as Marx notably claimed. It has the potential to awaken a revolutionary attitude that seeks a new and better day, energizing and sustaining a hope for something more.

It is important to note that Metz's retrieval of Scripture as a resource for doing theology entailed more than an appropriation of new images and categories supplied by the biblical tradition. Indeed, this turn toward Scripture related directly to his growing concern with the limitations of metaphysical speculation. As we have seen, Metz feared that the philosophical presuppositions of neoscholastic and transcendental theologies veil the possibilities of the future, compromising the openness of world history. In particular, although transcendental theology offers an analysis of the conditions for the possibility of history, it is removed from the flux of history itself. In seeking this ahistorical vantage point, the historicity of human existence can be taken into account and the existential freedom of

---

49. Ibid.
50. "Controversy about the Future of Man," 227.

the individual can be secured, but at the price of delimiting the indefinable potential of history in advance. As early as 1966, Metz acknowledged that his early reflections on secularization as history theologically construed betrayed this same limitation.[51] History "no longer reveals anything of a radically new nature," he wrote in 1962.[52] History was transcendentally determined, prematurely circumscribing what was deemed possible for the future. Engaging the ideas of Bloch had heightened Metz's attention to the consequences of such a project.

Even Metz's early effort to engage secularization, however, revealed an already operative concern, if underdeveloped, to theologize self-consciously from within a particular historical setting. Though his argumentation relied on transcendental reflection, we have seen that it was never detached from the specific context in which he worked. His project was directed explicitly toward addressing the modern person's experience of secularization. Notably, as early as 1961, Metz had warned that the Christian's faith "comes historically" by "way of actuality that is not deducible from within, that is, transcendentally. . . . [I]t is not the product of deductive reflection. It must be learned from history."[53] If only tentatively, then, he already had recognized that history itself must be the basis of Christian theology. By now taking up the narratives recounted in the Bible of God's saving promise in world history, stories of the particular and historical relationships between God and Abraham, Isaac, Jacob, and, most importantly, Jesus, Metz located the resource that would allow him to place human history at the center of theological reflection and avoid the consequences of transcendental

51. "Church and the World," 78.
52. *TW*, 33.
53. Metz, "The Theological World and the Metaphysical World," *Philosophy Today* 10/4 (1966): 258. First published as "Theologische und metaphysische Ordnung," *Zeitschrift für Katholische Theologie* 83 (1961).

speculation abstracted from concrete historical reality. As we will see in chapter 5, this nascent methodological turn would play a significant role in his future writings, where human history rather than the historicity of the human person becomes the governing arena of theological reflections.

A Deprivatized and Practical Hope in God's Promise

Bloch had presented Metz with a radicalized understanding of the future as well as the resources needed to apply a messianic hermeneutic to the reading of the Bible. Evidence of these ideas quickly appeared in Metz's developing project. He began arguing that the biblical message inscribes a fundamentally eschatological character to the Christian faith. Moreover, he sought to clarify the specific contours of that character in order to correct what he believed were inadequate conceptualizations of eschatology in contemporary theology. He criticized modern theology for failing to recognize that the biblical message bespeaks a radical trust in the promise of a new day that orients the Christian's hope toward a genuine future. On the one hand, then, Christian eschatology cannot presume a detemporalized and objectivist cosmological worldview in which transcendence and temporality are rent asunder. A faith that looks to the future as the locus of God's promise cannot be directed toward a disembodied other-world positioned somewhere "above" or outside of history. Writing in 1966, Metz argued,

> From the viewpoint of the future the often used—perhaps too often used—distinction between the natural and supernatural recedes into the background. In our relationship to the future we cannot be satisfied with a distinction which separates the natural future of the world from the supernatural future of the faith. . . . In other words, since the hope of the Christian faith is oriented toward the future, it cannot fulfill itself by bypassing the world and the future of the world.[54]

Here, the Christian's hope for the future is ultimately held in vain; salvation resides wholly outside of time and history. Only by ignoring the promise proclaimed in the Scriptures themselves, he believed, could the temporality of God's eschatological promise be dismissed so easily.

On the other hand, Metz warned that the Christian's eschatological hope cannot be exhausted by the mere possibilities of temporality reduced to the present. Like Bloch, he aggressively criticized the demythologization of the biblical message, taking sure aim at the work of Rudolf Bultmann.[55] Metz feared that, having been exposed to such a reading, "its contents of hope would be emptied to become a symbolic paraphrase of the human question as such."[56] Demythologization so construed presumes an existential interpretation that neglects the unknown of the future in lieu of a faith decision in the here and now, short-circuiting the hope-filled power of God's promise. As we have seen, transcendental theologies likewise succumb to this error. Along with his own early work, Metz also pointed to the limitations inherent in the work of his mentor, Karl Rahner. He greatly respected Rahner's efforts to introduce human existence and subjectivity into his reflections on the Christian faith, agreeing with him that the human person lives within the transcendent horizon of God's promise. He countered, however, that that horizon should not be ascribed to the precognitive, transcendental structure of the individual. Rather, the transcendent horizon of God's promise is the future.[57] History itself is the arena in which the human person responds to God's promise of salvation. It is by failing to account for this that transcendental theology

---

54. "Church and the World," 79.
55. Metz would criticize Bultmann's project on multiple occasions. For an early instance, see ibid., 74.
56. "Controversy about the Future of Man," 227.
57. See "Church and the World," 70–71.

prematurely delimits what is deemed possible in history. Again, the unintended consequence of this is the loss of hope. But Metz would extend his criticism even further. Not only do existential and transcendental theologies truncate the historical and evacuate a genuine future from eschatology, but they also inevitably collapse the promise of this "future" into the personal decisions and private possibilities of the individual. Indeed, these two concerns are dialectically related. Precisely because contemporary theology abstracts the human person from concrete history, the individual's faith becomes a private affair. Conversely, precisely because of its privatizing tendency, contemporary theology is apt to abstract the individual from concrete, historical existence.[58] Theological reflection performed with its back to history, he warned, veils the future in a merely presential and privatized eschatology, compromising the efficacy of Christian hope.

We have seen already, though, that Metz had identified the means by which to begin correcting this misstep. If theology was to avoid relegating hope to the private and sheltered domain of human subjectivity, the future promised could not be presumed to be available in the present as an object of speculative contemplation. It must be mediated in history and be made known practically. Metz would avoid, however, artificially importing Bloch's emphasis on practical reason into the theological task. Rather, he argued that practical reason arises out of the Christian faith itself. The eschatological faith of the people of the promise is itself a creative and militant hope and, thus, must emerge as a productive eschatology. A productive eschatology is "primarily not a doctrine," Metz insisted, "but an initiative for the passionate innovating and changing of the world toward the Kingdom of God."[59] The future in which

58. Ibid.
59. Ibid., 81.

Christians hope is not already in existence but merely concealed and out of sight for the time being. This would be no future at all, as Bloch and now Metz argued. Rather, it is an emergent reality being made by those whose hope is ultimately founded upon and awakened by God's promise of a genuinely new day: "This heavenly city does not lie ahead of us as a distant and hidden goal, which only needs to be revealed. The eschatological City of God is now coming into existence, for our hopeful approach builds this city. We are workers building this future, and not just interpreters of this future."[60] This work of building the future is animated by an expectation that exceeds present reality yet is engaged intimately and unavoidably in world history: "The Christian understands his relationship to transcendence itself eschatologically: he awaits the 'beyond' as something to come historically, and history itself as something to be transformed into the one kingdom of God and man."[61] Eschatological hope is not a flight out of history, Metz averred, but a flight forward in history, actively and creatively hoping for the fulfillment of God's promise. It cannot be aloof and indifferent to the dynamics of history.

By attending to the creative and militant character of Christian hope, Metz created the space in which the social character of the biblical promise of salvation could come into view. The excessively private and individualistic character of hope as framed by a temporally dipolar objectivist cosmology or within existential-actual eschatologies obscured the sociopolitical dimension of God's promised kingdom. The salvation for which Christians hope is not primarily the salvation of the individual's soul or the satisfaction of existential alienation. Surely, it is a profoundly personal promise, but it most decidedly is not a private affair. It is, rather, the promise

60. Ibid., 82.
61. "Theological World and the Metaphysical World," 263n24.

of a peaceable kingdom, a new universal order of reconciliation, freedom, and justice in which the individual necessarily stands in relation to others and which, consequently, is impossible to privatize without distortion. For this reason, Metz famously argued, a creative and militant eschatology must be a "political theology." The future that such an eschatology seeks to build surpasses a straightforward conversion of the individual abstracted from his or her societal context. It seeks the conversion of the sociopolitical order and looks to create the conditions in which peace, freedom, and justice flourish. Society is not an ancillary or subsequent concern for theology; it is the essential medium by which eschatological hope is realized. Therefore, in working to bring about the promised kingdom, a creative eschatology must place "itself in communication with the prevailing political, social and technical utopias and with the contemporary maturing promises of a universal peace and justice."[62]

As we will see, Metz certainly wants to do more than mark a simple identity between the militant hope of Christianity and the progressive optimism of modern society. Nevertheless, he warned Christians not to withdraw to the isolated margins of society under the pretense of their hope in the coming of a new day. The deprivatizing of theology would be a primary task of his political theology. If Christian hope is to make true in history the promise of God's kingdom, that hope cannot be hermetically located within the private sphere. Eschatology must become a liberating and critical force within the world. We return, then, to Metz's concern with the crisis caused by secularization and the consequences of his political turn for eschatological hope.

62. "Church and the World," 83.

Consequences of the Political Turn for a Secularization Thesis and Eschatological Hope

Repositioning the Secularization Thesis from an Eschatological Perspective

The promotion of a political theology and the corresponding intensification of the eschatological that began to emerge in Metz's thought during this period did not signal a departure from his concern with the process of secularization and the crisis he sensed it had initiated in the faith life of many Christians. To the contrary, it must be recognized first of all as an effort to reaffirm once more that secularization need not be experienced as contrary to a Christian understanding of the world. Indeed, in a 1966 essay in which he explored the need for a creative and productive eschatology, "The Responsibility of Hope," he explicitly framed his position as an attempt to engage and legitimate the modern situation in the midst of modern doubts.[63] In this essay, Metz again was eager to show the fundamentally Christian character of secularization. He reengaged secularization, though now from the perspective not of protology and Christology but of eschatology. In his earliest writings, it was creation and the incarnation that allowed for the emergence of a hominized–anthropocentric experience of the world. Here, he would seek to engage and affirm an increasingly secularized society, to make theological sense of the modern experience, by concentrating on its relationship to the eschatological hope rooted in the promise of God.

By undertaking this task, Metz had the opportunity to develop further his earlier characterization of secularization by now attending more deliberately to the relationship between hominization, anthropocentrism, and an emerging awareness of the primacy of

---

63. "Responsibility of Hope."

the future. "The phenomenon called 'secularization' and the primacy given to the future are really of one piece," he wrote. "The light of what is above the world, what is more than earth, seems to have burned out. What stirs the modern man is not involvement in a world above but involvement in the future."[64] A fascination with the future lies at the heart of modern culture, Metz now believed. It is this that most tellingly distinguishes the modern person's experience of secularization. An orientation toward the future allows for the world to be experienced not as static or fixed nature but as the arena and material of as yet unrealized historical possibilities. It is the striving for a new and better world, a "golden age" now believed to lie in the future rather than in the past or in a detemporalized reality located "above" and outside history, that marks modern human existence.

According to Metz, however, the necessary condition for this modern experience of hope and the primacy of the future is the promise of a genuinely novel future. That is to say, the experience of the world as history is possible only in that the world is experienced under an eschatological horizon of hope. "The modern orientation to the future, with its understanding of the world as history," he claimed, "is founded on biblical faith in the promise."[65] Once again, then, Metz affirmed the inner connection between secularization and the Christian faith. Secularization is not contrary to the Christian understanding of the world; indeed, it presumes God's promise revealed in the Bible. Nevertheless, he did not develop this claim in the same detail, and certainly not in the same manner, with which he had earlier established the origins of secularization upon creation and the incarnation.

For the origins of this process, Metz now would point to the Israelites' foundational experience of the world as history upon

64. Ibid., 281.
65. Ibid., 283.

receiving God's promise. Here, it now can be affirmed correctly, secularization was the result of an event historically realized and communicated. It was the power of a promise offered and mediated within history, not the transcendental structure of history itself, by which he now affirmed the Christian provenance of secularization. It was the story of the covenantal relationship remembered and passed down through time that constituted and made possible the modern experience of the world.

But Metz cautioned his reader against defending this position simply as a history of ideas. Rather, he challenged Christians to demonstrate its veracity practically, by critically sharing in the responsibility for the present world. What he clearly avoided developing here, then, was a transcendental-linear theology of history paralleling the one he put forth in his earlier writings, in which a Christic transcendental subject is coming to be in history through the process of secularization. Such a modification in argumentation is important to note, because it illustrates a significant transformation in Metz's theology of history, that is, the way he envisioned the eschatological character of history.

A Reconsidered Theology of History

When engaging secularization from the perspective of the incarnation, Metz's earliest theological understanding of history came to support an eschatological vision of the world in which what is hoped for is directly continuous with what has been realized in history already. The world, he wrote, "must itself become what it already is through the deed of Jesus Christ." The past is wholly determinate of the future. Nothing radically new is revealed in history, for everything is drawn from the incarnation of Jesus Christ. During this earlier period of Metz's work, secularization was an eschatological event in that through it history becomes what it already is in the incarnation. This, of course, was precisely the conception of history problematized by Bloch. What Metz found in Bloch's ontology of history was a resource for understanding history as something more than "the story of the origin of the present."[66] History as the possibility of something genuinely new, as the possibility of an authentic hope, requires an open and novel future. The freedom and flourishing of humanity are dependent upon the promise of a new day. The creative and active longing for a better day so characteristic of modern men and women cannot be sustained if their expectations are exhausted from the outset by the delimiting possibilities of the past and present. Metz's eschatological vision of history had changed in response to these emerging insights. Turning to an expression suggested by his former student Francis Fiorenza, he came to articulate a "utopic" theology of history in which the world is drawn toward a transcendent and genuinely novel future.[67] Continuity is not the mark of an eschatologically charged history. The eschatological character of history, and thus the Christian's hope, is predicated upon a radically new and discontinuous future, not an irreversibly emerging past.

Coupled with his engagement with secularization, it was the radical sense of the "new" introduced by Bloch that made possible the transformation in Metz's understanding of history and enabled him to identify the productive and creative character of Christian hope. At the same time, it would be in defense of the productive character of hope that he subsequently challenged Bloch's atheistic notion of a transcendent future as a yet-unrealized utopia fashioned by humans alone.[68] Metz feared that Bloch's "transcending without

---

66. "Responsibility of Hope," 282.
67. See Fiorenza, "Thought of J. B. Metz," 250.
68. "Gott vor uns," 227–31.

transcendence" was ultimately unable to overcome the very circumscription of history he sought to avoid. The liberating power of a transcendent future resides, he countered, in the radical transcendence of a God who stands before us as the power of the future. Only such a future "is based upon itself and belongs to itself, a future which does not arise from the potentialities of human freedom and action but summons our freedom to its historical possibilities. For only a future that is more than a projection of our own capabilities can free us to something really 'new.'"[69] If there is to be an authentic and sustainable hope for the future, that hope cannot be exhausted by the limits of what the human person envisages as progress. If that were the case, nothing genuinely new could be hoped for the future, because the human alone would be the lone subject of history. Creative and militant hope will collapse all too quickly under the limitations of human finitude, Metz warned, if a transcendent God, the Lord and subject of history, is not the guarantor of an absolute and gratuitously given future.

Paradoxically, it was precisely by speaking of God as the transcendent subject of history and the guarantor of the future that Metz was able to affirm a transcendent and self-possessed future at the same time that he recognized the human person as the author of that future. As he did in his earlier writings when speaking of the God of creation, he once again affirmed that God's transcendence guarantees human autonomy and freedom. The building of God's promised new day is not the solitary work of humans, but men and women can participate in God's creative activity and become "coworkers" with the God who summons them toward a freely given future.[70] This participation is not such that humans rely on

---

69. "Responsibility of Hope," 284.
70. Ibid., 286. In using the expression "coworker," Metz cites the Second Vatican Council's *Lumen Gentium*.

their own capabilities until they have been utilized fully and only then turn to God for what yet remains; the kingdom is wholly the work of the God who is the creative power of history. The excess of God's promise fundamentally transcends human potentialities and consequently must be called forth from the future in its entirety rather than erected from the present. This is "a future which does not arise from the potentialities of human freedom and action but summons our freedom to its historical possibilities." Thus, as we have seen, the summons of the future is offered gratuitously but must not be received passively. God's promise truly lies ahead and, as such, needs to be actively constructed rather than contemplated: "The orthodoxy of a Christian faith must constantly *make itself* true in the 'orthopraxy' of [a person's] actions oriented toward the final future, because the promised *truth* is a truth which must be made."[71] For Metz, our building of the future and God's sovereignty over history are not competing or conflicting dynamics. The Christian freely responds to the summons of the future by building a new and better day, revealing God as the subject of history by making true God's promise in history.

An Emerging Appreciation for the Critical Character of Eschatology

Here, we return to Metz's apologetic interest in developing a theological response and foundation for the Christian's bewildering experience of secularization. Again, he maintained, Christians need not find a modern culture seemingly in control of the world and its future a challenge to their faith. True, God is no longer to be found within a directly divinized and numinous nature. But through

---

71. "Church and the World," 82.

the unfolding of history itself, modern men and women can find God's saving activity mediated and revealed in the world.[72] Within a culture now oriented toward a future in the making, a creative and productive eschatological hope renders Christianity relevant and meaningful. Despite strident claims to the contrary, secularization does not liquidate the validity of the Christian's faith. In Metz's project, the theological category of eschatology effectively established a relationship between Christianity and the modern world, just as the category of incarnation functioned in his earlier writings. In turn, through this reevaluation of the basis on which this relationship was established, the category of eschatology had moved to the center of Metz's theology.

The development in Metz's thought during this period, however, entailed more than a modification in the privileged doctrinal locus of his project. More fundamentally, it entailed a change in his understanding of that doctrine, a change in his understanding of history. As we have seen, within his transcendental-linear theology of history, the identification of incarnation and secularization, though ambiguous, presumed an essential continuity that inadvertently compromised the Christian voice in addressing the modern world. Of course, his understanding of eschatology during this period was defined by his operative understanding of history and thus shared in the same limitation. Continuity was the mark of an eschatologically charged history. Metz's earlier project could engage and affirm the challenge of secularization but was not well situated to challenge it. From the perspective of a utopic theology of history, though,

---

72. "Because the world itself, as a result of hominization, loses its numinous character, it does not follow that its connection with the numinous completely disappears. There simply appears a new, as it were 'anthropocentric' place in which the numinous is experienced: no longer the comprehensive openness of the pre-given world, but the freedom that acts on this world; no longer all-embracing nature, but the history of this hominized nature, taken in hand by men, in its free futurity" (*TW*, 69).

Metz now was better positioned to locate within the category of eschatology a critical resource with the capacity to move beyond engaging and affirming secularization.

Though, at this stage in his career, this still appeared to be his primary apologetic interest, an eschatological hope in the God who is the power of a transcendent future now would be seen also to possess an intrinsic critical reserve capable of challenging not only the truncation of hope in prevailing theological paradigms and the corresponding privatization of the Christian faith, but also reductive presumptions imbedded in the prevailing culture. His critique of Bloch's call for a transcending without transcendence, considered earlier, illustrates this defiant power peculiar to the Christian's inexhaustible hope. Though indebted to Bloch's ontology of history, Metz took a posture toward his Marxist interlocutor that was simultaneously critical and theologically judicious. While seeking to show the manner in which Christian eschatological hope accounts for a neo-Marxist criticism of religion, he simultaneously positioned that hope as a criticism of Bloch's still-reductive account of the future. As we now will see, Metz's embrace of a utopic theology of history brought to the fore and ultimately liberated the critical function of Christian eschatology, allowing him to attend more earnestly to the contradictions and incongruities that exist between the Christian faith and modern culture, in addition to the continuities already affirmed.

Not surprisingly, Metz warned against locating the critical force of eschatological hope in an "omniscient" surplus of knowledge, a privileged prescience or blueprint of the promised future not yet realized. This, of course, would bring the future into the present, inadvertently deflating the possibility of an ever-greater hope for history. In its place, he argued that the transcendent and genuinely novel character of God's promised future establishes a "poverty" of knowledge.[73] Eschatological expectation construes Christian theology as a *theologia negativa* of the future; it cultivates what could be described as an "apophatic" eschatology, which firmly and faithfully refuses to know too much. Rather than deflating hope, however, Metz argued that it is precisely the Christian's poverty of knowledge that leaves open a genuinely new and indefinable future, thus securing the historical freedom that makes human hope possible. It fosters a creative expectation that resists premature circumscription

This apophatic eschatology, Metz argued, fosters a negative awareness that what is known in the present is not that which the world has been promised still lies ahead. Again, we see that although the two cannot be identified, for Metz, world history is coextensive with the history of salvation. But heightened attention was now being given to the provisional character of this inner-relationship. Describing his position, Rebecca Chopp writes, "God is the fulfillment of history and yet God is neither totally within history nor totally apart from history, but always dialectically related to history from the future."[74] The future of the promise, then, continuously stays out in front of even the modern world's most successful efforts to plan and construct a better tomorrow. It will necessarily reject every form of premature and positivist speculation that exhausts the progressive optimism characteristic of the time upon the capabilities of humans alone. Here, we see Metz extending his criticism of Bloch to the operative presumptions of modern culture at large. "The Christian's militant hope is not simply a 'militant optimism.' Nor does it canonize man's own progress," he wrote. "His hope is rather a hope against every hope which we place in the man-made idols of our secular society."[75] By accepting the poverty of knowledge that an

73. "Church and the World," 84.
74. Chopp, *Praxis of Suffering*, 68.
75. "Church and the World," 84.

apophatic eschatology demands, the Christian's expectation for the future will persistently resist the overidentification of the present with the promised future.

Christians rightfully support and engage in social, political, and technical projects that promise progress toward an ever more humane future. Such action, we have seen, is a constitutive feature of a creative and productive hope that seeks to participate in the inbreaking of God's promised kingdom. In describing his call for a political theology in 1966, Metz insisted, "It must come to terms with the great political, social and technological utopias, with modern society's promises of universal peace, universal justice, and universal human freedom. For the salvation to which Christian hope refers is not primarily the salvation of the individual."[76] But, here, Metz was more deliberately insisting that this same hope concurrently makes conditional and relativizes these ambitious modern endeavors: "Of course, the promises that shine forth in Christ are a spur to all our struggling efforts for the future, but likewise a thorn that cannot permit these efforts for the future to proceed in a simple, militant world optimism, but must also chafe them, resist them critically."[77] An apophatic eschatology reveals the inescapable insufficiency of all human plans and programs; it reveals as overextended the confidence of the day and, in doing so, places a corrective "thorn" in the pretense of self-sufficiency.

At a meeting of the Paulusgesellschaft in 1965, Metz carefully outlined, through a series of destabilizing questions, the limitations of such a pretense, challenging an atheistic humanism that places in the hands of humans alone the responsibility of constructing a more humane future. He asked, "Are there not rather forms of man's self-alienation which cannot be removed by a release from economic-

76. "Responsibility of Hope," 286.
77. "Controversy about the Future of Man," 229.

social situations, however successful, and from which man will always draw the 'sorrow of finiteness'? Are there not forms of self-alienation that cannot simply be dissolved into social-utopian expectation?"[78] What about the problem of guilt, a seemingly inescapable human experience, in light of our heightened sense of responsibility for the world? What about the problem of concupiscence, that relentless discrepancy between what we plan for the future and our subsequent actions? Surely, Metz asserted, these experiences complicate and even resist a purely immanent solution. And, what about our ever-pending death? Does not the experience of death most acutely expose as absurd the assumption that all forms of estrangement can be overcome through social, political, and technological progress? Metz warned that if we are to maintain hope in the face of even death, before which all progress necessarily ceases, then human capacities must not be allowed to delimit the boundaries of our hope.[79]

Metz's presentation to the Paulusgesellschaft interweaves his commitment to stimulating the Christian's participation in the struggle for a more humane future with his refusal to reduce the Christian's hope to a naive world-optimism. Attending to the inherent limitations of Bloch's transcending without transcendence facilitated this effort. The eschatological hope of Christianity resists identification with the reductive hope of contemporary culture. It is important to note, though, that in this address Metz's critique was not limited to the claim that Christianity offers a more extensive and thus qualifying promise. We also see in this essay a concern that modernity's truncation of hope risked distorting the very character of human hope. Expressing a position examined earlier in this chapter, Metz again emphasized that the hominization of the world has not unequivocally fostered humanization. This observation, though, was

78. Ibid., 231.
79. See ibid., 230–32.

now accompanied by an additional observation. Metz now warned that by our attempting to locate in the human person alone the means of human flourishing, the suffering that accompanies the failure to bring about greater humanization is "leveled down into everyday experience which is always ready for compromise. We experience the fact that pain, too, does not change us, that we seek and find a bourgeois way of getting along with it."[80] The inexhaustible depth of hope, then, or at least the hope of those who suffer, seemed to be systematically absorbed and "leveled down" by the operative presumptions of modern society. We will return to this underdeveloped but critical observation in chapter 5, where Metz will explore it much more extensively as he further refines his analysis of the prevailing historical context. Already, however, it illustrates his increasing unease with modernity and its consequences for the vitality of human hope.

Conclusion

In this chapter, we have seen that Metz's eschatological project developed out of his theological analysis of the modern process of secularization, was initially constrained by his transcendental-linear theology of history, and gradually emerged as a practical-critical hope for the future. It was with his heightened awareness of the critical potential of Christian hope, when he began to underline more deliberately the critical distance rather than the intimate proximity that correlates that hope with all that humans plan for the present and future, that the reader could see most clearly what was an ongoing shift in Metz's posture toward the process of secularization and the assumptions of late modernity. As this chapter has shown, even after

---

80. Ibid., 231–32. Metz referenced Albert Camus when sounding this concern.

Metz adopted a clearly eschatological perspective in his writings, in 1965–1966, he continued to concentrate on offering a theologically positive interpretation of secularization that could establish the Christian provenance of the primacy of the future that seemingly characterized European culture in the middle of the twentieth century. Though this was now affirmed by a hope mediated within history rather than the transcendental structure of history itself, the apologetic task still was one of supporting those Christians who experienced the modern world as an alien threat and challenge to their faith by affirming the continuity between the life of Christian hope and the cultural dynamics of Europe at the time.

At the same time, however, and without prejudice to his apologetic intent, we also have seen that Metz located within the Christian's eschatological hope an inherent resource that radically resists a simple identity between eschatology and the future-oriented dynamic that came to the fore with modernity. Detached from the gratuitous and inexhaustible promises of the transcendent, the pursuit of historical advancement could come only at the expense of a genuine hope in the future. As the texts cited in the chapter have demonstrated, Metz's approach to the apologetic task was in transition. Surely aware in even his earliest writings that the hope of Christianity and the hope of modern culture are not the same, his increasing sensitivity to this nonidentity would only intensify further as he engaged new interlocutors and continued to refine his theological project. After 1966, as we will see in chapter 5, these developments would alter even further his estimation of the modern world, his conceptualization of the apologetic task, and would once again transform his understanding of the eschatological character of history in a far more apocalyptic key. Before investigating this turn to apocalyptic in Metz's later writings, we turn first to the early writings of his Belgian colleague. As we shall see in the next three chapters, Edward

Schillebeeckx also revised his initial evaluation of secularization in his later work, but in a way that differed significantly from that of Metz.

2

Schillebeecks's Response to Secularization

From a Merciful Dispensation to Latent Eschatological Hope

In chapter 1, we saw that Metz's eschatological project developed out of his theological analysis of the modern process of secularization, was unduly limited by his transcendental-linear theology of history, and gradually emerged as a practical-critical hope for the future. Now, turning to Edward Schillebeeckx's efforts to address the apologetic consequences of secularization during the late 1950s through the mid-1960s, we will trace similar developments that unfold over significantly different terrain; Schillebeeckx offered a distinctive response to the same historical challenges, yet during this period the doctrine of eschatology also would move to the center of his theological project.

The first section of this chapter examines Schillebeeckx's early interpretation (1958–1964) of secularization as a historical opening for purifying the Christian faith, a "merciful dispensation" by which

Christians can reclaim a more authentic understanding of God as Creator. Despite the notable advantages of such a tack, however, we will see that he ultimately was led to discover that a defense of his view of secularization grounded on creation faith would require an eschatological vision of history if it was to secure the elemental value of the world and human participation in history.

As with Metz, then, by engaging the process of secularization, Schillebeeckx was drawn to the apologetic significance of the doctrine of eschatology. Moreover, and again like Metz, Schillebeeckx began to argue that the Christian's eschatological expectations underwrite the processes of secularization. In the second section of this chapter, we will examine the Belgian's claim that Christians can recognize a latent eschatological hope contained within that desire to create a better future that, by the mid-1960s, he identified with the modern process of secularization. We shall see that it was precisely this manner of engagement that allowed Schillebeeckx to advance the practical character of eschatology. The distinctly modern route by which he retrieved the doctrine of eschatology would allow him to affirm the enthusiasm of modern culture while repositioning the Christian hope as an "active hope."

The third section of the chapter highlights the developments in Schillebeeckx's understanding of history and the Christian's hope that unfolded during this period. By the mid-1960s, Schillebeeckx would locate in the doctrine of eschatology a resource for affirming the Christian claim for the meaningfulness of history while more critically affirming that that meaning remains outstanding and a task for the future. This insight, with its corresponding understanding of God as "the God who is to come," placed greater emphasis on the indeterminacy and openness of history. Like Metz, Schillebeeckx had reevaluated the manner in which he understood history theologically. He, too, began to discover within the Christian's eschatological hope a theological vantage point that radically resists a simple identity between eschatology and the future-oriented dynamic he associated with the times. This heightened awareness of the critical character of the Christian's eschatological hope initiated what would be a gradual shift in Schillebeeckx's posture toward the course and prospects of late modernity.

Coupled with chapter 1, this chapter reveals the important relationship between the theological engagement with mid-twentieth-century interpretations of secularization and developments in the doctrine of eschatology, the emergence of practical eschatology in Catholic theology, and, ultimately, the beginnings of a more critical employment of Christian eschatological hope as it meets the challenges of a modern world. In doing so, the chapter underscores the remarkable parallels between Metz's and Schillebeeckx's projects evident by the mid-1960s while simultaneously preparing us for engaging each theologian's mature eschatology in the following chapters. As we shall see, for both men, the attention paid to the critical function of eschatological hope would only continue to develop as they began to uncover more clearly an underside to the modern world, an underside that optimism and progress had forgotten.

Secularization as Merciful Dispensation

God in Dry Dock

Just as he was transitioning to his new position as professor of dogmatic and historical theology at the University of Nijmegen in the late 1950s, Schillebeeckx also began to address the process of secularization and its impact on Western European culture.[1] Like Metz, Schillebeeckx took for granted that by the middle of the twentieth century, Europe had entered into this process and would only continue along that course. He, too, was concerned with the crisis of faith among Christians that seemed to accompany this emerging phenomenon.[2] And, reaching beyond the boundaries of the church, he also felt accountable to those who denied the existence of God in response to their experience of an increasingly secularized society.[3] Again, then, the question at hand was, what challenges

1. In 1958 and 1959, Schillebeeckx published a number of articles on the topic: "Dialogue with God and Christian Secularity," first appeared under the title "God en de mens," in *Verslagboek van de Theologische week over de mens* (Nijmegen, Neth., 1959), 3–21, reprinted in *God and Man*, trans. Edward Fitzgerald and Peter Tomlinson (New York: Sheed & Ward, 1969), 210–33; "The Intellectual's Responsibility for the Future," originally a lecture given to the Roland Society of Nijmegen University in November 1958 and first published as "De verantwoordelijkheid van de intellectueel voor de toekomst" in *Roeping* 34 (1958): 390–99, reprinted in *World and Church*, trans. N. D. Smith (New York: Sheed & Ward, 1971), 269–81; "The Search for the Living God," delivered as Schillebeeckx's inaugural address at Nijmegen University in 1958, reprinted in *God and Man*, 18–40; "God in Dry Dock," first published in *Tijdschrift voor Geestelijk Leven* 15 (1959): 397–409 and in *Opvpeding* 9 (1959): 90–95, reprinted in *God and Man*, 3–17. "Supernaturalism, Unchristian and Christian Expectations of the Future," first published as "De plaag van onchristelijke toekomstverwachtingen" in *Kultuurleven* 26 (1959): 504–51, reprinted in *World and Church*, 163–76; and "The Catholic Hospital and Health Service," first published as "Het katholieke ziekenhuis en de katholieke gezondheidszorg" in *Ons Ziekenhuis* 20 (1958): 317–25, reprinted in *World and Church*, 213–29. These writings will provide the textual basis for our evaluation of Schillebeeckx's early engagement with the phenomenon of secularization. This period of intense work on the subject was itself preceded by less explicit exploratory studies written in the 1940s and early 1950s, including a collection of the following essays: "Christelijke situatie," three consecutive articles in *Kultuurleven* 12 (1945): 82–95, 229–42, 585–611; "Humble Humanism," first published as "Nederig humanisme" in *Kultuurleven* 16, no. 1 (1949): 12–21, reprinted in *World and Church*, 19–31; "Religion and the World: Renewing the Face of the Earth," first published as "Godsdienst en wereld: Het aanschijn der aarde vernieuwen" in *Het geestelijk leven van de leek* (Tilburg, Neth.: Drakenburgh-conferenties, 1951), 7–27, reprinted in *World and Church*, 1–18; "Priest and Layman in a Secular World," an essay based on talks given to young Dominicans in 1952 and 1953 and previously printed in a magazine circulating among Dominican candidates for the priesthood; the Dutch title was 'Het kerkelijk apostolaat in verband met de situatie, 1945–1954"; the original article was slightly shortened when reprinted in *World and Church*, 32–76.

2. "Intellectual's Responsibility for the Future,"270. In 1966, Schillebeeckx developed this more fully in "The Sorrow of the Experience of God's Concealment," an essay first delivered in a lecture at a congress of Dutch-speaking student unions and theology faculties and published under the title 'Het leed der ervaring van Gods verborgenheid' in *Kerugma* 9, no. 4 (1966), reprinted in *World and Church*, 77–95.

3. "God in Dry Dock," 8.

does the secularization of society present Christianity, and what does Christian theology have to say in response?

From the onset, it is important to make clear that at this early stage in his writing, Schillebeeckx was working with a very different notion of secularization from the one that Metz developed only a few years later.[4] As we have seen, Metz, on the one hand, offered a theologically "positive interpretation of this permanent and growing secularity of the world." The process of secularization not only is fundamentally Christian in character and provenance but also is the historical continuation of the incarnation. Schillebeeckx, on the other hand, claimed that secularization had arisen neither from within nor against the Christian faith. In fact, he did not yet attempt to locate its origins. It was, he admitted, historically related to the development of an atheistic culture in modern Europe. He went on to argue, though, that this was not inherent to the process of secularization itself but was rather the consequence of the process having been understood against distorted notions of God. Employing a nautical metaphor, Schillebeeckx subsequently claimed that the secularization process was pressing the idea of God into "dry dock." Safe and well-worn assumptions about God would need to be lifted out of murky waters and carefully reexamined. He insisted, however, that this was best approached as an opportunity for the church rather than an obstacle. The process of secularization had the potential to create a space in which Christians could begin to purify their distorted notions of God that had arisen in times of unchallenged confidence. It was

---

4. To that point, when Metz revised the essay from 1962 (examined in chapter 1) for compilation in *Theology of the World*, he included Schillebeeckx, along with other prominent theologians, including his mentor, Rahner, in his criticism that common to alternative theological efforts to address the modern situation was the "the fundamental rejection of the secularization of the world." See Metz, *Theology of the World* (New York: Herder & Herder, 1969), 15 (hereafter abbreviated *TW*). As we will see, this criticism does not recognize the precise character of Schillebeeckx's early engagement with secularization. Nonetheless, it does highlight the disparity in the two theologians' projects at this time.

precisely here, then, that Schillebeeckx would engage secularization as a theologically fruitful phenomenon. Although not itself a theologically positive event, it presented a unique moment of renewal, a "merciful dispensation" through which the Christian faith could purge itself of deceptive and even idolatrous understandings of God, the world, and, as we will see, human history.[5]

At this early stage in his reflections on the subject, Schillebeeckx had not yet developed a well-defined historical account of the modern emergence of the secularization process, though he would come to do that in time.[6] In this period, he spoke more generally of a process in which nature, history, values, and even the human person were made sensible and given meaning without recourse to the divine. Identifying the same cultural developments noted by Metz, Schillebeeckx observed a world now understood to function according to the laws of nature rather than divine intervention, with humans freely employing such laws in order to fashion the future, and values secured by the freedom of the individual and the effective ordering of society rather than ecclesial authority. Secularization, Schillebeeckx would write, was concerned with "the worldly maturity of modern man, who has taken the ordering of this secular sphere into his own hands."[7]

Schillebeeckx was concerned, though, that Christians frequently experienced this as a process in which God was being edged out of the world. In 1959, he warned that modern developments had "gradually advanced into those formerly hidden domains whose obscure inaccessibility for the human mind was once regarded as

---

5. "God in Dry Dock," 8.
6. In 1967, Schillebeeckx identified four historical "turning points" in which he traced the development of modern secular consciousness. See "Secularization and Christian Belief in God," in *God the Future of Man*, trans. N. D. Smith (New York: Sheed and Ward, 1968), 57–62. See also "Theology of Renewal Talks about God," in *Revelation and Theology*, vol. 2, *The Concept of Truth and Theological Renewal* (London: Sheed & Ward, 1968), 84–90.
7. "Search for the Living God," 22.

identical with the mystery in which God came into tangible contact with the world. But nowadays, for every step forward man takes, God has to take a step backwards."[8] Because God's existence had frequently been identified with those areas of life and world that at the time eluded explanation, scientific progress and the technological achievements of modernity now appeared to confirm God's nonexistence. The inexplicable "gaps" through which God once seemed to intervene in the world had disappeared. This was to say that the expansion of human responsibility directly corresponded with the shrinking of God's domain, precisely the dynamic envisaged by proponents of the zero-sum theory of secularization. Nevertheless, Schillebeeckx embraced the advancements of science and technology that explained and manipulated the natural cycles of the world without reference to God.[9] He celebrated the "translation of values" that reframed what were once the church's demands for charity as inalienable human rights protected by the state.[10] Schillebeeckx responded to these modern developments in this way because he was eager to show that the intervening god who was being "edged out of the world" was not the God of Christian faith.

In addition to fostering this "almost existential experience" of God's nonexistence within modern culture,[11] Schillebeeckx also credited the process of secularization with bringing to light a regrettable passivity among Christians in the face of political, economic, and social responsibilities. If God's nonexistence seemed to be confirmed by the steady march of progress, then belief in God would quite predictably be regarded as an obstacle to that progress. In the idiom of existential phenomenology, which strongly influenced Schillebeeckx's writing during this period, the human person is free

8. "God in Dry Dock," 4.
9. "Search for the Living God," 19. See also "God in Dry Dock," 6.
10. "Search for the Living God," 20–21.
11. Ibid., 18.

to create meaning in the world and history only if the future is an open question and a personal risk. Critics such as Jean-Paul Sartre and Maurice Merleau-Ponty argued that faith in the supernatural or suprahistorical misdirects the individual's responsibility from the world.[12] Such faith is "the final remnant of a certain attitude towards life in which man does not dare to tackle life for himself and therefore projects a solution of the historical mystery into the hereafter—into eternity."[13] Christians, it was being argued, abandon history for the suprahistorical. Secularization stood as a challenge to the Christian faith, then, not just by edging God out of the world but also in revealing an irresponsible indifference to the world that appeared to be inherent to the faith. Schillebeeckx himself asked, "Hasn't atheism perhaps got a point when it calls on the evidence of history to show that believers use their beliefs as an excuse for their own sloth and timidity and their refusal to face the urgent problems of the day?"[14] Nonetheless, Schillebeeckx embraced this challenge. In his judgment, it, too, provided Christians the opportunity to reconsider erroneous ideas about God that distorted the faith, allowing for the renewal of a more fully orthodox articulation of Christianity that could respond to the perceived theological implications of secularization.

Thus, Schillebeeckx's engagement with secularization, like that of Metz's, is best approached as a project in apologetics. He recognized that men and women had experienced this modern phenomenon as a crisis of faith, leading frequently to the denial of God's very existence. Nevertheless, from Schillebeeckx's perspective, this crisis provided an opportunity for purifying the Christian theological vision. The

---

12. At this stage in his work, Schillebeeckx repeatedly engaged influential existentialist readings of the human situation and their corresponding critiques of religious faith. See his responses to Merleau-Ponty and Sartre found in the essays published in *God and Man* and, in particular, "God in Dry Dock," 7n2.

13. "God in Dry Dock," 7.

14. Ibid.

idea of God could be put in dry dock, lifted out of dark waters and reconsidered in light of the challenging questions posed by the process of secularization. Has the inexplicable been explained, edging God out of the world? Do faith in God and hope in the eternal nullify the value of the world and history? In attempting to respond to these questions, Schillebeeckx, again like Metz, would turn to the theological categories of protology and Christology.[15] There, he found resources for his earliest response to the challenges posed by secularization.

Creation Faith in Light of Secularization

Even a brief look at Schillebeeckx's early work reveals his methodological commitment to mining the Christian theological tradition in the hope of offering an authentic reading of the faith for a new historical context.[16] In his doctoral thesis, entitled *De Sacramentele Heilseconomie*, for example, he developed a reading of Thomas Aquinas's sacramental theology in view of the prevailing phenomenological emphases on the person as being-in-the-world and on human encounter as mediated by bodily presence.[17] The subtitle he gave to this work illustrates his practice: *Theologische bezinning op S. Thomas' sacramentenleer in het licht van de traditie envan de hedendeaagse sacramentsproblematiek* ("The Sacramental Economy of Salvation: Theological Reflection on S. Thomas' Teachings on the Sacraments in Light of the Tradition and Present-Day Sacramental Problems").[18] During this period, then, the unambiguous starting

---

15. Ibid., 12–13.
16. For a helpful study of Schillebeeckx's early theological method, see Mary Catherine Hilkert, "Hermeneutics of History in the Theology of Edward Schillebeeckx," *Thomist* 51 (1987): 99–106.
17. See Cornelius Ernst's foreword to Schillebeeckx, *Christ the Sacrament of the Encounter with God*, trans. Paul Barrett (Franklin, WI: Sheed & Ward, 1999), xv.

point of Schillebeeckx's work was the church's doctrinal teaching, especially as articulated by Aquinas. At the same time, the contemporary situation was self-consciously allowed to play a significant role. The light of the present-day situation, as the preceding subtitle suggests, was permitted to illumine traditional expressions of the faith. "In a sense he made an attempt at a literary effect," observed Erik Borgman of *De Sacramentele Heilseconomie*. "He presented Thomas in such a way that the question of the place of the sacraments in his work almost coincided with the question of the place of the sacraments in the life of [contemporary] Catholics."[19] As we will see, this same methodological decision also would structure Schillebeeckx's apologetic response to secularization. Again, he offered an internal return to traditional Christian sources from the vantage point of contemporary thought, only now he would develop a reading of Thomistic protology in light of the distressing concerns surrounding the process of secularization. He responded to the modern experience of God's nonexistence and explored the Christian's responsibility for the world in such a way that these challenges posed by secularization seemed to "almost coincide" with the questions addressed by Aquinas's metaphysics of creation.

Briefly stated, in Aquinas's massive scholastic synthesis, it is incorrect to speak of God as a being (*ens*) more or less distinguishable from created beings. Only a creature is properly described as a being. God is not an essence (*essentia*) that possesses an existence, but the very act of existence (*esse*). That is, God is being itself, whereas all

---

18. *De Sacramentele Heilseconomie: Theologische bezinning op S. Thomas' sacramentenleer in het licht van de traditie envan de hedendeaagse sacramentsproblematiek* (Antwerp, Belg.: 't Groeit; Bilthoven, Neth.: Nelissen, 1952). In addition to examining the thought of Aquinas, Schillebeeckx's thesis also examined contributions made by a variety of patristic sources. A shorter and less technical version of this work was published in English as *Christ the Sacrament of the Encounter with God*.

19. Erik Borgman, *Edward Schillebeeckx: A Theologian in His History,* vol. 1, *A Catholic Theology of Culture (1914–1965),* trans. John Bowden (London: Continuum), 207.

creation possesses being by continuously participating in God's sheer act of existence.[20] It is fair to say that Schillebeeckx's theology would self-consciously presume this nondualistic ontological framework throughout his career, though frequently with a fair amount of license.[21] Studying under innovative teachers such as Dominicus De Petter and M. Dominique Chenu,[22] Schillebeeckx was deeply immersed in Aquinas's project during his philosophical and theological training with the Dominicans and grew rather adept at repositioning Aquinas's thought in response to emerging pastoral and intellectual challenges.[23] In answering the concerns posed by secularization, then, it is not surprising that his first response was to transpose this Thomistic ontology of creation into an anthropological register. Humans are called into existence and continually receive their being from the infinite and transcendent God. At the same time, they are truly their own, free and independent beings of this world. Precisely as created, they are finite and that which is not God. At the same time, humans are wholly from God the Creator, constantly dependent on another for their very existence. This anthropological

20. See Thomas Aquinas, *Summa theologiae* Ia, q. 44, a.1, as well as *Thomas Aquinas on Being and Essence*, trans. Armand Maurer (Toronto: Pontifical Institute of Medieval Studies, 1968). For a brief introduction to Schillebeeckx's appropriation of Aquinas's metaphysics of creation, see Philip Kennedy, "God and Creation," in *The Praxis of the Reign of God*, ed. Mary Catherine Hilkert and Robert J. Schreiter, 2nd ed. (New York: Fordham University Press, 2002), 37–58.

21. Philip Kennedy traces this theme in Schillebeeckx's work from his unpublished lectures given in the mid-1950s through his most mature writings, in *Deus Humanissimus: The Knowability of God in the Theology of Edward Schillebeeckx* (Fribourg, Switz.: University Press, 1993).

22. For an introduction to the influence of the elder Dominicans on Schillebeeckx's early work, see Borgman, *Edward Schillebeeckx*, 191–99.

23. For example, Schillebeeckx's Thomistic understanding of creation underlies the "perspectivalist" epistemology he developed under the influence of De Petter during the 1950s and early 1960s, by which he sought to account for the truth status of the church's dogmatic statements while avoiding both the abstract conceptualism of neo-scholasticism and the subjectivist relativism associated with modernist theology. See "The Non-Conceptual Intellectual Dimension of Our Knowledge of God according to Aquinas," *Revelation and Theology*, vol. 2, trans. N. D. Smith, 30–53. For an account of this project, see Daniel Speed Thompson, *The Language of Dissent: Edward Schillebeeckx on the Crisis of Authority in the Catholic Church* (Notre Dame, IN: University of Notre Dame Press, 2003), 13–22. For another helpful example, note Schillebeeckx's reflection on the sacramental economy referenced earlier.

dynamic of freedom through dependence, Schillebeeckx claimed, is at the center of Christian creation faith. Christians confess that the human person's "whole life is lived within the vast sphere of the personal God who embraces us. It is therefore pointless to seek him in isolation *somewhere* in this world."[24] God is the One *in* whom we exist; as a result, God cannot be located *in* the world.

The apologetic value of this understanding of creation for addressing the modern experience of God's nonexistence should be apparent. Relying on this protological vision, Schillebeeckx was able to argue that the "god" edged out of the world through the advances of secularization is not the God of Christian faith. The God of Christian faith cannot be identified with those areas of life and world which until recently eluded explanation. God does not "intervene" in the world and is not one among many finite and tangible beings who can be circumscribed and "edged out." Accordingly, Schillebeeckx could maintain that there was no need for the crisis of faith surrounding modern progress; such a crisis was just the consequence of a distorted understanding of God. In the end, the advances of secularization merely "dislodge a pseudo-God" while simultaneously, if inadvertently, cautioning Christians against domesticating a God who is infinite mystery and the very ground of human existence.[25]

Schillebeeckx would also employ this vision of creation as he explored the relationship of Christians to the world. By doing this, he hoped to respond to the aforementioned critique that Christians devalue the world and fail to accept responsibility for history. He began by further transposing Aquinas's thought, now into the existential-phenomenological key of encounter or dialogue between God and humanity. His understanding of the anthropological dynamic of freedom and dependence provided the foundation that

24. "God in Dry Dock," 9.
25. Ibid., 11.

allowed him to speak of the human person as engaged in a dialogue with both God and the world. In the radical experience of contingency, he argued, humans are unable to find in themselves the reason or cause of their own being. A theological understanding of the human person will recognize in this experience of contingency, the sheer gratuitousness of existence, an existential orientation toward self-transcendence.[26] This orientation bespeaks the human person's fundamental dependence upon God for sustained existence. Such dependence upon God is not an ancillary aspect of being human but instead is the foundation and provides the very meaning of being human. Humans are created for relationship with their Creator; the human person is "a being with a superhuman or supernatural potentiality."[27] Precisely because of their finitude, however, humans cannot fulfill this potentiality through their own powers. In grace, the transcendent God reaches out and enters into a personal and immediate relationship, becoming immanently present in and through human finitude and making possible the very relationship for which humans are created. Schillebeeckx spoke of this relationship as the "theologal" relationship, a personal dialogue between the finite person and the transcendent God.[28] Moreover, he insisted that this intimate intersubjectivity with God is the purpose and "primary task of life."[29] It alone provides the ultimate meaning of human existence.

Such a claim would seem to confirm the suspicions of Christianity's critics who argued that religious faith redirects attention from the worldly to the supernatural. If the primary task of life is our dialogical relationship with God, where does that leave the very human tasks

---

26. "Search for the Living God," 23.
27. "Dialogue with God and Christian Secularity,"215.
28. On Schillebeeckx's use of the term *theologal*, see *Christ the Sacrament*, 16n14, as well as "Faith Functioning in Human Self-Understanding," in *The Word in History*, ed. Patrick Burke (New York: Sheed & Ward, 1966), 59n1.
29. "Dialogue with God and Christian Secularity," 217.

and duties of life in the world? In response, Schillebeeckx affirmed that creation establishes the human as autonomous and free as well as wholly dependent upon God: "On the one hand I am really and truly myself; I stand freely and courageously in this world and take my life in my own hands, arranging it according to what I in my freedom choose. . . . On the other hand, in this whole being I am at the same time, and into the finest warp and woof of my being, wholly from God."[30] A theologically orthodox understanding of the human person, he argued, recognizes not only the person's fundamental orientation toward intimate relationship with God but also the fact that the human person is essentially of this world. Humans are inherently embodied and situated creatures, by their very creation participating in a dialogue with the world as well as oriented toward dialogue with God. Thus, to live theologally, in such a way that intersubjectivity with God is given priority, cannot compromise the person's relationship to the world. On the contrary, the living out of Christian creation faith fundamentally requires that one freely and creatively engage the world. Precisely as creation, the world is finite and that which is not God. It possesses a value and significance of its own. As such, all humans, religious and nonreligious alike, share in the task of ordering secular affairs.

This dialogue with the world should not be understood, though, as occurring outside the context of the human person's dialogue with God. Schillebeeckx argued that the human person's essential embodiment does not merely stand alongside and remain uninformed by a fundamental orientation toward relationship with God. Rather, when approached from the vantage point of theologal intimacy, the person's free and creative ordering of the secular is taken up into the relationship with God. The world is thus approached as the very place in which dialogue with God takes

30. "God in Dry Dock," 9.

form; the proper and humane ordering of the world mediates and becomes the embodiment of our love for God and God's gratuitous love for humanity: "As believers we live with God in this world, which we construct into a home worthy of human habitation in which, moreover, the incarnation of our personal communion with God is expressed."[31] Secular life partakes in and reveals the theologal life. It possesses a meaning and significance of its own, Schillebeeckx reaffirmed. Yet, for the human person theologically defined such that the relationship is given priority, the ultimate meaning of the secular is realized in that it becomes the arena in which human dialogue with God finds expression. Dialogue with the world, therefore, attains its full significance and value in the context of the person's dialogue with God. Only as such does it become the embodiment of personal communion with God. Both successful attempts at humanizing the world and even those that can be described only as fiascoes mediate and express the human person's relationship with God.[32]

Once again, the apologetic value of Schillebeeckx's understanding of creation should be apparent. Christian faith need not minimize the value of the world, attending to the supernatural at the expense of the natural. Properly understood, Christian creation faith in effect guarantees the value of the person's participation in the world. Indeed, Schillebeeckx could write that the church's "latter-day saints" are those "who carry the dogma of creation into practice instead of leaving the ordering of secular affairs in the hands of unbelievers."[33] By responding to the challenge posed by secularization in this way, Schillebeeckx made an important distinction between a Christian mode of engaging the world and a nonreligious mode of

---

31. "Dialogue with God and Christian Secularity," 227.
32. Ibid., 232. At the time, Schillebeeckx did not explore the peculiar manner in which "fiascos" embody this divine–human relationship. As we will see in chapter 4, with much greater attention he would return to this claim in his later writings.
33. "God in Dry Dock," 15.

engagement. *Secularization,* he ultimately claimed, is a theologically ambiguous term.[34] There is, on the one hand, the possibility of a Christian secularization in which the believer recognizes and engages the world within the context of a life of faith. The world mediates and embodies the divine–human relationship. Affirmed and engaged responsibly, it is precisely the locale in which we enter into dialogue with God. This, Schillebeeckx assured, is a secularization that the church need not fear. It is a mode of secularization inherent to the creation faith of the tradition and cannot be accused of abandoning this world for another. There is, on the other hand, the secularization of the atheist, for whom the world itself exhausts the possibility of meaning. This is a secularization that detaches life in the world from the context of life with God: "Exclusively secular or atheistic laicization is an *hairesis,* a tearing away of profane or secular reality from the whole into which it fits, the existential relationship of faith with the living God."[35] As we will now see, Schillebeeckx would argue that, ironically, it is this atheistic secularization that is, in the end, unable to secure the human person's meaningful and responsible participation in history as well as the ultimate value of the world.

The Salvific Character of History: The Possibility of Human Responsibility

It is here that Schillebeeckx's protological response to secularization converged with his understanding of the theological character of

---

34. "Christians and Non-Christians, 2: Practical Cooperation," in *World and Church,* 217.

35. "Dialogue with God and Christian Secularity," 224. Here, Schillebeeckx used the language of "laicization" rather than "secularization," a term that came out of discussions in France regarding the relationship of the church and the world. These terms appear to have been used synonymously in this essay, though I would suggest that *laicization* was the more appropriate term for the intra-ecclesial discussion regarding the role of Christians in the world, whereas *secularization* was better suited for the more fundamental question of the value of the transcendent in what was perceived to be an increasingly secular culture.

history. It is a convergence, we shall see, that ultimately takes place in the person of Jesus Christ. As the historical manifestation of the fullness of the theologal life, the incarnation stands at the center of time: "It was only in Christ that God fully expressed the meaning of human life and history."[36] Christ is the eschaton; he is the fulfillment of time. It was through his death and resurrection that the ultimate meaning of history and world were established. Prior to the incarnation, Schillebeeckx maintained, the very meaning of history remained an open question; it was a history that was still becoming. It was already a history of salvation, he acknowledged, but only in that it was inwardly oriented toward a "God who was to come."[37] Following the incarnation, however, the salvific character of history was definitively realized and established. By interpreting history in this way, Schillebeeckx was not proposing the existence of two different, if successive, histories, one presalvific and the other salvific. He was also not positing two parallel but separate histories, one profane and the other salvific. His nondualistic understanding of the divine–human dialogue established in creation would make such dualistic interpretations of God's saving activity in the world unintelligible. Rather, he was looking to affirm that Christ had marked history in a definitive manner. Indeed, with language similar to that used by Metz only a few years later, Schillebeeckx could write, "History is already at an end in Christ."[38] That is to say, the universal and total meaning of history is closed, because the salvific character of history has been realized fully in the incarnation.

Schillebeeckx was aware that this characterization of history as closed was intimately related to the concerns of the secular culture he was seeking to address. Is it not just such a construal of history

36. "Supernaturalism," 168.
37. Ibid., 167.
38. Ibid., 169. See also Metz, *TW*, 25.

that allows Christians to shirk their responsibilities and secular duties? Does this narration of history allow Christians to remain indifferent to the present precisely because of an already-determined future? In response to such questions, Schillebeeckx once again insisted upon the freedom of the human person grounded in creation. But now, he would recalibrate that anthropological claim in a temporal key and correlate the essentially incarnate or embodied character of human existence with the irreducible temporality of human life. The freedom granted in creation offers the possibility of an authentic hope or expectation for history; to be free is to stand before an open and indeterminate future.[39] A history "closed in Christ," then, will not discount the history-making capacity of human expectations for the future. "The end of time is, on the one hand, an accomplished fact," Schillebeeckx wrote, "and, on the other hand, it still has a history."[40] He insisted that the future remains unknown and under construction even as its meaning has already been established. Human freedom fashions world history, we order and put our secular stamp on it, but what we make of that history occurs within the structure of its salvific character established in Christ. History remains soteriologically ambiguous, but it is no longer soteriologically neutral or pending. That is to say, history is freely fashioned, but in that its ultimate meaning has been established, it is fashioned as a history of salvation or of judgment.

In 1958, in an essay entitled "The Intellectual's Responsibility for the Future," Schillebeeckx responded to efforts that sought to frame human freedom and expectations for the future in such a way as to detach them from the context of salvation history. Here, he took up the argument of the French existential phenomenologist Maurice Merleau-Ponty, who insisted that only apart from this Christian

39. "Intellectual's Responsibility for the Future," 269.
40. "Supernaturalism," 169.

86

theology of history could the freedom of the human person be secured in a history with a genuine future.[41] Continuing to approach secularization as a "merciful dispensation," Schillebeeckx once again looked to identify a corrective contribution in his interlocutor's critique. He acknowledged that Christians had frequently narrated history in such a way as to eliminate the unknown of historical life, blunting the very real risks inherent to human freedom with a passive confidence that all would come to its preordained and proper end. In doing so, Christians failed to recognize that the salvific character of history affirmed in faith does not reveal the content of history but rather establishes its ultimate meaning and structure. "We do not simply possess the future," he wrote. "Expectation of the future is only a name for *hoping*."[42] The content of the future remains in the dark for the believer as well as for the atheist.[43] According to Schillebeeckx, it was precisely the kind of misguided eschatological confidence too often avowed by Christians that correctly called down the judgment of a critic such as Merleau-Ponty. Nevertheless, he warned that such criticism should not prevent believers from confessing that human freedom, which makes hope and an expectation for the future possible, indeed subsists within a history already established as salvific, for it is precisely with this confession that meaningful activity in the world is made possible.

Rather than dulling the Christian's commitment to the future, Schillebeeckx insisted that it is within the context of salvation history that human *expectation* for the future becomes *responsibility* for the future. In fact, he feared that outside of this context, history, and therefore human hope, remains dangerously directionless.[44] Here, we see him affirm what his fellow Dominican Servais Pinckaers has

---

41. "Intellectual's Responsibility for the Future," 270.
42. Ibid., 281 (original emphasis).
43. "God in Dry Dock," 16.
44. "Search for the Living God," 22.

described as Aquinas's "freedom for excellence" in lieu of a "freedom of indifference."[45] If history has no purpose or meaning, the vitality of our participation in the world and hope for the future will be compromised. It is Christ who gives history universal meaning, and that meaning provides human hope or our expectation for the future a particular direction and end. The salvific character of history places human freedom in the context of vocation; it renders freedom and hope as responsibility by providing them purpose and task. Thus, Christian hope for the future is fundamentally directed toward theologal salvation established in Christ. And it is this hope that establishes and animates the Christian's responsibility for the future of this world.

Such a future comes as gift, Schillebeeckx affirmed; it is gratuitously given rather than self-achieved. We have already seen, however, that the relationship established in creation locates the human person in a dialogical partnership with God, through which the human person's free ordering of the world can mediate and embody God's gratuitous love. Schillebeeckx was now concerned to explain that the salvific character of history established in Christ renders this possibility a graced responsibility through which the human person participates with God in freely bringing the world and history to share in the eschaton: "The world therefore has an ultimate meaning which is more than simply worldly, a meaning which it does not need to have in itself, but which our being called to responsibility must give it. Our ordering of life within this world . . . is thus a participation in the eschatology of mankind."[46] God's grace coming from the future is received in the present and structures the Christian's dialogue with the world. The salvific character of history

---

45. Servais Pinckaers, *The Sources of Christian Ethics*, trans. Mary Thomas Noble (Washington, DC: Catholic University of America Press, 1995).
46. "Intellectual's Responsibility for the Future," 275.

allows the believer to take responsibility for a future gratuitously given. And in so doing, "world history grows slowly from within towards the end of time."[47] Schillebeeckx did not elaborate further during this period on the relationship between our taking responsibility for the future and the coming of the eschatological kingdom. He was already clear, however, that the ultimate meaning of history has been definitively established in Christ, and in and through our graced engagement, world history begins to participate in eschatological glorification.

We can see that in Schillebeeckx's earliest effort to address the challenges of secularization, he took up the traditional language of Christian creation faith as his first response. The category of protology was asked to bear the brunt of the theological work. It is important to note that this tack functioned fundamentally as a defense of the tradition, seeking to soothe the fears of those who had experienced secularization as a crisis of faith. In taking up the category of eschatology, however, Schillebeeckx's response went on the offensive. Secularization was still seen as a merciful dispensation in which traditional expressions of the faith could be reexamined. But, from the vantage point of eschatology, he located a more robust position from which not only to defend Christianity but also to challenge its critics. He discovered that a defense against the challenges of secularization grounded on creation faith required an eschatological vision of history if it was to secure the deepest dimension and ultimate value of the world and human participation in history. Such a defense was founded upon a theological position Schillebeeckx directly affirmed: creation and the eschaton ultimately converge "in the very historical fact of the mystery of Christ and as a consequence and in light of this . . . in the contemporary fact of our created human existence as men who make history and

47. "Supernaturalism," 172.

89

who are subject to God's call to salvation."[48] Protology remained the privileged theological category for his apologetic project, but he found it to be intimately related through the incarnation to the eschatological hope of Christian faith. As we will now see, changes in his understanding of the process of secularization would allow him to reconsider further his apologetic tack and, in turn, to advance even more aggressively an eschatological account of Christian life in the world.

Secularization as Latent Eschatological Hope

A New Response to Secularization

Schillebeeckx continued to rely on the same creation-centered theological argument throughout the early 1960s when addressing the phenomenon of secularization. In 1963 and 1964, for example, he wrote two articles responding to John A. T. Robinson's enormously popular reflection on secularization entitled *Honest to God*.[49] In these articles, we clearly see Schillebeeckx's decision to privilege the apologetic force of Christian creation faith. His response focused almost exclusively upon what he saw to be Robinson's failure to account adequately for the anthropological dynamic of dependence and freedom we have already considered.[50] Significantly, in

---

48. Ibid., 167.

49. See "Evangelische zuiverheid en menselijke waarachtigheid," *Tijdschrift voor Theologie* 3 (1963): 283–325, and "Herinterpretatie van het geloof in het licht van de seculariteit," *Tijdschrift voor Theologie* 4 (1964): 109–50. These articles were edited and published as "Life in God and Life in the World" in *God and Man*, 85–160. See also John A. T. Robinson, *Honest to God* (Louisville, KY: Westminster, 1963).

50. Schillebeeckx criticized Robinson for giving the appearance of collapsing the human person's dialogue with God (vertical relationship) into the person's dialogue with the world (horizontal relationship). Ultimately, he was concerned that despite his claims to the contrary, Robinson had given the reader a defense of an atheistic secularization under the guise of theological discourse.

Schillebeeckx's extensive evaluation of the book, he only briefly challenged Robinson to consider more fully the place of eschatology in his engagement with secularization. Schillebeeckx devoted less than a page to the topic.[51]

But starting in 1966, Schillebeeckx began to formulate a more nuanced account of the process of secularization.[52] Rather than approach secularization as primarily a theological challenge in which God is edged out of the world, as he did in his earlier writing, Schillebeeckx came to frame secularization as fundamentally a sociological phenomenon. It is, above all, a new interpretation of the world and the human person. Citing, among other texts, Metz's "The Future of Faith in a Hominized World," Schillebeeckx also started writing about a presecular experience of "nature" as a numinous reality that inspired an overwhelming sense of reverence or fear. The human person dwelled in a directly divinized world, beset by outside powers bringing about both good and ill: "[A]ncient man experienced God's anger or his blessing in the thunder and lightning, in the tempest and in the blowing of the wind."[53] The mysterious forces of nature were seen as a reflection of God's power, establishing a world in which the human was vulnerable and powerless.

51. "Life in God," 158.
52. Schillebeeckx wrote two articles in 1966 in which he explored a new approach to secularization and the role of eschatological faith in modern culture. See "Sorrow of the Experience"; and "Is the Church Adrift?," in *The Mission of the Church*, trans. N. D. Smith (New York: Seabury, 1973), 20–42. In 1967, he would further this work in "Christian Faith and Man's Expectation for the Future on Earth," in *Mission of the Church*, 51–89; "Religious Life in a Secularized World," in *Mission of the Church*, 132–70; and the first five chapters of *God the Future of Man*, which were originally delivered throughout the United States during a lecture tour. Because of the transitional character of the final chapter of *God the Future of Man*, that text will be examined more closely in chapter 3. The essays mentioned here will provide the textual basis for our analysis of Schillebeeckx's work during this short but important period of development in his thought. "Is the Church Adrift?" was first published in *Tijdschrift voor Geestelijk Leven* 22 (1966): 533–54. "Christian Faith and Man's Expectation for the Future on Earth" was first published in *De kerk in de wereld van deze tijd* (Hilversum, Neth.: Brand, 1967), 78–109. "Religious Life in a Secularized World" was first published in *Tijdschrift voor Theologie* 7 (1967): 1–27 and was entitled "Het nieuwe mens- en Godsbeeld in conflict met het religieuze leven."
53. "Sorrow of the Experience," 79.

Secularization marked a shift in this attitude toward the world. In a secular culture, nature is experienced no longer as the pregiven world in which humans find themselves but as that which can be transformed by human hands. The world can be conquered and planned; it is the object of human control. The need for a God to make sense of the world's chaos disappears. The world displays no longer the *vestigia Dei* but the *vestigia hominis*.

Schillebeeckx went on to observe that this changed attitude toward the world corresponded with a change in the human person's self-understanding. Now aware that the world does not operate according to the incontestable whims of the divine, humans found themselves free to shape the world according to their own skills and needs. The person "becomes the subject, the demiurge of the form of his existence on earth."[54] In relating to the world in this new way, Schillebeeckx believed that humans ultimately recognized the historicity of human existence and the possibility of a future. They came to see themselves as in control of what the world was to become. They discovered their capacity to create a world and future that better fulfill the needs of humanity: "What man wants to do is to build up a new world on this earth and this is above all a project for the future, in contrast to the view of man and the world that he had in the past, in which the norm was provided and the form determined."[55] The world became a project for the future through the process of secularization, and, in turn, humans found themselves oriented toward the future as its creator or author.

It bears repeating that Schillebeeckx now stressed that this process was, on the first order, a sociocultural phenomenon. Secularization was primarily a change in our understanding of world and person. Of course, this change can subsequently be evaluated theologically.

54. "Religious Life in a Secularized World," 138.
55. Ibid., 137.

And though carefully acknowledging that historically the process of secularization developed within an antireligious atmosphere that frequently fostered an atheistic interpretation of the event, he insisted that this need not be its theological interpretation. Once more relying on Christian creation faith, he affirmed the created character of the world as autonomous and as that which is nondivine. In addition, he proposed a christological position similar to the one that Metz had articulated a few years earlier, construing the incarnation as God's acceptance of the secularity of the world, not its deification.[56] Thus, on the basis of the faith itself, Schillebeeckx now concluded that the sociological process of secularization is essentially a "consequence" of Christianity. Indeed, it is a confession of the faith: "The Christianisation of the world—an essential part of the Christian's task—therefore means making the world secular, making it human and, in light of faith, letting it be world."[57] Having repositioned secularization from primarily a theological question to primarily a sociological one, Schillebeeckx no longer needed to define the phenomenon negatively, as a merciful dispensation in which the church is given the opportunity to renew its theological vision. Though he did not develop his argument as extensively, he now had arrived at the position put forth by Metz. Secularization is not theologically fruitful merely as an oppositional or corrective force. It is in itself a theologically positive event, even if ambiguously so because of the religious interpretation that is only subsequently offered.[58]

In light of his now-positive account of the secularization process, Schillebeeckx can be seen embracing rather eagerly the progressive optimism of his surrounding culture. His writings from this period

---

56. Ibid., 139–40. Schillebeeckx had developed a similar position in *Christ the Sacrament*, 215–16.
57. "Religious Life in a Secularized World," 140–41. Schillebeeckx acknowledges Metz, as well as Friedrich Gogarten, for previously developing this position, on 235n47.
58. Ibid., 139.

portray a theologian plainly sharing in the confidence so characteristic of the time. In 1967, he would write, "Mankind as a whole is at this moment experiencing an almost irresistible desire to make this world a better place for all men to live in and to improve the welfare of all men so that everyone can thrive in a climate of solidarity, justice and love."[59] Secularization repositioned the relationship of humans to the world. Historical progress became a real possibility. It had freed men and women to work for a more humane world with a better future. Schillebeeckx was surprisingly convinced that this was precisely what was under way in history as the course of secularization unfolded.

At the same time, and his sanguinity notwithstanding, Schillebeeckx remained concerned that this process continued to be experienced by many Christians as a crisis of faith. Religion had become for them a "useless hypothesis" no longer helpful in making sense of the world.[60] But because he now approached this challenge with a sociocultural understanding of secularization, he recognized the need to reconsider the way in which he responded to the crisis: "Many people experience this new interpretation of the world and of man directly as a crisis in their religious life. We can say and are indeed bound to say that they should not, but, if we say this, we are misjudging the religious relevance of this event, which is not . . . the original datum, but a natural consequence of this datum."[61] In his earlier work, Schillebeeckx had framed secularization as a fundamentally religious phenomenon and in turn responded to the concerns surrounding the process with the traditional language of Christian creation faith. And as we have just noted, even as his thought developed, he continued to offer a protological and

59. Ibid., 135.
60. "Sorrow of the Experience," 81.
61. Ibid.

christological defense of secularization as a process inherently affirmed by the faith. But, while continuing to affirm the theological veracity of this position, he now recognized that such a response misjudged the significance of secularization. His apologetic tack needed to change if he was to speak meaningfully to this crisis.

It is here that we can identify an important transition in Schillebeeckx's methodological approach. We have seen that in his earlier writings, Schillebeeckx mined the Christian theological tradition in order to re-present the church's doctrinal teachings in a new context. In particular, the dogma of creation was his point of departure in responding to the concerns surrounding secularization. By the mid-1960s, however, he would conclude that the concrete historical context needed to become the starting point, not just the backdrop, for theological reflection.[62] The meaningfulness of conventional theological discourse and categories could no longer be presumed in the wake of secularization.

Consequently, Schillebeeckx's dogmatic starting point would give way during this period to an explicitly hermeneutical project that self-consciously recognized "that faith is never entirely dissociated from a historically conditioned view of man and the world."[63] That is to say, the way in which we speak and think of God is codetermined by our contemporary interpretive framework; there is a fundamental correlation between our images of the world and self and our image of God. Because humans have access to God only as mediated in and through the world, Schillebeeckx now argued, "I can only speak about the God of my salvation with the profane words, images and

---

62. See Hilkert, "Hermeneutics of History," 116.

63. "Is the Church Adrift?," 26. Schillebeeckx developed this position more fully in "Towards a Catholic Use of Hermeneutics," delivered as a lecture in 1967 and published in *God the Future of Man* (1–50) in 1968. Particularly in this essay, Schillebeeckx draws heavily from the work of Hans-George Gadamer. Schillebeeckx also would associate his newly articulated methodological approach with John XXIII's call for *aggiornamento* within the church in the opening speech of the Second Vatican Council. See "Is the Church Adrift?," 25–28.

concepts derived from my interpretation of myself and my world-view."[64] Thus, while believing that secularization is fundamentally a sociological event, Schillebeeckx nonetheless insisted that it has profound theological implications. Development in modern persons' understandings of the human and the world necessarily requires a change in persons' understanding of God. If secularization marks a shift in our understanding of the self and the world, then our understanding of God also will need to undergo change if it is to remain meaningful.

Secularization, it can therefore be said, undermines conventional ways of thinking and speaking about God.[65] It moves the historically contingent character of human understanding to the fore, affirming in a very practical manner that every image of the transcendent God is ultimately inadequate. Secularization fosters crisis; it creates an experience of dissonance as our approach to the world and self undergoes significant change while our understanding of God continues to be expressed in concepts from an earlier era. Schillebeeckx came to believe that presenting traditional theological concepts as a response to this crisis misjudged the significance of secularization. Such concepts have become alien and unintelligible in contemporary consciousness. Affirming the compatibility of secularization with the creation faith of Christianity does not assist Christians in making sense of their faith in a new cultural milieu. Such an approach, it could be said, provides a "correct" answer to the "wrong" question. While remaining aware that every concept of God will need to be superseded, theology must assist the church in finding a new way to speak and think of God with concepts and images meaningful in a new secular context.

64. "Sorrow of the Experience," 82.
65. "Secularization and Christian Belief in God," 61.

God the Ground of Hope

How, then, are Christians to speak and think of God in a secularized world? How can we speak meaningfully of God at a time when the divine has become a "useless hypothesis" no longer needed to make sense of the world? Has the "death of God" established an inescapable silence, as Schillebeeckx feared was suggested by the now widely forgotten but then popular American theological movement?[66] Is the God of Christian faith more than an unintelligible and irrelevant superstructure unrelated to modern life? Taking up these questions, Schillebeeckx deliberately eschewed any manner of "fideism" that seeks to isolate and extricate human experience from the Christian faith. In order to speak of God in a meaningful way, he argued, theologians must attend to the fundamental experiences of concrete human life. If such experiences are not carefully considered, our words and images for God register as only alien and incoherent. Such a concern was not new to Schillebeeckx's thought. As we have seen, in his earlier writings he identified the experience of radical contingency as an existential orientation toward self-transcendence that bespeaks the human person's fundamental dependence upon God for sustained existence. To speak of God as the ground of being, then, addressed the underlying basis and condition of possibility for this experience of the sheer gratuitousness of existence. What is new to Schillebeeckx's thought during this period, however, is his attention to the contemporary pervasiveness of the experience. "It has become clear to me," he wrote, "that even a so-called 'meaningful' answer to a question that cannot be justified remains, of course, meaningless."[67] In his effort to engage a secular culture, Schillebeeckx reconsidered the fundamental experience through which he sought

66. Ibid., 65.
67. Ibid., 73. Schillebeeckx would reflect on this problem at a later date in light of Wittgensteinian linguistic analysis in "Correlation between Human Question and Christian Answer," in *The*

to make God-talk intelligible. He would begin attending to the prevailing experience of trust in the future rather than in human contingency alone.[68] In his judgment, an experience of hope and confidence in the future characterized life in the wake of secularization. This phenomenon, he argued, provides an opportunity for meaningful God-talk.

Such God-talk would be made possible by demonstrating that this experience of hope itself inwardly refers to the God of Christian faith. What must be sought and named is that which grounds our existential trust in the meaningfulness of the future. Why are men and women working to build a new world, trusting that the future promises to be something other than a surd? What is the basis of their radical, hope-filled "yes" given to their fellow humans as they work for a better tomorrow? To what does this hope point? Schillebeeckx believed that these were the legitimate or "correct" questions to which the theologian now must attend. He acknowledged that such hope could be interpreted as no more than illusion, wishful thinking with no grounds in reality. Christians, however, see in this trust in the meaningfulness of the future the acceptance of history as "a promise of salvation which cannot be explained in the light of man's concrete being."[69] Indeed, interpreted through the lens of faith, this self-transcending hope for a better future offers a new "natural theology," according to Schillebeeckx; it presents no "proof" or "guarantee" of a meaningful future, but it bespeaks a God who is the ground of human hope.[70]

Understanding of Faith: Interpretation and Criticism, trans. N. D. Smith (New York: Seabury, 1974), 85–86, published in Dutch in *Tijdschrift voor Theologie* 10 (1970): 1–22.

68. As we shall see, Schillebeeckx would retrieve the apologetic value of experiences of contingency in his later work. See *Church: The Human Story of God,* trans. John Bowden (New York: Crossroad, 1994), 84–85.

69. "Secularization and Christian Belief in God," 75.

70. Ibid., 73.

By the mid-1960s, Schillebeeckx had begun to look for the language needed to speak of God as the ground of hope and the promise of a better future, language that meaningfully addresses and authenticates the secular experience. And, like Metz, he found in the language and concepts of the Old Testament important resources for this project. He offered a reflection on Exod. 3:14 in which the divine name is first translated as "I, God, am your salvation" before ultimately being rendered as "I am the eternal lover of man, for man I am the future, absolute future."[71] During this period, he also began to explore the imagery of "promise," and "God as Promise" to the world. God is the promise of salvation for humanity, and as such, our hope in a better tomorrow is grounded in God's very self. These images culled from Scripture, which Schillebeeckx regarded as normative for authentic Christian God-talk,[72] allowed him to move toward speaking of a God who not only is intelligible from the perspective of a secular world but also guarantees the meaningfulness of the secular experience. God is "man's future."[73] Such a God provides the underlying basis and condition of possibility for an authentic experience of hope in the future.

In turn, the Christian will recognize an at least implicit trust in the promise of God contained within the "irresistible desire" to create a better future that Schillebeeckx now so enthusiastically identified with the process of secularization. In Schillebeeckx's reading, the faith that humankind has a future carries an implicit trust that there is some ground or objective basis for that hope: "Not to lose faith in man in all his activities, despite all evil experiences, reveals itself, on closer analysis, as a latent, unconditional trust in God, a faith that human existence is a promise of salvation."[74] The hope-filled human "yes" to

---

71. "Sorrow of the Experience," 88–89.
72. "Towards a Catholic Use of Hermeneutics," 8. See also "Religious Life in a Secularized World," 144.
73. "Secularization and Christian Belief in God," 75.

the future that is characteristic of secular culture reveals, Schillebeeckx now argued, a profound trust in the unfulfilled yet absolute "yes" that is God's promise of salvation to humanity. Our "yes" to the future is an anonymous confession of God's "yes" to the world.[75]

Conversely, Schillebeeckx also claimed that to deny the meaningfulness and promise of the future reveals a fundamental refusal of God as humanity's future, even if it is never made explicitly. Such a refusal, however, received very little of Schillebeeckx's attention during this period. His embrace of secularization left little room for such a concern. It was a culture oriented toward the future and committed to a better world that had captured his imagination. His enthusiasm was evident when, in 1966, he wrote,

> Never before in history has God's presence in the world been so intimate and so tangibly real as now, in our own time, yet we do nothing but proclaim his absence everywhere, as though God were not really and most significantly present precisely at a time when impartial commitment to our fellow-men, service to others, is becoming a fundamental project in life. . . . God has consequently come infinitely more close to us now than he was in the past.[76]

Schillebeeckx's extraordinary optimism soon would be tested. And as we now will see, he certainly looked to do more than mark a simple identity between the eschatological hope of Christianity and the progressive optimism of modern society. His remarks, however, illustrate the significance of his changing understanding of God. By speaking of God as the promise of humanity's future, Schillebeeckx now saw Christian faith as affirming and authenticating the meaningfulness of the secular experience, and the life of faith manifesting itself as a new hope for humanity and the world.

74. Ibid., 77.
75. "Sorrow of the Experience," 94.
76. Ibid., 78.

The Relativization and Radicalization of Hope

It was here that the doctrine of eschatology moved to the very center of Schillebeeckx's theological project. He embraced secular culture's new hope for humanity and the world, allowing it to transform the way in which he thought and spoke of God. He allowed the contemporary experience of secularization to shed light on a God who, as the promise of salvation, is the ground of human hope. And by doing this, the future of this world became a profoundly theological concern for Schillebeeckx: "[T]heology has become eschatology in confrontation with the building of the 'city of man.'"[77] Subsequently, Schillebeeckx recognized that the critical question confronting theology as it meets this new situation concerns the relationship between human efforts to build up a new world and God's gratuitous promise of definitive salvation. How is our work to create a better future here on earth informed by and related to the Christian hope in an eschatological kingdom?

In an essay written in 1967 entitled "Man's Expectation for the Future on Earth," Schillebeeckx sought to situate this question within the context of the definitive and absolute character of God's eschatological promise. The eschaton for which Christians hope is not a self-made future but an incomprehensible mystery freely given by God. It is a transcendent and gratuitously given future that, according to Schillebeeckx, necessarily calls into question and *relativizes* all that is accomplished in history. At the same time, he also argued that it is precisely the absolute character of the eschaton that animates Christian efforts to build a better world. It *radicalizes* human action to seek an always-better future; it stimulates a hope that can never grow content with what men and women have achieved or even will achieve. This tensive relationship between the relativization

---

77. "Christian Faith," 82.

and radicalization of human efforts to build a new world need not confound Christian hope but can empower an active hope to participate in the coming of God's kingdom.

Schillebeeckx began his reflections on this tensive relationship by considering that singular human reality which uniquely evokes the eschatological question: death. He stressed that the reality of death illuminates the contingency of human life and confronts every human hope for the future. Death relativizes every effort to build a better world, because before it all progress necessarily ceases. It makes clear that no present or self-constructed future can be definitively identified with that for which Christian's hope, for that hope seeks a world in which death has lost its grip: "The ultimate world that is fully worthy of man can only be given to us as a gift of God beyond the frontiers of death, that is, in the act in which we ultimately confess our impotence to make this world truly human, in our explicit and effective recognition that the 'new world' cannot be the result of human planning."[78] In the experience of contingency, then, not only are humans unable to find in themselves the reason or cause of their existence, they are also unable to find in themselves the means for their own salvation. Death confirms the gratuitous character of salvation. It places an impassable gap between the human person's capabilities and the Christian's hope.

It is precisely the inadequacy of our work toward a definitively humane world, however, that reveals the truly radical character of the Christian life, according to Schillebeeckx. The Christian trusts that what is impossible for us is nonetheless made possible. An eschatologically charged commitment to a better world can never grow content, despite the impossibility of ultimate success on earth. The impotency of dull satisfaction is avoided, because that for which Christians hope continuously stays out in front, ceaselessly

78. Ibid., 84–85.

stimulating a desire to bring about something better. The trust in the promise of an absolute future sends men and women out again and again in radical commitment to the world, despite death's reminder that these efforts will always come up short. Christian hope is not a self-deceiving optimism, nor is it naive foolishness. Christian hope recognizes the inherent and insurmountable limitations of human effort. And it is precisely in the face of this wide-eyed assessment of the human situation that Christian eschatological faith cultivates a radical "hope against hope," a daring wager that a love for this world is not held in vain.

Because of the incomprehensible mystery of the future in which Christians hope, what is achieved in this world can never be identified with eschatological fulfillment. At the same time, Christian faith in this ultimate end stimulates a radical love committed to renewing this world. Schillebeeckx went on to argue in "Man's Expectation for the Future on Earth" that it is precisely through this radical, incomprehensible love "that the very essence of the kingdom of God breaks through into our world."[79] Through an active hope in God's eschatological promise, "the eschaton itself is already shaping history."[80] Again, the divine–human relationship established in creation, and now framed temporally, allows for the human person to enter into a partnership with God through which our free and graced ordering of the world communicates and embodies God's gratuitous love. Commitment to building a world of love, justice, and peace becomes a revelation of what the final future will be. This breakthrough of the kingdom surely remains vague, for this world is not the kingdom itself. But through an active commitment to building a better world, God's promise begins to be realized within history. The God of the future, the God who is to come, makes

---

79. Ibid., 89.
80. "Church, Magisterium, and Politics," in *God the Future of Man,* 145.

meaningful all that death appears to make meaningless: "Only the form of this present world passes, nothing of what has been achieved in the world by man's radical love."[81] What is achieved in the world, and those who achieve it, mediates a kingdom freely given by God.

Theological Consequences of Rethinking Secularization

Developments in Schillebeeckx's Understanding of History and Hope

It is at this point in our study that we can identify important developments in Schillebeeckx's writings from the late 1950s considered earlier in this chapter. In 1958's "The Intellectual's Responsibility for the Future," Schillebeeckx responded to Merleau-Ponty's concern that Christian eschatological hope fosters an indifference to the things of this world. He argued that it was precisely the eschatological hope of Christian faith that allows human expectation for the future to become a responsibility for the future, bringing the world and history to share in the eschaton and securing their ultimate value and deepest dimension. There is a clear relationship between this argument and the writings presently under consideration. In both periods, Schillebeeckx was eager to reconcile the Christian's understanding of history and the Christian's social activity. Having now placed eschatology at the center of his theological project, however, he notably changed his understanding of the salvific character of history.

In Schillebeeckx's earlier thought, it was only prior to the incarnation that history was oriented toward a "God who *was* to come."[82] Following the incarnation, the salvific character of history

---

81. "Christian Faith," 89.
82. "Supernaturalism," 167 (emphasis mine).

was established. In his later work, he again argued that the salvific character of history was established in the incarnation, but he now would speak of it as being established in the mode of promise: "Christ is the completed promise, but he is still the *promise* to make all things new."[83] As such, history continues to be oriented toward "the God who *is* to come, who goes ahead of us towards a future."[84] In making this modification, Schillebeeckx altered more than the way in which he spoke of God. He was implicitly modifying his theological understanding of history, though this would fully come to light only in the succeeding years. Secularization had pushed the historically contingent character of theology to the fore. A dogmatic and nonhistorical determination of history as already salvific could no longer be proclaimed meaningfully in a culture profoundly oriented toward a future-in-the-making. More fundamentally, however, secularization had fostered an increased awareness of human temporality and the contingencies of history itself. Consequently, Schillebeeckx now began speaking of eschatological history as oriented toward a promised future still to come, rather than as "closed" and at its "end." A heightened emphasis was landing on the indeterminate openness of history. The future remains on the way, and although Christians believe that its meaningfulness has been established in Jesus, this meaning exists in the mode of promise and remains yet a hope.[85] Christians, it could therefore be said, are those who hope in a future that can and will be made meaningful. It was this emerging understanding of history that came to distinguish Schillebeeckx's characterization of Christian hope.

With this development in his understanding of the eschatological character of history, Schillebeeckx was better situated to articulate the

---

83. "Sorrow of the Experience," 93.
84. "Secularization and Christian Belief in God," 81 (emphasis mine).
85. Ibid.

unique nature of a hope founded upon the God who is humanity's future. In 1967's "Christian Faith and Man's Expectation for the Future on Earth," Schillebeeckx again responded to Merleau-Ponty's critique, but this time with an even more aggressive defense of the Christian's commitment to the world.[86] A "responsibility" for the future no longer adequately characterized Schillebeeckx's understanding of Christian hope. Indeed, he now argued, if only tentatively, that eschatological hope promoted a fundamentally constructive and creative practice. With Metz, he no longer envisioned the future for which Christians hope as being already in existence, merely concealed and out of sight for the time being. Rather than participating responsibly in a meaningful history construed as already realized, and doing so precisely *because* it is construed as already realized, an eschatological hope actively trusts in a promise that history can and will be made meaningful. It looks to build a future that is only now coming into existence within history. Christian hope is a radical, love-filled commitment to tomorrow that never grows content, even in the face of death itself. It is a hope directed toward a future that stays just out of reach, ceaselessly stimulating a desire to make true in history that for which it longs. It is an inexplicable, relentless hope that, according to Schillebeeckx, constructively mediates in history the very essence of eschatological salvation.

This is more than a rhetorical development. It was here that the practical character of Christian faith began to take a privileged place in Schillebeeckx's thought. The persuasive force of his earlier response to Christianity's secular critics focused on presenting a correct understanding of the Christian faith. Properly understood doctrines of creation, Christ, and history allowed for responsible

---

86. "Christian Faith," 85.

participation in the world. Orthodoxy, right thinking, bore the weight of his apologetic defense against those who accused Christians of abandoning the world for the supernatural and history for the suprahistorical. As we have seen, Schillebeeckx's future-oriented reinterpretation of Christianity itself was offered as an apologetic response to such misunderstandings of the faith. In these later writings from the mid-1960s, however, he can also be seen asking, though cautiously, an alternative line of questions: Can an interpretation, even one attentive to the concrete historical context and existential situation of the interpreter and interlocutor, offer a meaningful defense of eschatological faith? If the eschatological structure of faith imposes on the Christian the task of reaching toward and building the future, is a new interpretation an adequate proclamation?[87]

In response, Schillebeeckx took his first steps toward privileging what he referred to as "orthopraxis," that is, Christian hope properly performed or practiced, as the best defense of the Christian's eschatological faith.[88] Christians, he argued, are not merely to understand or interpret the future differently from others. The future cannot be elucidated theoretically. Thus, through a radical trust in God's promise, Christians must transform the world, actively constructing God's eschatological kingdom: "The future is not, of course, to be interpreted, but it certainly has to be realized and, what is more, it should bring something new into being."[89] First and foremost, then, an eschatological hope must be an *active* hope:

---

87. "Towards a Catholic Use of Hermeneutics," 35–38.

88. Ibid., 38. See also "Is the Church Adrift?," 42. Erik Borgman notes that Schillebeeckx's use of this term follows upon Metz's writings in "Van cultuurtheologie naar theologie als onderdeel van de cultuur," *Tijdschrift voor Theologie* 34 (1994), 350.

89. "Towards a Catholic Use of Hermeneutics," 36. As with Metz, during this period Schillebeeckx frequently turned to language reminiscent of Marx's eleventh thesis against Feuerbach to describe the practical character of Christian theology. For additional examples, see "Sorrow of the Experience," 93–94, and "Christian Faith," 88.

"Christian hope in God, who is man's future, is not a theory, but an active hope which only becomes a reality in man's working for a better future on earth."[90] Schillebeeckx would now warn that hope confessed at the level of theory alone could function as nothing more than an extrinsic and foreign creed unrelated to human reality. But confessed as an active hope, it becomes a meaningful, though obscure, manifestation of God's promised future. An active hope constructively fashions a future that we have been promised is on the way but is not yet here. Such a hope offers a practical defense of eschatological faith by making God's promise true in history. Our hope in action becomes the proving ground for that in which we hope, making credible our hope in the eschaton by making manifest the eschaton in history.

An Emerging Appreciation for the Critical Character of Eschatology

As we have seen, in his earliest writings, Schillebeeckx was already comfortable with speaking of the world and history as mediating and participating in eschatological salvation. Salvation is established in Christ as a historical event that emerges in and through the created world. His eschatological reflections were directed toward neither a detemporalized and disembodied otherworld nor a private and internal existential state. Moreover, whereas Metz intentionally engaged in critiques of these explicitly theological positions, Schillebeeckx did so only rarely during this period.[91] Thus, as we have seen, when pressing for the sociopolitical dimension of a militant hope, Metz argued his position by speaking to the social character of

90. "Christian Faith," 86.
91. See "Supernaturalism," 163–66, as well as Borgman's survey of Schillebeeckx's lectures at the Dominican House in Louvain from the 1940s and 1950s, in *Edward Schillebeeckx*, 241–52.

the biblical promise of salvation. The challenge at hand was plainly theological, and he responded accordingly. It was not as critical for Schillebeeckx to develop a similar response as he too began to reflect on the sociopolitical scope and significance of Christian hope. His interlocutors had posed different challenges,[92] and his theological project was already well positioned to account for the sociohistorical dimension of human salvation.[93]

Nevertheless, Schillebeeckx did provide an interesting additional observation regarding the theological effort to attend more carefully to this dimension of salvation. It was the process of secularization, he noted, that had created an awareness of the contingent character of the social order. Only in the wake of secularization could social and economic structures be seen as human constructs rather than divinely established realities. It was this process, therefore, that would foster a more expansive vision of the scope in which an active eschatological hope could potentially engage the world. The Christian tradition had shown great concern for charity in the private sphere of interpersonal encounter, and an active hope would surely seek the transformation

92. Metz, for example, appeared to be concerned especially with intra-ecclesial projects, such as Bultmann's "demythologization" and the "transcendentalism" of his teacher Rahner. Though Schillebeeckx also criticized positions taken by Bultmann and other theologians, he seemed to be interested primarily in "secular" challenges coming from outside the church, such as the critique presented by Merleau-Ponty. This difference can be explained, in part, by the dominant strains of Enlightenment thought that the two theologians were exposed to during their studies. Although the German Enlightenment consistently maintained an interest, though critical, in issues of religion and Christian theology, the French Enlightenment presented a much more hostile opposition to questions of religion.

93. This may be explained in part by Schillebeeckx's early appropriation of a phenomenological Thomism in which an implicit intuition of absolute reality, theologically framed as the unthematized (nonconceptual) and direct element of human knowledge of God, is located in the objective dynamism of that which is known rather than the subjective dynamism of the human spirit as knower. That is to say, his early work was methodologically less vulnerable to disembodied and privatized understandings of God's activity in the world. Though modified as he engaged modern hermeneutics, Schillebeeckx's position developed in dialogue with that of his philosophical mentor, Dominicus De Petter, whereas the latter position is related to the work of Joseph Maréchal, whose transcendental Thomism influenced both Rahner and the early Metz. See Thompson, *Language of Dissent*, 13–22.

of damaged or harmful relationships. But because the social order could now be seen as self-constructed rather than eternally established, Schillebeeckx claimed that Christians now should recognize their role in transforming the sociopolitical sphere as well.[94] Recognizing that systematic change at the social and economic level is possible extends the Christian's unquenchable eschatological thirst for a more just world into the political sphere.

Schillebeeckx was careful, however, to draw the reader's attention once again to the relativizing function of eschatological hope. And it is here that we begin to see his gradually emerging appreciation for its critical promise. He cautioned that the ineffable character of the eschaton provides no direct program for sociopolitical action. It is, rather, "socially and politically relevant in an indirect way, namely, in a 'utopian' sense."[95] He identified Christian hope in the eschaton as a utopian horizon, that is, as a standard by which the established situation can be evaluated. And because of the definitive and inexhaustible character of this horizon, this hope necessarily functions as a permanent criticism of every attempt to absolutize a particular moment or project within history. An eschatological hope will resist every effort to identify a particular political order or social structure with the future for which Christians hope. "Historically we can never say *this* is the promised future," Schillebeeckx warned.[96] Metz, of course, had also begun to investigate and employ this critical function of Christian hope, and Schillebeeckx remarked on the similarities between their thought.[97] Inspired in part by this work, Schillebeeckx likewise began to leverage the proposition that a hope

94. "Church, Magisterium, and Politics," 155.
95. Ibid., 157.
96. Ibid. (original emphasis).
97. Ibid., 159. Schillebeeckx cites Metz's essay "The Church and the World," delivered at the St. Xavier Symposium they both attended in 1966, in *The Word in History*, ed. Patrick Burke (New York: Sheed & Ward, 1966), 69–85.

directed toward God's promise will inherently oppose every effort to identify the current order with God's eschatological order, even as that hope sends us out in the present to create a more humane society.

Schillebeeckx examined this indirect, critical relationship between the eschatological hope of Christianity and the political order in a 1967 article entitled "Church, Magisterium, and Politics." It was in the same article that he first began to explore the theological significance of what he referred to as "contrast-experiences." We will consider the central place contrast experiences hold in Schillebeeckx's maturing thought in the next two chapters. For our purposes here, this nascent concept is helpful in that it further illustrates his emerging appreciation for the critical character of eschatological hope. A contrast experience occurs when a disordered or unjust situation is experienced with resistance, with a protesting "no" that this situation cannot continue. The critical force of this experience is realized, according to Schillebeeckx, in that the disordered situation is encountered temporally against a utopian horizon.[98] A "no" in the face of injustice or suffering indirectly discloses an eschatological hope that is the basis of the opposition. As we have seen, it was only one year earlier, in 1966, when seeking to secure the meaningfulness of Christian faith in a secular culture, that Schillebeeckx had spoken of the human person's "yes" to the future as disclosing the eschatological horizon that is God's "yes" to humanity.[99] In both articles, he was concerned with establishing a relationship between an active hope in the world and an eschatological hope in God's promise, between the process of secularization and the Christian faith. Although both formulations were able to secure such a relationship, it was the negative formulation of the relationship as a contrast experience that simultaneously accounted for the

98. "Church, Magisterium, and Politics," 159.
99. "Sorrow of the Experience," 94.

nonidentity between the present and the promised future. It is in the negative formulation that we see Schillebeeckx begin to rediscover the potential for Christian eschatology to do more than affirm modern culture.

Conclusion

As with Metz, this heightened awareness of the critical character of eschatological hope in Schillebeeckx's writing in the mid-1960s initiated what would be a gradual shift in his posture toward the course of late modernity. This shift, however, was only beginning and was not yet his foremost concern. His primary concern remained engaging the process of secularization. By placing eschatology at the center of the theological project, Schillebeeckx had identified a way in which not only to proclaim the Christian faith in a meaningful manner from a new context but also to affirm the future-oriented hope characteristic of secular culture as disclosing an eschatological horizon. Christians need not experience secularization as a crisis of faith, for it is a process that illumines God as humanity's future. It was by doing this, however, that he also located within the category of eschatology a resource to move beyond engaging and affirming secularization. He found that the Christian faith's affirmation of a secular culture is necessarily relative. Within eschatological hope resides an inherent impulse that will prophetically challenge every effort to identify the present order with that for which Christians hope. The promise established in Christ of a definitively meaningful future is precisely that, a promise; it has not yet been fully realized in history. As we will now see, Schillebeeckx's attention to this prophetic function of eschatological hope would only continue to develop as he began to uncover more fully an underside to the modern world, an underside that optimism and progress had forgotten.

3

Schillebeeckx Contends with a History Marked by Suffering

Contrast Experiences and a Search for Eschatological Hope's Positive Orientation

In the preceding two chapters, we examined the turn to eschatology in the writings of Metz and Schillebeeckx as they attempted to respond to the cultural pressures faced by the European church in the 1960s. Initially, their distinctly modern approaches to eschatology allowed both theologians to champion a practical eschatology that operated rather comfortably within the wider cultural context. As we observed, however, it was not long before both theologians grew increasingly sensitive to the subsequent overidentification of the hope of Christianity with the hope of modern culture. This sensitivity to the nonidentity of eschatological and societal hope only would increase as their thought matured and, as we now will see, would foster significant developments in their eschatological projects.

The first section of this chapter underscores the emerging contours of these developments in Schillebeeckx's later eschatology as they are woven into the epilogue of *God the Future of Man*, a text from 1968 that represents an important transition in his eschatological writings.[1] After noting Schillebeeckx's reaffirmation of the correlation between the practical character of Christian hope and the new concept of God that he believed more adequately resonates with the experiences of modern men and women, we will identify two important developments in his project related to his early engagement with the writings of Frankfurt theorists. First, it was in this text that Schillebeeckx returned to the concept of contrast experiences and reflected more fully on the critical negativity and positive practical character of the Christian eschatological hope. Second, it was here that he began to reevaluate the cultural analysis that had initiated his turn to eschatology, now warning that the very freedom that seemed to have been gained with the rise of secularization risked disappearing in its aftermath. As we shall see, these developments allowed Schillebeeckx to extend his earlier intuitions examined at the end of chapter 2 and to locate in eschatology a privileged vantage point from which to resist the dangerous consequences of modernity's distorted ambitions.

The next section of the chapter traces Schillebeeckx's more sustained engagement with critical theory as developed by Jürgen Habermas. Schillebeeckx's move beyond hermeneutics to critical theory was prompted by criticism of his earlier theology of secularization and is reflected in the shift in his eschatological

---

1. Many interpreters of Schillebeeckx have identified an important methodological transition in his "The New Image of God, Secularization, and Man's Future on Earth," the epilogue to *God the Future of Man*, trans. N. D. Smith (New York: Sheed & Ward, 1968), 169–203. For examples, see William Hill, "Schillebeeckx's New Look at Secularity: A Note," *Thomist* 33 (1969): 162–70; and Philip Kennedy, "Continuity Underlying Discontinuity: Schillebeeckx's Philosophical Background," *New Blackfriars* 70 (1989): 271.

writings from his earlier language of the need for an "active hope" to his later call for critical Christian praxis. Although Schillebeeckx's later writings on hermeneutics and history were significantly influenced by the writings of the first and second generations of critical theorists, in his view their insights remained inadequate for the task of articulating an adequate hope that could prompt action on behalf of human flourishing. Schillebeeckx remained convinced that Christianity's contribution to the work of emancipation required a positive orientation that was to be found in the life, death, and resurrection of Jesus. For that reason, the final section of this chapter will turn to Schillebeeckx's massive christological project, highlighting his argument that the story of the eschatological prophet provides the concrete contours of Christian hope and praxis.

Developments in Schillebeeckx's Practical Eschatology

The New Understanding of God and the Practical Character of Christian Hope

Schillebeeckx returned to Nijmegen at the end of 1967 after delivering a series of lectures in the United States concerning the intersection of Christian faith and the culture of secularization. His travels through America only confirmed for him the important role secularization was playing in reframing the Christian life and the urgent need for an effective theological response. He published the lectures from this trip in an English-language collection entitled *God the Future of Man*, which included many of the essays considered in chapter 2. We observed in these and his other essays written at that time that the future-oriented hope characteristic of modern culture nourished his appreciation for the eschatological character of Christian faith. It transformed the way he thought and talked of God. He assured Christians who had experienced the process of secularization as a crisis of faith that the hope associated with this sociocultural phenomenon was, in fact, a latent expression of eschatological faith. Indeed, that faith affirms and authenticates the meaningfulness of the secular experience.

On the one hand, then, Schillebeeckx was persuaded to locate eschatology at the center of his theological project after listening to the dominant experience of a people committed to the primacy of the future in both Europe and North America. On the other hand, we have seen that it was precisely by doing this that he also came to recognize, if only tentatively, that within Christian eschatology dwells an inherent reserve that resists an overidentification of eschatological hope with the confident and optimistic hope of modern Western culture. That is to say, a definitively meaningful future has been promised but is not yet fully realized in history. We observed early signs of this growing awareness at the end of chapter 2, even though it appears that Schillebeeckx's foremost concern remained engaging and affirming the course of secularization from an apologetic perspective. Turning now to an important article written in 1968 as an epilogue for *God the Future of Man*, we will see that Schillebeeckx would need to navigate a shifting situation in which he reaffirmed positions he developed in response to the pastoral crisis brought about by secularization at the same time that his more critical stance toward the process was intensifying as he engaged in new conversations and further reexamined the implications of an eschatological faith.

In the epilogue "The New Image of God, Secularization, and Man's Future on Earth," Schillebeeckx began by reaffirming the theological value of the "new concept of God" emerging from contemporary culture. In the preceding years, he had searched for a way to speak meaningfully of God in a modern context. The very title of this collection of articles illustrates that project. In the epilogue to the book, however, he would further develop this new concept of God by speaking of a shift in the contemporary Christian's understanding of divine transcendence, an idea already introduced by Metz. Transcendence emerged in modernity, Schillebeeckx now argued, as a temporal category as well as an ontological category as it acquired an affinity with the indeterminateness of history. The radical transcendence of God was gradually being recognized as a claim about the "wholly New" rather than an exclusively static claim about God's ontological distinctiveness as the "wholly Other." Consequently, a new image of God as the promise of salvation and the ground of hope was coming to the fore, and it was this image, Schillebeeckx once again insisted, that would allow for meaningful God-talk in the wake of secularization.

Schillebeeckx also went on to reaffirm that it was this new eschatological image of God that allowed for "the surprising rediscovery of the fact that the God of the promise again gives us the task of setting out towards the promised land, a land that we ourselves, trusting in the promise, must reclaim and cultivate, as Israel did in the past."[2] It was precisely the new concept of God that informed the growing commitment by Christians to join with their neighbors in building a better future. Faith in God who is the promise of the future is the spring from which arises a hope that longs to prove itself true within history. Christian hope does not, therefore, function on the level of theory alone; it "has to make this believed promise come true in history and has to do this precisely by making this history new."[3] A temporally charged hope, a hope in the divine promise of eschatological fulfillment, will be an active hope capable of rewriting human history as a history of salvation.

2. "New Image of God," 181–82.
3. Ibid., 183.

Here again, we see Schillebeeckx emphasize the practical character of Christian hope. It is likely that by this time, he already had started reading the writings of Jürgen Habermas, though Habermas is not yet cited.[4] It was still three years before Schillebeeckx would expressly take up Habermas's ideas in a number of important articles that will be considered later in this chapter. But already, Schillebeeckx appeared more nuanced when speaking of eschatological hope as an active hope. In 1967, he had written, "Christian hope in God, who is man's future, is not a theory, but an active hope."[5] In 1968, however, he warned against an eschatological understanding of history that falls victim to the "fatal division" between theoretical and practical reason.[6] Though now convinced that the practical character of eschatological hope is more than an ethical application or responsibility that follows from a particular theoretical understanding of history, Schillebeeckx was also concerned with the reduction of eschatological hope to unreflective activity. An eschatological understanding of history is itself a practical understanding; it is a performative profession of hope founded upon a divine promise that makes true in history that for which it hopes.

This more judicious approach to speaking of practical hope notwithstanding, thus far in this article, Schillebeeckx primarily reaffirmed positions that he had already developed in the earlier articles of *God the Future of Man*. He once again argued that the future-consciousness of secular culture renewed the eschatological center of theology, fostering a new image of God and enjoining

---

4. In Ted Schoof's review of Schillebeeckx's years of teaching at Nijmegen, Schoof notes that Schillebeeckx lectured on proponents of "ideology critique" in his classroom in 1968, but Schoof does not mention Habermas by name. Schoof does confirm that by 1969, Schillebeeckx had begun lecturing on Habermas in preparation for the two articles that he published in 1971. See Ted Schoof, "Edward Schillebeeckx: Twenty-Five Years in Nijmegen," *Theology Digest* (Winter 1990): 326–28.

5. "Christian Faith and Man's Expectation for the Future on Earth," in *The Mission of the Church*, trans. N. D. Smith (New York: Seabury, 1973), 86.

6. "New Image of God," 185.

Christians to participate in the modern project of building a new world. As we have seen, he came to these positions looking for a suitable way to speak of God in his new, secular context. This search was at the heart of the theological enterprise as Schillebeeckx understood it. Such a search, however, would also bring to the surface pressing hermeneutical questions that needed to be addressed. Did Schillebeeckx risk identifying the Christian faith with the culture he sought to engage? Did he compromise that which is uniquely Christian in exchange for contemporary significance?[7]

Developments in a Practical-Critical Eschatology

Schillebeeckx recognized that his eschatological understanding of God and Christian hope raised such concerns. He reminded the reader that this new concept of God was profoundly biblical. The modern historical context merely provided the opportunity to rediscover the scriptural image of God as "our future," especially in the books of the Old Testament.[8] He also reiterated that his intent was not the identification of faith and culture but the integration of Christian faith with Christian efforts to humanize a broken world. He sought to reenvision the way Christians understand God in order to "prevent anyone who is wholeheartedly taking part in the new culture from letting faith remain an attitude that cannot be realized, something that alienates him from the world because it forces him

---

7. William Portier suggests this concern in "Edward Schillebeeckx as Critical Theorist: The Impact of Neo-Marxist Social Thought on His Recent Theology," *Thomist* 48 (1984): 353. Portier made a similar suggestion in "Interpretation and Method," in *The Praxis of the Reign of God*, ed. Mary Catherine Hilkert and Robert J. Schreiter, 2nd ed. (New York: Fordham University Press, 2002), 30. In the earlier essay, he described this period of Schillebeeckx's writing as a "prolonged flirtation with the theology of secularization and the over-identification with modern Western culture it implied." Interestingly, in the later essay, he described this period as a "brief flirtation," a modification that revealed, presumably self-consciously, the importance of historical perspective when evaluating the contours of an author's career.
8. "New Image of God," 188.

to live in two worlds, the world of science and technology . . . and a world of fantasy which he has to enter in his faith."[9] The weight of the objection to Schillebeeckx's project, however, lay precisely in the manner in which this integration of Christian faith and social activity occurred. Did he collapse Christian hope into the future-oriented efforts of secular culture? Is there a distinctively Christian contribution to humanity's active search for a better future? In what way does the eschatological structure of Christian faith define the character of Christian hope? These questions would take center stage in the epilogue.

The Influence of Adorno:
Negative Contrast Experience

It is here, and with an eye to these questions, that we return to the idea of a contrast experience examined at the end of chapter 2. Kathleen McManus has written that Schillebeeckx himself did not know the origins of this concept.[10] Others frequently note the influence of figures as diverse as Theodor Adorno and Paul Ricoeur in his writing on the concept.[11] Although it is helpful to keep these ambiguous origins in mind, it is still important to examine the development of this idea in Schillebeeckx's thought in order to identify more exactly his understanding of a distinctively eschatological hope. As we have seen, the idea of a contrast experience first appeared in his writing in 1967. At that time, he referenced remarks made by Joseph Cardinal Cardijn, crediting him

---

9. Ibid., 187.
10. Kathleen Anne McManus, citing a personal interview, in *Unbroken Communion: The Place of Meaning and Suffering in the Theology of Edward Schillebeeckx* (Lanham, MD: Rowman & Littlefield, 2003), 26.
11. Vince Miller has even suggested the influence of Karl Barth, though he did not explore the claim further, in "Tradition and Experience in Edward Schillebeeckx's Theology of Revelation" (PhD diss., University of Notre Dame, 1997), 193.

with coining the expression.[12] Cardijn had described his commitment
to the social problems of his day as a response that emerged from
his experience of fellow workers' resenting his privileged access to
education. His opportunity stood in contrast with, and thus shed
light upon, the injustice that was their lack of opportunity. In
Schillebeeckx's telling, the inequity of the situation promoted a
pretheoretical experience of ethical conscientiousness. It engendered
a response of protest that preceded any explicitly formulated ethical
principle, fostering both the workers' resentment and Cardijn's social
commitment. Schillebeeckx did not comment extensively on the
influence of Cardijn's remarks in this essay or anywhere else. He did,
however, take Cardijn's rather intuitive observation and proceed to
situate experiences of contrast within the context of Christianity's
eschatological hope. He claimed that the pretheoretical critical force
of a contrast experience is realized because the disordered situation
is encountered against an eschatological horizon. A protesting "no"
in the face of injustice and suffering indirectly discloses an
eschatological hope that is the basis of the opposition.

In 1968's epilogue, Schillebeeckx returned to the topic, identifying
the explicit protest or the "critical negativity" of a contrast experience
as the specifically Christian contribution that Christians bring to their
activity in the world. What he intended by this claim is what needs to
be examined. The expression "critical negativity" is borrowed from
the Frankfurt theorist Theodor Adorno.[13] Like his contemporary
Ernst Bloch, Adorno was concerned by the failure of Marxist theory

---

12. Joseph Cardijn was the Flemish founder of Young Christian Workers, a youth organization
associated with Catholic Action. Prominent throughout Europe during the nineteenth and
the first half of the twentieth centuries, the Catholic Action movement sought to extend the
church's influence within society by integrating Catholic laity into the work of the hierarchy.
Although following the Second Vatican Council a new emphasis was placed on the baptismal
character of the lay vocation in the world, this movement anticipated the interest in extending
the Christian's participation in social and political life evident in Schillebeeckx's work.

13. Theodor W. Adorno, *Negative Dialectics*, trans. E. B. Ashton (New York: Continuum, 1973).
For an introduction to Adorno's negative dialectics, see Susan Buck-Morss, *The Origin of*

to effect the social transformation it had once promised. He recognized that Marx's project could not account for the widespread resignation that continued to exist in the face of ongoing economic and political repression. The lack of resistance to the rise of National Socialism in his native Germany openly exposed the horror of an ethical paralysis that had enveloped Western society. In search of the cause of such acquiescence, Adorno would eventually stray far from the economic analysis and historical materialism of Marx. Along with others associated with the "Frankfurt school," he came to believe that the source of this resignation was a creeping epistemological positivism that uncritically identified the reasonable with present reality. Social analysis had been confused with scientific analysis, consequently suppressing the contingent character of social existence and establishing the repressive paralysis of an entrenched and thus concealed cultural hegemony.[14] Adorno feared, again like Bloch, that traditional theories, particularly metaphysical theories, could not provide the critical leverage needed to overcome the stagnation of such hegemonic thinking.[15] He developed his negative dialectics in response.

Schillebeeckx would rely heavily on this work by Adorno to develop further his understanding of the critical function of a contrast experience in the epilogue.[16] He turned to the German's principle of nonidentity or negative dialectics to help articulate a framework that could account for and even privilege the epistemological value of

Negative Dialectics: Theodor W. Adorno, Walter Benjamin, and the Frankfurt Institute (New York: Free Press, 1977).

14. A heightened recognition of the contingent character of history was, of course, precisely the advance Schillebeeckx believed was gained through the process of secularization.

15. Adorno develops his criticism of "metaphysics" in "The Actuality of Philosophy," *Telos* 31 (Spring 1977): 120–33.

16. For discussions of Adorno's influence on Schillebeeckx, see Elizabeth Tillar, "The Influence of Social Critical Theory on Edward Schillebeeckx's Theology of Suffering for Others," *Heythrop Journal* 42 (2001): 148–72; and William Portier, "Schillebeeckx' Dialogue with Critical Theory," *Ecumenist,* January–February 1983, 20–27.

such an experience. Designed to prevent the closed and authoritarian claims on meaning offered by positivist theories, Adorno's negative dialectics deliberately attends to the essential inequality of concepts and objects.[17] He argued that the epistemological presumption for equality or identity of concept and object found in traditional theories inevitably represses particularity, suppressing that which is unique in exchange for the circumscribable. Identity-thought inscribes conformity, on the one hand, by privileging either the knowing subject or the known object in such a way that one overwhelms and dominates the other. An epistemological principle of nonidentity, on the other hand, seeks to take advantage of the inequality of concept and object in order to perceive dialectically the particularities and surplus meaning that exist in the gap between the two. Adorno's negative dialectics does this not with a Hegelian concern to then bring about a new and totalizing conceptual synthesis but in order to guard against the impression that the totality of an object has been grasped, a comprehension that would leave nothing in remainder and unmastered.

Adorno's investigation of the concept and social reality of human freedom illustrates particularly well the critical value of the principle of nonidentity. He observed that the judgment that persons within a society are free requires an operative concept of freedom. Such a concept is the standard by which the judgment can be made. But the content of that concept, Adorno carefully noted, is never actually operative in the world; it is never wholly realized. The concept of

17. Miller ("Tradition and Experience," 193) has suggested that Schillebeeckx's perspectivalist epistemology, in which an implicit, nonconceptual knowledge of the whole of reality is presumed given in the objective dynamism of every act of knowing, shared an affinity with the negative dialectics he encountered in Adorno. Indeed, Schillebeeckx's earliest reference to critical negativity cited not Adorno's negative dialectics but his own articles on the nonconceptual element of knowledge. See "The Church as the Sacrament of Dialogue," in *God the Future of Man*, 125. In this chapter, we will be examining Schillebeeckx's attempt to distance himself from both his earlier position and Adorno's as this relates to his developing understanding of eschatology.

freedom "feeds on the idea of a condition in which individuals would have qualities not to be ascribed to anyone here and now."[18] There is a surplus of meaning in the concept that cannot be accounted for by means of any currently realized freedom. It is in confrontation with the present reality of deficient freedom, in confrontation with repression and injustice, that this surplus of meaning subsequently fashions a negative knowledge of an as yet unrealized freedom. This negation of the concept of freedom sheds light on impediments to freedom in the present order while simultaneously creating a dialectical awareness of excess meaning in the concept itself. Negative dialectics thus resists collapsing or identifying the possibilities of human freedom with the limited meaning ascribed to it in the present; it affirms that freedom cannot be conceived adequately under current conditions. The potentiality of human freedom is therefore protected from being prematurely delimited or narrowly applied according to inadequate preconceptions. The possibility of an always-greater freedom is in turn held open.

Schillebeeckx's description of contrast experiences in this article clearly reveals the influence of Adorno's negative dialectics. A protesting "no" in the face of injustice and suffering, Schillebeeckx argued, relies upon a concept of what is "humanly desirable."[19] The content of that concept, that which is humanly desirable, cannot be formulated positively under present conditions. To do so would be to circumscribe prematurely the scope of what is objectively desirable. It can, nevertheless, be known negatively through experiences of contrast: "In the long run, situations which are unworthy of man give

---

18. Adorno, *Negative Dialectics*, 150.
19. Here, Schillebeeckx draws on an expression used by Paul Ricoeur. See "New Image of God," 191. Schillebeeckx credited Ricoeur with indirectly influencing his use of critical negativity, making reference to the article "Tâches de l'éducator politique," *Esprit* 33 (1965): 78–93 (translated as "The Tasks of the Political Educator Today," *Philosophy Today* 17 [1973]: 142–52). James Wiseman surveys Ricoeur's influence upon Schillebeeckx with regard to this issue in "Schillebeeckx and the Ecclesial Function of Critical Negativity," *Thomist* 34 (1971): 207–46.

rise to explicit protest, not in the name of a concept of what would here and now have been worthy of man which is already positively defined, but in the name of human values still being sought, and revealed in a negative manner in the contrast-experiences of situations unworthy of man."[20] A negative knowledge of what is humanly desirable is disclosed in confrontation with present realities that are undesirable. The Christian has "as little positive idea" as the non-Christian of what is humanly desirable.[21] It is by protesting against inhumane situations currently in existence that both the Christian and the non-Christian anticipate dialectically an as yet unrealized reality more humane than the present. It is only the Christian, however, who will understand this negatively known unrealized reality within the context of eschatological faith.

The Positive Contribution of Christian Hope

Schillebeeckx's debt to Adorno's negative dialectics is unmistakable. Adorno provided an epistemological framework that could account for the value and critical function of the indirect and negative knowledge that Schillebeeckx came to associate with experiences of contrast. Both men affirmed that in spite of our inability to conceptualize in the present what human life should be, it is nonetheless possible to know what it should not be. It was most likely because of the visibility of this affinity, however, that starting in this article Schillebeeckx repeatedly drew his reader's attention to an important divergence in his and Adorno's thought. He warned that Adorno's commitment to negative dialectics was restricted to the deferment of meaning exclusively. Although not fairly described as nihilistic, Adorno's principle of nonidentity, on the one hand,

20. "New Image of God," 191.
21. Ibid.

was limited to the deconstruction of circumscribed meaning and the destabilization of all positive claims to purpose. He sought to uncover surplus significance in order to break down the domination of identity-thought, not to expose open and immeasurable meaning. That, he feared, would risk greater and even more precarious hegemonic identification. Schillebeeckx, on the other hand, feared that such an absolute negativity, or "system of the non-system,"[22] was ultimately impotent, "incapable of providing any positive contribution to the improvement of the condition of mankind."[23] Such negativity could not account for the meaning of world and history affirmed by Christian faith. Thus, it is here we see Schillebeeckx return to the question of what is uniquely Christian in the Christian's activity in the world.

Schillebeeckx responded by deliberately positioning "critical negativity" and "contrast-experiences" within the eschatological structure of history. That is, the explicit protest of a contrast experience occurs because "the reality of the present contradicts the fullness promised."[24] He avowed a positive sphere of meaning dialectically known in experiences of contrast and associated it with the eschatological promise for which Christians hope. The definite content of this hope cannot be formulated. The kingdom of God remains unavailable to positive conceptual knowledge; Christians can make no claim to a special gnosis or blueprint of the future. Disregarding this, as Adorno warned, risks authoritarian hegemony in the present by delimiting what is deemed possible in the future. It can, nonetheless, be known dialectically in confrontation with the "antikingdom." It can be defined negatively, Schillebeeckx noted, as a kingdom in which "neither shall there be mourning, nor crying nor

22. Ibid., 205n8.
23. Ibid., 193.
24. Robert Schreiter, "Edward Schillebeeckx: An Orientation to His Thought," in *The Schillebeeckx Reader,* ed. Robert Schreiter (New York: Crossroad, 1984), 18.

pain any more."[25] This eschatological reality negatively known is not one currently in existence though veiled; it is a definitively promised reality dialectically disclosed and vaguely perceived in contrastive experiences of injustice and suffering.

Moreover—and here Schillebeeckx further distinguished his project from Adorno's—this negative knowledge of a promised reality establishes the basis of "a positive power which continues to exert constant pressure in order to bring about a better world."[26] This positive and prophetic "pressure" is precisely what Adorno refused to account for in his project and is language Schillebeeckx borrowed from Paul Ricoeur, whose writing on the role of the church as countercultural critic Schillebeeckx also credited with influencing his thought in this article.[27] Anticipation of the eschaton stimulates and provides positive purpose to the Christian's activity in the world, even if that purpose cannot be formulated positively. The critical negativity of Christian faith subsequently identifies and criticizes the gap between the present order and God's eschatological order. It protests every existing situation that stands in conflict with God's eschatological promise. Empowered by a negative knowledge, critical negativity opposes the justification of current inequities in the name of an already-established order. At the same time, it can resist the sacrificing of individuals in the name of positive and totalizing utopian projects. Critical negativity is the function of Christian faith; it offers a constant protest against all that would offend eschatological hope.

---

25. Schillebeeckx referred to Rev. 21:4 in multiple essays to illustrate the negative character of eschatological hope. For examples, see "New Image of God," 184, and "Theological Criteria," in *The Understanding of Faith: Interpretation and Criticism*, trans. N. D. Smith (New York: Seabury, 1974), 65, first published in the Dutch in *Tijdschrift voor Theologie* 9 (1969): 125–50.
26. "New Image of God," 191.
27. Ricoeur, "Tasks of the Political Educator Today," 150.

Schillebeeckx ascribed the unique vitality of Christianity's critical negativity to its fundamental grounding in the gratuitous character of the eschaton. Christian hope is not limited to the possibilities of human achievement. Salvation is a promise and gift. As we have seen, an eschatological hope is surely not passive, but neither is it self-redemptive. We cannot construct our own salvation, and our hope need not be exhausted by the capabilities of humans alone. Schillebeeckx warned that dismissing this gratuitous character of God's eschatological promise risks compromising the critical force of our hope: "Without the dynamism of Christian hope straining towards an absolute future we are left with an ideological design of man which limits what is 'humanly desirable' in advance."[28] Negativity detached from the eschatological hope of Christianity will ultimately be found sterile. It is the infinite surplus of meaning negatively anticipated in the promise of eschatological salvation that keeps open the possibility of definitive human flourishing. And it is such a horizon, as we will now see, that can destabilize an optimism that limits its hope to the possibilities of scientific and technological advancement.

Secularization and a Flight from the Future

The more fully developed reflection on the eschatological character of contrast experiences presented in the epilogue allowed Schillebeeckx to establish with greater clarity the critical dynamic of Christian hope. No longer was his foremost concern the affirmation of secularization and the progressive optimism of modern culture. Over the preceding years, encouraging Christian participation in this culture's "flight towards the future" had been at the center of his

28. "New Image of God," 197.

theological agenda. His enthusiasm for the direction of this culture was now waning. This is not to say that he had ever embraced the course of secularization without reservation. He was sure to remind the reader in even his earliest writings that human abilities could never exhaust that for which Christians hope; death confronts us with the inadequacy of even the best-laid plans. But he was now being guided by the critical function of eschatological faith. The critical negativity of Christian hope heightened Schillebeeckx's sensitivity to the possibility of not just this proportional inequity but also an explicit conflict between the modern project for the future and the insatiable hope embedded in eschatological faith. He discovered that eschatological hope is best suited for identifying fissures between the present order and God's order. Certainly, his eschatological reflections continued to commit the Christian to a positive, constructive role in shaping history, even if it was unclear what that would look like after being influenced by the profound negativity of Adorno. He now recognized, however, that the Christian's hope could not uncritically affirm the course of secularization, nor could it merely caution reserve in the face of inevitable death; rather, it would need to provide a vantage point from which to resist the consequences of the modern world's unrestrained ambition.

It is not surprising, then, that Schillebeeckx can be seen engaging more critical accounts of modern culture in the epilogue. He appears to have been influenced in particular by the work of another critical theorist associated with the Frankfurt school, Herbert Marcuse, who originally worked alongside Adorno at the Institute of Social Sciences but remained in the United States after escaping Germany during the Second World War. Marcuse developed an important cultural analysis of his adopted country that integrated insights from critical theory with that unique perspective often fashioned in the experience of emigration.[29] It is likely that Schillebeeckx found this work under discussion during his lecture tour of the United States in 1967. In any case, it is only upon his return that we find reference to Marcuse's writings. Coupled with the influence of Adorno's insights, it is in the epilogue that we see Schillebeeckx significantly modify his own cultural analysis and develop his concern that the very freedom for the future ushered in with the process of secularization was placing human freedom in jeopardy and compromising the vitality of hope.[30]

Though undoubtedly informed by the "dialectic of Enlightenment" associated with the Frankfurt theorists, Schillebeeckx's analysis of culture in this article remained visibly marked by the language he used in engaging the process of secularization. It was this process, he had already argued, that allowed for the world to be identified as the object of human control and planning. The technical or instrumental reason appropriate to such a task prioritized efficiency and domination as it worked to shape the world according to human design. This mode of rationality was given priority in the wake of secularization and could point to an explosion of scientific and technological advancements in the modern era as evidence of its productivity and promise. Along with other social critics, however, Marcuse warned those enchanted by these successes that such rationality is dangerously "one-dimensional," all too ready to objectify humans as mere extensions of the world and unable to value anything but progress as it is narrowly defined by science. Adorno, as we have seen, also feared the consequences of applying unqualified scientific rationality to social realities.

29. Schillebeeckx cites Marcuse twice in ibid., 204–6nn3, 15. See Herbert Marcuse, *One-Dimensional Man* (Boston: Beacon, 1964).

30. It once again should be noted that the origins of Schillebeeckx's developing ideas are diffuse, and he credited a variety of writers with influencing a shift in his assessment of late modernity, including Ricoeur. In fact, he had already cited Ricoeur in an earlier article, published in *God the Future of Man,* where he observed that the process of secularization, and particularly the primacy of instrumental rationalization, was beginning to produce within contemporary society a widely experienced anxiety and even a fear of the future. At that time, however, he was unable to expand on the observation. See "Secularization and Christian Belief in God," 63.

Schillebeeckx could now be seen offering a similar warning: "The
constraint imposed by rationality—the principle which is above all
operative in the designing of a new society and a new future—is
threatening to reduce man himself and the future to the level of
things—mere material for objective analysis and planning."[31] In such
an environment, the human person becomes the object rather than
the subject of reason's domination and planning. The very freedom
that seemed to have been gained with the rise of secularization
disappears in its aftermath. Men and women once again find
themselves enslaved to an external and foreign force, freed from the
mysterious whims of a directly divinized nature only to submit to the
incontestable logic of technical reason.

The significance of these insights for Schillebeeckx's eschatological
project was evident. Schillebeeckx was afraid that this paradoxical
loss of freedom was beginning to extinguish the human capacity
for hope: "The constraint of universal rationality under which the
individual person and society are forced to live in an age subject
to the rule of 'scientific reason'—in other words, scientific
omnipotence—can quickly become unendurable, giving rise to
uncertainty about this self-made world."[32] Less and less he spoke of
a culture marked by confidence and an "irresistible desire to make
this world a better place."[33] He now warned of a "fear of the future"
and a corresponding loss of purpose and agency.[34] The primacy
of the future threatened to become a debilitating yoke, an elusive
weight borne by the modern person: "Human freedom is so heavily
burdened by it that there is real danger, no longer of a flight from
the world, but of a flight from the future."[35] Schillebeeckx had

31. "New Image of God," 176.
32. Ibid.
33. "Religious Life in a Secularized World," in *Mission of the Church*, 135.
34. "New Image of God," 199.
35. Ibid., 177.

profoundly transformed his reading of culture. It was not the Christian's aloof indifference to the world that was in need of address but a myopic technological progress that advances at the expense of the human person.

What is the value and role of Christian eschatology in such a culture? In keeping with his earlier efforts to affirm culture precisely by way of the Christian's eschatological hope, Schillebeeckx still held modern culture out as a fitting and even indispensable point of engagement. But he was now being guided by the critical function of eschatological faith. It would engage men and women not in order to affirm the course of secularization and to encourage participation in the progress of the modern world but to destabilize the hegemony that accompanies a one-dimensional notion of progress. He believed that the critical negativity of eschatological hope possesses a capacity to disrupt a positively defined mechanistic vision of the future that limits in advance what that future may hold. It refuses to delimit the contours of God's promise by identifying what is possible with what is "reasonable." It provides a distinctive hope that cannot be positively defined and, precisely because of that, cannot be reduced to even the best of political activity or technological planning. By refusing to close the door to definitive human flourishing in the future, God's eschatological promise can empower a constant and active criticism of a culture that would instrumentalize or even sweep away the human person in the name of progress.

Schillebeeckx concluded the epilogue to his book with a warning that the Christian's distinctive hope needs to be cultivated continuously if it is to escape the suffocating logic of technical rationality. The church risks making its mission and message indistinguishable from that of the surrounding culture if it fails to proclaim a gratuitous promise that surpasses the narrow promises of efficiency and productivity. To fail at this would be to stifle the very breadth and range of human hope. Although the church, too, will actively seek to establish a more "humanly desirable" future, particularly in impoverished and underdeveloped regions of the world, Schillebeeckx cautioned that it must do so in such a way that simultaneously announces God's eschatological promise, or such efforts will simply reinscribe the anxious despair that he now feared afflicted the modern world: "The Christian who provides help for the emergent countries without bringing the Christian message is simply transplanting the problems of the West into the 'third world.'"[36] However, it is fair to say that, having offered this warning, Schillebeeckx was not well positioned to address how the Christian's hope could ultimately avoid capitulating to the creeping logic of technical rationality. By what means can an eschatological hope be cultivated? Are there positive resources for sustaining such a hope? The critical negativity of the Christian faith developed in this article could oppose the oppressive claims of a one-dimensional society but offered little in the way of nourishing an alternative.

The Influence of Habermas:
Orthopraxis as Integral to Eschatology

Challenges to Schillebeeckx's Theology of Secularization

The writings of the first-generation Frankfurt theorists Adorno and Marcuse opened Schillebeeckx's eyes to the dangerous excesses of

36. Ibid., 202. Schillebeeckx had warned of a similar danger a year earlier: "If the Church becomes identical with 'the world' and 'improving the world' and means nothing more than this, she has already ceased to bring a message to the world. She has nothing more to say to the world and can only echo what the world discovered long since" ("Secularization and Christian Belief in God," 79). Notably, this earlier warning regarded the loss of an original voice, not a critical voice. At the time, he did not explore the need for the church to say something against Western culture and that which it had "long since discovered," even if it was important to supplement that hope by saying something above and beyond it. This position, of course, was precisely what was changing in the epilogue.

modernity. They offered him entrance into the categories of critical theory while confronting him, if inadvertently, with limitations in his own theological agenda. As we have seen, the implications of this encounter were already clearly visible in the epilogue of 1968. Nevertheless, they existed in that article right alongside the reaffirmation of theological positions that emerged from Schillebeeckx's earlier and more sanguine engagement with secularization. He appeared, in the article, rather unsure whether hope or fear most urgently marked the contemporary context. It is not surprising, then, that the most appropriate theological response also remained an open question: Does the eschatological faith of Christianity affirm and authenticate secularization, or does it stand as an ardent and even prophetic critic? Because of this ambiguity, the epilogue can read as an innovative though somewhat fragmented exercise in transition.

Following the publication of *God the Future of Man*, however, Schillebeeckx was introduced to the writings of a circle of theologians who were explicitly directing the insights of critical theory toward Christian theologizing and the church. These theologians exposed his work to a much more direct challenge and initiated a series of articles written between 1969 and 1973 in which he would reflect more systematically upon the interplay of critical theory and theology.[37] Schillebeeckx associated these theologians with interrelated movements he referred to as "Kritischer Katholizismus" and "Tegenspraak," both of which were titles of now-defunct journals published during this period in German and Dutch, respectively.[38] In spite of the presence of influential Dutch thinkers

---

37. Originally published in *Tijdschrift voor Theologie* and *Concilium* between 1969 and 1973, these articles are found in *The Understanding of Faith: Interpretation and Criticism*, trans. N. D. Smith (New York: Seabury, 1974).

38. For Schillebeeckx's reference to these movements, see the introduction to *Understanding of Faith*, xiii. Schillebeeckx's criticism of these movements, from which he exempts Xhauflaire, can be

within these critical movements, including former Dominican Karl
Derksen, the theologian within this circle repeatedly cited by
Schillebeeckx was the Belgian Marcel Xhaufflaire, who wrote his
dissertation under Metz at the University of Münster.[39] Schillebeeckx
made it clear that insights from this dissertation, initially published
in 1970 as *Feuerbach et la théologie de la sécularisation*, played an
important role in reorienting his approach to theology.

Xhauffaire's study warned that contemporary theologies of
secularization, to which both Schillebeeckx and Metz had certainly
contributed during the 1960s, uncritically capitulated to modern
culture in a manner not unlike Ludwig Feuerbach's a century earlier.
Whereas Feuerbach looked to exhume the anthropological relevance
of Christianity, and in doing so emptied it of theological
consequence, theologies of secularization looked to give Christianity
a secular relevance by offering a culturally meaningful
reinterpretation of the faith. Xhauffaire argued that these theologies
unfortunately came to a similar end as Feuerbach's, because the
hermeneutical strategies employed merely reinscribed secular mores
and reflected the dominant culture. Theologians produced uncritical
reinterpretations in which modern experience once again
overwhelmed and swept away the particularity of Christian faith.
Xhauffaire did not remark on the connection, but the imperious

found in "The New Critical Theory and Theological Hermeneutics," in *Understanding of Faith*,
136–42, first published in *Tijdschrift voor Theologie* 11 (1971): 113–39. For a survey of these
movements published in the same journal, which Schillebeeckx edited at the time, see Henk
Meeuws, "Tegenspraak of Kontradikue," *Tijdschrift voor Theologie* 13 (1973): 203–12. For a
short introduction to these movements in English, see Charles Davis, "Theology and Praxis,"
Cross Currents 23 (1973): 154–68. See also Portier, "Edward Schillebeeckx as Critical Theorist,"
350–52.

39. Marcel Xhauffaire, *Feuerbach et la théologie de la sécularization* (Paris: Cerf, 1970). See also the
collection of essays, edited by Xhauffaire and Karl Derksen, *Les Deux visages de théologie de
la sécularization* (Tournai, Belg.: Casterman, 1970). The influence of Xhauffaire is particularly
evident in Schillebeeckx's "The New Critical Theory and Theological Hermeneutics" and
"The New Critical Theory," in *Understanding of Faith*, originally published in *Tijdschrift voor
Theologie* 11 (1971): 30–50.

consequences of identity-thought, well articulated by Adorno, could be seen at work. Theologians had accepted modern culture with too little reserve, unintentionally permitting culture to structure and dictate the expression of faith. They affirmed the progressive optimism of secularization, offering what amounted to something of a theological endorsement. And by simply echoing conventional wisdom, they in fact legitimated the destructive excesses of modernity. Though it is unclear whether Schillebeeckx ultimately identified his own writings with this critique,[40] Xhaufflaire directly challenged him to attend further to the concerns of "postidealist" philosophy and its implications for his theological project in order to overcome such a methodological misstep.[41] It appears to have been through this exchange that Schillebeeckx came to recognize that a hermeneutical retrieval of the faith would need to be critical as well as contemporaneous and creative.

The Eschatological Warrant for a Critical Hermeneutic of Praxis

It was exposure to Xhaufflaire and the "theology of contestation" that prompted Schillebeeckx to begin his more extensive study of critical theory via the ideas of Jürgen Habermas, the "second-generation" Frankfurt theorist and student of Adorno whose work had significantly influenced Xhaufflaire. Frequent references to both men can be found in the two articles Schillebeeckx dedicated to critical theory in 1971, which were later translated in *The Understanding of Faith* as "The New Critical Theory" and "The New Critical Theory and Theological Hermeneutics." In these articles, we see

---

40. In "Theological Criteria," Schillebeeckx did recognize Bultmann and Gogarten in this critique, and wrote, "[T]he theology of secularization is therefore basically a new ideology" (see 67–68).

41. Xhaufflaire directed a similar critique toward Metz. See the German translation *Feuerbach und die Theologie der Säkularisation* (Mainz, Ger.: Grünewald, 1970), 14–15.

Schillebeeckx respond to the methodological warning offered by Xhaufflaire by submitting modern hermeneutical theology to Habermas's critical analysis. As we will see, the result of this interaction, which was very much informed by the celebrated debate between Habermas and Hans-Georg Gadamer in Heidelberg, allowed Schillebeeckx to articulate a "critical theology" without entirely discarding the advantages of theological hermeneutics.[42] Moreover, and particularly germane to our purposes, it also allowed him to articulate a more critical understanding of history that would build upon that which his earlier eschatological reflections only cautiously uncovered.

Schillebeeckx affirmed in these articles the value of a hermeneutic tradition that looks to overcome the interruptions in communication that occur as a result of historical, cultural, or linguistic development. Such a tradition, which found its classical expression in Gadamer, rightfully looks to make present again that which was meaningful in the past. According to Schillebeeckx, this task is essential to Christian theology, "because it attempts to make the meaning that has been proclaimed in history present here and now in our contemporary existence."[43] In fact, he argued that regardless of whether the methodological choice is made explicitly, the Christian theologian cannot avoid the hermeneutical obligation to proclaim for every new age God's salvific work in history. This is precisely what Schillebeeckx himself attempted to do when he offered a future-oriented reinterpretation of the Christian faith in the effort to think and speak of God in the unfamiliar context of secularization. Of course, the often-unspoken presupposition of such a project is "that

---

42. Schillebeeckx's account of the relationship between post-Heideggerian hermeneutics and Habermas's critical theory, particularly in the second article, is heavily indebted to Albrecht Wellmer's discussion of the Habermas–Gadamer debate in *Critical Theory of Society*, trans. John Cumming (New York: Herder & Herder, 1971), 41–62.
43. "New Critical Theory and Theological Hermeneutics," 128–29.

what is handed down in tradition, and especially the Christian tradition, is always meaningful, and that this meaning only has to be deciphered hermeneutically and made present and actual."[44] It is this presupposition that Habermas looked to problematize.

Schillebeeckx's study of critical theory concentrated on two corrective extensions of the hermeneutical project found in Habermas's analysis of the historical process of communication. The first was the importance of attending to the role of ideological biases in the construction and retrieval of the past. Classical hermeneutics, he cautioned, are well equipped to "discover breakdowns of communication in the dialogue with history which are the result of original differences in the sphere of understanding, but not those which are the result of repressive and violent power structures that already exist as given in any society."[45] Habermas's suspicion of hermeneutics, then, was based in large part on what today is a well-accepted position. Much of the refraction that occurs in the handing down of the past occurs not because of historical aporias but because of ideological biases that systematically distort in order to maintain existing social structures and narratives that benefit those responsible for constructing and handing the past down.[46] He warned that because traditional hermeneutics deliberately looks to make the meaning discoverable in history once again present, it is poorly equipped to identify the meaningless in history. It is structurally blinded to the untruth of the past and is, therefore, ineffective in putting right subsequent breakdowns in communication.

44. Ibid., 130.
45. Ibid.
46. Schillebeeckx recognized alternative and even positive meanings ascribed to the term *ideology* but generally limited his use of the term to describe "a false consciousness or speculative assertion for which no empirical or historical basis can be provided and which therefore has a broken relationship with reality." See ibid., 163n90. In *The Idea of a Critical Theory: Habermas and the Frankfurt School* (New York: Cambridge University Press, 1981), 4–26, Raymond Guess presents a helpful survey of descriptive, positive, and pejorative applications of the term. This short book offers a fine introduction to Habermas's thought.

Consequently, in attempting to retrieve the past, an ideology critique is needed in order to detect that which appears to be true and meaningful in history but which in fact only serves the purposes of meaning makers.[47] The absurd of history needs to be unmasked lest it be reinscribed in contemporary reinterpretation.

In addition to Xhaufflaire's parallel criticism, Schillebeeckx recognized in Habermas's corrective an important challenge to the way theology was done. Attention would need to be given to the ideological biases carried within theological mediations of meaning from the past to the present. The value of an ideology critique resides in its ability to open the theologian's eyes to the often-veiled aspects of history that have too easily been overlooked when attempting to make the tradition present. It draws attention to "the fact that tradition is not only a source of truth and unanimity, but also a source of untruth, repression and violence."[48] Discovering the nonsense of history, then, and not just what is sensible, should be an important task of theological hermeneutics. The ambiguity of history, an "insane complex" in which meaning and meaninglessness lie side by side, is disregarded at the price of ideological capitulation. Theologians need to keep before themselves precisely that which is so tempting to ignore: a history marked by suffering and oppression. They must not make an abstraction of the faith, dismissing the violence and suffering in history as if the tradition could be passed down smoothly and without interruption "as a kind of history of ideas."[49] Schillebeeckx challenged theologians to stop working within

---

47. In *Idea of a Critical Theory*, 26–44, Guess examines three modes of ideology critique (*Ideologiekritik*) employed by Habermas: epistemic, genetic, and functional. Although Schillebeeckx never offered a precise methodological description of ideology critique, even regarding his own writings, his studies in the historical development of ministry exemplify his use of genetic critique, in this case with regard to ecclesial structures of pastoral authority. See *Ministry: Leadership in the Community of Jesus Christ*, trans. John Bowden (New York: Crossroad, 1981).

48. "New Critical Theory and Theological Hermeneutics," 130.

49. Ibid., 131.

"a barely concealed idealist concept of history" and to attend to the concrete elements of distortion ever present in the emergence and transmission of the faith.[50]

This call for a postidealist form of theology provides the transition to Habermas's second significant contribution to hermeneutics considered by Schillebeeckx: the extension of hermeneutics from "pure" interpretation to practical actualization. Along with Schillebeeckx, Habermas lamented the inability of Adorno's critical negativity to provide a positive and practical force for change. Adorno, on the one hand, feared that linking theory with practice risked the same hegemonic domination and authoritarian totalitarianism that accompanies the identification of concept and object.[51] Thus, the endless deferment of meaning anchored upon an absolute negativity could critique inhumane situations but could make no practical contribution to the creation of a more humane situation. No warrant or positive claim to meaning was deemed available by which to determine innocuously such action.

Habermas, on the other hand, feared that such a project inadvertently legitimated the status quo by leaving the world as it is, functioning as little more than a "new ideology."[52] He readily received from Adorno and other Frankfurt theorists a suspicion of positivist theories, including metaphysical theories. He, too, was concerned with the uncritical identification of existing reality and truth, the identification of the present with that which is possible. As we have seen, an ideology critique looks to expose the conflation of what has been with what is true. It seeks to demonstrate that what seems to be inevitable given existing social structures and narratives is

50. Ibid.
51. See Tillar, "Influence of Social Critical Theory," 164. For a helpful analysis of Adorno's position, see J. A. Colombo, *An Essay on Theology and History: Studies in Pannenberg, Metz, and the Frankfurt School* (Atlanta: Scholars Press, 1990), 226.
52. "New Critical Theory," 105.

in fact contingent and therefore changeable. Nonetheless, Habermas believed that if critical theory remained at the level of theory alone, even if critical, it would never achieve the emancipation it looked to effect. Unlike Adorno, he would wager that "a practical transformation of the whole social structure can in fact make what is objectively possible cease to be in fact impossible."[53]

In his work from this period, Habermas tried to overcome the impotency of a definitively negative theory by attending to the intrinsic relationship between theoretical and practical reason.[54] He did this by first challenging the notion that methods of human knowing are objective or value-free. Both scientific-analytic and hermeneutic-historical knowledge, he argued, are informed by a fundamental concern for human emancipation. Specifically, the search for hermeneutical knowledge is rooted in and bent toward a human interest in communicative freedom. Interpretation presupposes and is directed toward what he described as an "ideal speech situation" in which communication is absolutely unlimited and free from coercion.[55] By hypothesizing this ideal speech situation, Habermas located a "quasi-transcendental" criterion by which he could not only offer a critique of controlling ideologies but also go beyond negativity and make positive proposals aimed at the enhancement of such a situation. Indeed, the unmasking of controlling ideologies itself should be seen as aimed at the enhancement of such a situation. The very structure of communication, therefore, provides a ground that extends the hermeneutical project toward the construction of those conditions

---

53. Ibid., 117.
54. See especially Jürgen Habermas, *Theory and Practice*, trans. John Viertel (Boston: Beacon, 1973), and *Knowledge and Human Interests*, trans. Jeremy J. Shapiro (Boston: Beacon, 1972). It should be noted that Schillebeeckx limited his use of Habermas to writings from early in Habermas's career.
55. Guess examines the work done by this concept in Habermas's project in *Idea of a Critical Theory*, 65–70.

which make communication and knowledge possible. Consequently, emancipative action is an essential element of the hermeneutical process that is inherently directed toward actualized liberation from repressive situations rather than the "pure" communication of meaning.

It was by developing this position that Habermas recalibrated the relationship between theory and praxis. Following in the tradition of Marx, his very use of the term *praxis* elucidates his epistemological proposal.[56] The term is meant to confound idealized notions of either unconcerned, presuppositionless theory or pure, unreflective technique: "Praxis is distinguished from mere practice by its reciprocal or co-constitutive relationship with theory likewise conceived."[57] Furthermore, and in opposition to traditional theories in which action is perceived to follow theoretical understanding, Habermas subordinated theory to praxis. If that which is objectively possible cannot be conceived adequately under current conditions, then a rational epistemological project needs to be concerned with establishing the conditions necessary for knowledge. That is to say, "emancipative or critical praxis is the only way in which what is possible and rational can be realized."[58] Praxis creates the conditions required for knowledge, whereas theory is bent toward human concern, itself oriented toward action: "In Habermas' opinion, praxis determines the conditions by which man may come to knowledge yet is also dependent upon those processes."[59] In his hands, critical theory becomes the consciousness of praxis, whereas praxis is infused with theory, which itself inevitably implies a way of acting.

56. In "Theology and Praxis," 158–60, Charles Davis briefly surveys the introduction of the Greek term *praxis* into modern philosophy, the importance of the term for Marx, and its eventual emergence in modern Christian theology.
57. Portier, "Schillebeeckx' Dialogue with Critical Theory," 23.
58. "New Critical Theory," 117.
59. Ibid., 108.

This reconciliation of the theoretical and practical lay behind Schillebeeckx's own decision during this period to transition from speaking of an "active hope" to speaking of "Christian praxis." He became convinced that an appreciation for the co-constitutive relationship between theory and praxis guards against the unraveling of the church's eschatological message from its work on behalf of those in need, which Schillebeeckx believed endangered human freedom by reinforcing the dominance of technical rationality. It negated the temptation to posit and isolate a purely theoretical theological position and disinterested technical action. More fundamentally, it afforded Schillebeeckx the opportunity to revisit the category of "orthopraxis" and to address the idealist tendencies he now recognized hindered much of modern theology.

Schillebeeckx had already recognized, if only tentatively, that the eschatological structure of Christianity imposed the task of constructing rather than interpreting the faith. What was new in his thought, then, was not a concern with moving beyond a purely theoretical hermeneutics, though he certainly grew even more critical of that position during this period. What was new was a greater appreciation for those contingent elements of bias and distortion present in the emergence and transmission of the faith. Theology makes an ideological abstraction of the faith when it willfully or naively ignores the often oppressive sociopolitical context in which it is constructed and actualized. It does this, as Xhaufflaire warned, at the risk of ideological accommodation. What was needed instead was orthopraxis, the authentic actualization of the faith as "a flesh and blood affair" in the world.[60] Praxis, Schillebeeckx argued, resists detaching the tradition from concrete human history by offering a nonidealist actualization of the faith that verifies (or

---

60. "New Critical Theory and Theological Hermeneutics," 132.

invalidates) its emancipative value and is, thus, less vulnerable to ideological distortion and application.

Schillebeeckx was deliberate, however, to establish once again the intrinsic link between the theoretical and practical by way of the eschatological structure of faith. That is, he identified a specifically theological charge for an ideologically critical hermeneutics of praxis. Note the ground on which he determined praxis to be an essential element of the hermeneutical process:

> It should not be forgotten that eschatological faith imposes on the present the task of transcending itself, not only theoretically, but also as a change to be realized. Only the critical attitude towards the present, and the resulting imperative to change and improve it, really open access to the coming truth. The basic hermeneutic problem of theology, then, is not so much the question of the relationship between the past and the present, but between theory and practice, and this relationship can no longer be solved idealistically, by a theory of Kantian pure reason from which consequences flow for the practical reason, but it will have to be shown in how the theory appears in the praxis itself.[61]

Here, we see that Schillebeeckx's appropriation of Habermas's project came with an important qualification. It is eschatology that provides the warrant for a critical stance toward the present and for privileging the actualization of Christian faith as praxis. He would not be content to determine Christian praxis on the rather thin and rationalistic notion of an ideal speech situation.

Schillebeeckx resisted grounding emancipative praxis upon an ideal speech situation on two counts. First, he believed that by directing praxis toward communicative freedom, Habermas betrayed an "optimism of reason" that presumes that the human person "can achieve a really emancipative history entirely and exclusively on his own initiative and power."[62] Lest this position silently take its

---

61. "Theological Criteria," 66.
62. "New Critical Theory and Theological Hermeneutics," 149.

place among the many other unexamined plausibility assumptions of
modern society, Schillebeeckx proposed testing it against the doctrine
of original sin, which confesses negatively the fundamentally
gratuitous character of the redemption and improvement of the
world.[63] Turning to a practice and formula he borrowed from Metz,
the doctrine serves as a "subversive memory," exposing what appears
to be incontestable as in fact open for dispute.[64] Can the "promise"
of an ideal speech situation, he asked, really underwrite human
liberation? Of course, behind that question lies a distinctly theological
understanding of human redemption not shared by Habermas, but
attending to the unique character of Christian hope was precisely
Schillebeeckx's concern. He charged Habermas with proffering a
"Pelagian interpretation to the emancipative praxis,"[65] and though he
did not develop his critique with regard to Habermas in particular,
we have already seen he feared that such a position would ultimately
be found sterile, caged within the limited sphere of what can be
achieved by purely human means.

Second, Schillebeeckx criticized Habermas's hypothetical ideal
speech situation as essentially abstract and devoid of positive content.
Communicative freedom presumes a modern notion of liberty
characteristic of the Enlightenment, liberty correctively construed
as freedom from coercion and limitation, which in its abstraction
and negativity is incapable of offering a positive orientation to
emancipative praxis.[66] Such a vague concept of freedom, he warned,

---

63. Ibid., 145–46.
64. Schillebeeckx cites Metz's "'Politische Theologie' in der Diskussion," in *Diskussion zur 'Politischen Theologie,"* ed. Helmut Peukert (Mainz, Ger.: Matthias-Grünewald, 1969); see Schillebeeckx, "New Critical Theory and Theological Hermeneutics," 148. In "Critical Theories and Christian Political Commitment," in *Political Commitment and Christian Community (Concilium* 84), ed. Alois Muller and Norbert Greinacher (New York: Herder & Herder, 1973), 57, Schillebeeckx credits Leszek Kolakowski with suggesting the applicability of the doctrine of original sin in this context, referencing an unidentified public congress held at Nijmegen.
65. "New Critical Theory and Theological Hermeneutics," 148.

does not offer an adequate ground for hope. Without providing some manner of definite direction, can such a principle really function as a constructive force for change? Empty of positive substance, is it capable of nourishing and sustaining the praxis of hope under the weight of structural repression and the omnipotence of instrumental rationalization? Schillebeeckx posed these questions to Habermas's project and concluded that, despite Habermas's intent, he had failed to overcome sufficiently the impotence of Adorno's critical negativity. In response, he looked once again to the promise of eschatological salvation in search of an "optimism of grace" that could augment and transcend the rationalistic and formless hope offered by critical theory.[67]

This is not to suggest that Schillebeeckx considered insights culled from the Frankfurt theorists only incidentally applicable to the eschatological faith of Christianity. In large measure, he attributed the emancipative impulse orienting critical theory to the Jewish heritage of its early advocates, including Adorno, finding in their work and those they influenced "the now secularized prophetic and critical tradition of the Old Testament and of the hope of the coming of a new, free, humane and just Kingdom of God."[68] Together with Christians, then, Jews shared a past that fostered a common hope for the redemption of the world and a prophetic refusal to identify the present with all that is genuinely possible. Nonetheless, Schillebeeckx believed that, in the end, the character and potency of their "secularized" hope had been deeply compromised. The consequence of disregarding the past by detaching a prophetic hope

66. "Critical Theories," 58. This criticism was similar to the one Schillebeeckx directed toward Merleau-Ponty in 1959, when Schillebeeckx relied on a Thomistic account of freedom to argue that without eschatological faith, human expectation for the future ultimately lacked vitality and orientation.

67. "New Critical Theory and Theological Hermeneutics," 149.

68. "Critical Theories," 51.

from the irreducible framework of a religious tradition was the loss
of that concrete content which gives vitality and positive direction to
liberating praxis.

Identifying a Positive Orientation for Eschatological Praxis:
The Christian Contribution

Reclaiming Past and Present as Dimensions
of an Eschatological Future

Here, we see Schillebeeckx begin to temper a position he developed
in the epilogue to *God the Future of Man* in 1968. When expressing
the dialectical character of the awareness of God's eschatological
promise, Schillebeeckx claimed that the Christian has "as little
positive idea as the non-Christian of what is worthy of man, either
ultimately or here and now."[69] Even at the time, it did not go
unnoticed that this claim placed him in a difficult situation. In an
essay written in 1969, William Hill noted, "[T]he reservation felt
towards Schillebeeckx's project is that it is not clear how it makes any
allowance for a positive contribution to the future that is Christian in
any specific and explicit way."[70] By taking this position, Schillebeeckx
found himself in a situation similar to the one he believed
encumbered Habermas. His account of God's eschatological promise,
though affirmed as a transcendent and therefore inexhaustible source
of hope, was itself abstract and devoid of content. Both the past and
present were regarded as problematic loci of that hope. As such, it was
difficult for him to account for a distinctively Christian contribution
to the future. There was little in the way of concrete content to
nourish the Christian's hope and give direction to Christian praxis.

---

69. "New Image of God," 191.
70. Hill, "Schillebeeckx's New Look at Secularity," 169.

Schillebeeckx recognized the need to address this lacuna even in 1968. At the time, his principal concern was to affirm that the kingdom of God remained unavailable to positive conceptual knowledge; Christians could make no claim to a road map or blueprint of the future. Disregarding this, he noted, risks authoritarian oppression in the present by delimiting what is deemed possible in the future. Still, he also worried that unless attention was given "to the present relationship with God and to Jesus' past, which the Spirit 'brings to our remembrance,' even the new idea of God appears to be in danger of becoming a new mythology."[71] Already, then, he was aware that the primacy given to the future in modern theology, though legitimate, was in jeopardy of becoming misleadingly one-sided. Indeed, he affirmed the centrality of Christology: "For Christianity the foundation, norm and criterion of every future expectation is its relationship with the past, i.e., with Jesus of Nazareth and what has taken place in him."[72] It is not surprising, though, that this statement received little further consideration at the time. Schillebeeckx's attention was turned decisively toward the idea of a contrast experience and the dialectical character of our knowledge of God's eschatological promise.

It was only one year later, however, that Schillebeeckx returned to these concerns. In an article published as "The Interpretation of the Future" in 1969, he once again reaffirmed the privileged place of the future in contemporary thought, though he now warned with far greater determination that the past and present "must not be sacrificed to the primacy of the future."[73] The irreducible historicity of human existence, he argued, means that each person necessarily lives from a past in the present toward an open future; that is, the

71. "New Image of God," 189.
72. Ibid.
73. "The Interpretation of the Future," in *Understanding of Faith*, 5.

future always starts from the present on the basis of the past. To forsake this essential threefold historical dynamic, he cautioned, was to partake in aimless "futuristic fantasies." Indeed, Schillebeeckx maintained that the normative source for the Christian's hope in the future is grounded and oriented by this fundamental dynamic. In the Scriptures, he claimed, "the interpretation of a past event always coincides with the announcement of a new expectation for the future. The past is 'read again' in a manner which makes it once more actual, and thus it becomes a guarantee for the hope of a new future."[74] Remembrance of the past and expectation for the future are essentially related. Meaningful events from history are remembered and associated with events in the present, each illuminating the other, so that the present itself tenders a new promise for the future and, in turn, history is interpreted as the gradual fulfillment of God's promise. The basis for the Christian's hope in the future, therefore, lies in the present actualization, if only partial, of a past promise remembered, once more affirming and pledging God's enduring fidelity.

According to Schillebeeckx, an understanding that our hope for the future always starts from the present on the basis of the past "rejects on the one hand any 'de-eschatologisation' of time (there is no room for a radical eschatology of the present) and on the other hand demands a rejection of all apocalyptic elements from the expectation of the future (apocalyptic thought thinks from the future to the present)."[75] We are by now familiar with the first

74. Ibid., 6. As an illustration, Schillebeeckx presented the biblical story of Joshua's victorious entrance into the land promised to Israel and the renewed hope entailed in that fulfilled promise for the future restoration of Israel following its defeat to the Assyrians, the event in response to which the biblical text itself was written.

75. Ibid., 7. Again, we can note that Schillebeeckx believed that this understanding of the future is grounded in the biblical structure of eschatological hope and a prophecy of the future. Also significant to note is that Schillebeeckx's description of apocalyptic thought is similar to that of Karl Rahner's in "The Hermeneutics of Eschatological Assertions," in *Theological Investigations* (London: Darton, Longman & Todd, 1966), 4:236–46. Schillebeeckx cited this essay later in his own article.

aspect of this warning. Reducing the future to the present inevitably legitimates hegemony, fostering both the loss of hope and the danger of repression. It was the second aspect of this warning, however, that especially interested Schillebeeckx in this article. Though he would revisit his critique of apocalypticism in later writings and further clarify what he understood by the term, in this article he was concerned to show that only an actual relationship with God in the present, itself informed by God's fidelity in the past, provides the hermeneutic context needed for belief in a transcendent eschatology. We can know nothing of the eschaton, he argued, except insofar as it is "already indicated in the course of historical events expressing the actual relationship between the God of the covenant and mankind, particularly in Christ."[76] Apocalyptic thought, he warned, mistakenly determines the present from the future rather than the future from the present. Disordered toward both the present and its past, allowed to float without tether, "interpretations" of the future subsequently dissolve into illusion. That is to say, apocalypticism severs the future from the present and past, making hope-filled expectation epistemologically impossible. "In this sense," Schillebeeckx wrote, "there can be no true eschatology of the future without a certain eschatology of the present."[77] To be embedded in a lived tradition, he countered, is the necessary context for hope in the future; it provides a reliable source for the belief that God's faithfulness transcends the present.

The emphasis on historical continuity is unmistakable in Schillebeeckx's eschatological writings: "The post-terrestrial eschaton is but a question of the manner in which what is already growing in the history of this world will receive its final fulfillment."[78] Although

76. "Interpretation of the Future," 10.
77. Ibid., 8. Schillebeeckx singled out Jürgen Moltmann in particular for having failed to account for this in his writings.
78. Ibid., 10.

the future cannot be identified with the present, neither is it "totally
new" or wholly discontinuous: "Although the future has an element
of 'not yet' in it, we cannot neglect the element of 'already.' In
fact, only the 'already' allows us to say anything meaningful about
the still unknown future."[79] Unless hope for the future is founded
upon God's past promises remembered and actualized in the present,
our expectations remain vague and directionless. In the person of
Jesus Christ, however, Christians find within history the basis for an
eschatological hope. In him, within history, Christians recognize a
"prophetic pointer" and the "last promise" of God's final fulfillment.
Indeed, in his resurrection, the world received an eschatological
promise proleptically embedded in history itself. "While the
apocalyptic approach puts the eschaton at the end of the history
of this world," Schillebeeckx wrote, "Christianity has put it within
history."[80] Detached from history, hope functions as sheer fantasy;
founded upon an eschatological event embedded in history, though,
hope is genuinely possible. Not surprisingly, Schillebeeckx warned
that we must speak only haltingly of the final eschatological
kingdom, and "mainly" in images and language that arise out of
contrast experiences.[81] But, clearly, a new emphasis was being placed
on the claim that, in the life, death, and resurrection of Jesus,
Christians find a historically concrete basis from which to hope that
even death can be defeated and human history renewed.

79. Ibid., 8.
80. Ibid., 11.
81. Ibid. In a later text, Schillebeeckx would identify in Scripture four "great metaphors" or images
   for speaking of the eschaton: the kingdom of God, the resurrection of the body, a new heaven
   and a new earth, and the Parousia. See *Church: The Human Story of God*, trans. John Bowden
   (New York: Crossroad, 1994), 133–34.

A Critical Retrieval of the Past for the Future:
The Centrality of Jesus and the Concrete Contours
of Christian Hope

In an attempt to reclaim or rehabilitate the past as a positive source of Christian hope, and having now grown frustrated with the dearth of concrete content and the corresponding inability to provide a positive orientation to Christian praxis, Schillebeeckx returned to these earlier observations in an article entitled "Critical Theories and Christian Political Commitment," published in 1973. It was in this article that he began advocating for the practice of "critically remembering," a practice in which select memories carefully culled from history, memories with the potential to support and animate emancipatory praxis, are identified and introduced as destabilizing alternatives to idealistically abstract or exclusively technical understandings of what is objectively possible for the future.[82] These memories are reclaimed from the "past not in order to make it present here and now, but rather to save for the future certain values which might otherwise have been lost in the past."[83] Filling out the somewhat abstract position he developed in the 1969 article, here Schillebeeckx argued that for Christians, the normative remembrance

82. Though he did not offer a textual citation, Schillebeeckx credited Ricoeur for advocating the value of "critically remembering" in "Critical Theories," 57. The critical value of looking to the past was also discussed, though briefly, in the article from 1971 in which Schillebeeckx used the language of "subversive memory," and the two ideas are notably similar. Along with recognizing Metz in that article, Schillebeeckx also cited Ricoeur, Bloch, Marcuse, and Adorno for having explored the "past as a subversive memory," though, again, he did not reference texts; see "New Critical Theory and Theological Hermeneutics," 134. In his survey of Schillebeeckx's lecture notes from Nijmegen, Ted Schoof argues that it was with the inclusion of Metz's *memoria* thesis in his lectures that Schillebeeckx first began to discuss the role of remembering in Christian theology; see Schoof, "Edward Schillebeeckx," 33.

83. "Critical Theories," 57. The critical value of this approach is clarified by Schillebeeckx in "Correlation between Human Question and Christian Answer," in *Understanding of Faith*. It is necessary to preserve, he explained, "the critical distance that we learn to acquire especially by remembering the past with a better future in mind. Without this critical distance, the present functions as an uncriticised pre-decision with regard to the Christian faith" (91).

for awakening hope and orienting emancipative praxis is the life, death, and resurrection of Jesus of Nazareth. It is in Jesus Christ that Christians find the subversive memory capable of reenvisioning an alternative and better future. In him, they discover the basis or source of their hope in God's eschatological promise, which in turn grounds their criticism of all repression and provides a positive practical orientation aimed at establishing human freedom.

This promise of freedom found in Jesus is no futuristic fantasy or vague abstraction. The basis of Christian praxis is not a thin and formless hypothetical ideal. Rather, that which it is oriented toward "has already been realized in a concrete historical form in the life praxis of Jesus, whose proclamation of the Kingdom of God is the thematization of this praxis."[84] Schillebeeckx located, then, a distinct example or prototype of emancipation, the positive content needed to offer a robust account of Christian praxis. To act for freedom is to conform one's life to Jesus', to follow in his own praxis. By critically remembering the life of Jesus, particularly through the liturgical celebrations in which his memory is reclaimed and in the small, critical communities in which his story is shared, the Christian locates a concrete hope that can sustain, nourish, and give direction to an authentically liberating Christian praxis. Here, we undoubtedly see the beginnings of Schillebeeckx's massive christological project, which he surely had begun writing by this time. The first volume was published only one year later and would open with this eschatological epigraph: "That you may not grieve as others do who have no hope" (1 Thess. 4:13). Schillebeeckx was convinced that remembering the life, death, and resurrection of Jesus provides sustenance for the Christian's praxis of hope. It offers positive direction and definite content. It was with this aim, then, that Schillebeeckx developed the Christology for which he would become most widely known. His

84. "Critical Theories," 58.

studies in Christology are not tangential to his earlier writings but illustrate an ambitious extension of his eschatological project. With this in mind, it is to this work that we now turn.

A Narrative Christology with a Practical Intent

Concurrent with his study of critical theory, Schillebeeckx had immersed himself in an intensive study of modern New Testament exegesis. Out of this research came *Jesus: An Experiment in Christology,* in 1974; *Christ: The Experience of Jesus as Lord,* in 1977; and *Interim Report on the Books "Jesus" and "Christ,"* in 1978.[85] In these works, Schillebeeckx synthesized a remarkable amount of secondary literature in an attempt to tell the "story of Jesus" in a way such that the modern person, deeply craving greater freedom but struggling to envisage a hope greater than technological progress, might hear and respond to the story anew. His focus in this project on promoting eschatological hope and practical action was clear. He wanted to awaken and animate a more robust hope, and he believed that narration or storytelling was particularly well suited to that end. Stories, he claimed, have a peculiar capacity to convey what is incommunicable by theoretical argumentation alone: "When . . . reason is no longer able theoretically to express in words what in fact there is still to be said, it is obliged to utter its elusive 'surplus-vested-in-reality' in stories and parables."[86] Moreover, he argued that stories possess a practical epistemological force; again, remembrance

---

85. *Jezus, het verhaal van een levende* (Bloemendaal, Neth.: Nelissen, 1974), translated as *Jesus: An Experiment in Christology,* trans. Hubert Hoskins (New York: Crossroad, 1995); *Gerechtigheid en liefde: Genade en bevrijding* (Bloemendaal, Neth.: Nelissen, 1977), translated as *Christ: The Experience of Christ as Lord,* trans. John Bowden (New York: Seabury, 1980); *Tussentijds verhaal over Jezus boeken* (Bloemendaal, Neth.: Nelissen, 1978), translated as *Interim Report on the Books "Jesus" and "Christ,"* trans. John Bowden (New York: Crossroad: 1981).
86. *Jesus,* 79.

and expectation are essentially related. Stories are to be told with an
eye to the future, thus inviting a practical response in the present
from, in this case, the reader.[87]

It will be of little surprise, though, that Schillebeeckx warned that
these stories must be remembered and retold with great care. No less
than a "pure" theory can, a story unhinged from concrete reality can
too easily degenerate into ideology, providing cover and legitimacy
for already-established powers.[88] Herein lies the highly weighted
commitment to the historical-critical study of the New Testament
that characterizes these books. While acknowledging problems
associated with a historical-critical approach to Scripture,[89]
Schillebeeckx anchored his work on this scholarship in order to create
a critical bulwark against the dangers of ideological mythologizing:
"If the Christian affirmation of Jesus' universal significance is not
ideological but is an assent to reality, something in the record of Jesus
must point in that direction."[90] Unfortunately, what then portended
to be critical remembering as historical narrative at times seemed to
function as the mere collection of historical data.[91] And, undoubtedly,

---

87. Regarding the practical epistemological power of narrative traditions, Schillebeeckx cited the
influence of Metz in "The 'God of Jesus' and the 'Jesus of God,'" in *Language of Faith: Essays
on Jesus, Theology, and the Church* (Maryknoll, NY: Orbis, 1995), 108. Illustrating his position
through narrative himself, Schillebeeckx recounted a story told by Martin Buber to great effect:
"My grandfather was paralyzed. One day he was asked to tell about something that happened
with his teacher—the great Baalschem. Then he told how saintly Baalschem used to leap about
and dance while he was at his prayers. As he went on with the story my grandfather stood up; he
was so carried away that he had to show how the master had done it, and started to caper about
and dance. From that moment on he was cured. That is how stories are to be told" (*Jesus*, 674).
Metz recounted the same story in "A Brief Apology for Narrative," in *The Crisis of Religious
Language* (*Concilium* 85), ed. Johann Baptist Metz and Jean-Pierre Jossua (New York: Herder &
Herder, 1973), 84–96. For an introduction to the relationship between narratives and theology
from a number of perspectives, including Metz's essay, see Stanley Hauerwas and L. Gregory
Jones, eds., *Why Narrative? Readings in Narrative Theology* (Grand Rapids, MI: Eerdmans, 1989).
88. *Jesus*, 76.
89. Ibid., 36–40.
90. Ibid., 611.
91. William Portier also offers this critique in "Edward Schillebeeckx as Critical Theorist," 367. For
a more favorable evaluation of Schillebeeckx's historical reconstruction as narrative, see Robert
A. Krieg, *Story-Shaped Christology* (New York: Paulist, 1988), 65–87.

it is difficult for fragments of data to quicken a genuinely liberating hope. Leaving aside the tactical success of his program, however, Schillebeeckx was now advocating the "critical and productive, liberating force" of the story of Jesus, and within his telling of that story emerged the unified thread of a cohesive narrative carrying important implications for his eschatological project.[92]

Before proceeding, it will help for us to consider briefly Schillebeeckx's own understanding of his project. He showed little patience for those who characterized his multivolume study as a neoliberal quest for a prekerygmatic or predogmatic Jesus to function as a fixed criterion for all Christology.[93] He insisted repeatedly that the irreducible particularity of every person necessarily exceeds scientific assessment, that the historical study of Jesus can never prove or rationalize completely the Christian faith, and that it is pointless to speak of a noninterpreted "Jesus in himself." His interest, then, was not the establishment of a secure foundation for the faith by means of the historical-critical method. What he hoped to do, rather, was invite his reader on a journey following alongside the earliest Christians as they recognized and struggled to articulate in the idiom of their day the experience of renewed life and definitive salvation found in Jesus of Nazareth. In the first volume, Schillebeeckx tried to identify those features of the "historical Jesus" that may have led the earliest Christians to confess this experience. He hoped to detect "possible signs in the critical historical reconstructed image of Jesus which could direct the human question of salvation toward the Christian offer of an answer which points to a special saving activity of God in this Jesus."[94] In the second volume, his attention

---

92. *Interim Report*, 131.

93. The usually irenic Schillebeeckx claimed that such an accusation was "absurd" and described those who put it forward as "blind." See ibid., 27–35.

94. "Verrijzenis en geloofservaring in het 'Verhaal van een levende,'" *Kultuurleven* 42 (1975): 81; translated by Robert Schreiter in *The Schillebeeckx Reader* (New York: Crossroad, 1984), 124.

shifted to the ongoing confession of salvation-in-Jesus elaborated by early Christians in the New Testament itself. In both books, though, Schillebeeckx's fundamental concern was the profound longing for freedom that remains unfulfilled in the alienation and suffering of a modern technocratic society.[95] He wanted readers to find themselves caught up in the Christian story of salvation, to discover anew a credible promise capable of shattering narrowly defined plausibility assumptions and of opening up the possibility of an ever-greater hope. Schillebeeckx was engaged once again, then, in the task of Christian "apologetics," offering an account and point of entry into the Christian hope even if now he preferred describing this work as the "pastoral task."[96]

Remembering the Life, Death, and Resurrection of Jesus

In his first book, Schillebeeckx excavated diverse strains of theological tradition in the New Testament in an effort to trace the christological commitments of the earliest Christian generation. Relying heavily on the exegetical work of Helmut Koester, he identified four basic pre–New Testament creeds confessed by early Christians about Jesus: a maranatha or parousia creed, a wonder-worker creed, variations on a wisdom creed, and an Easter creed.[97] Each of these trajectories, he

95. See *Jesus*, 19–26; and *Christ*, 653–70.

96. *Interim Report*, 35. Though he did not provide an explanation, it is likely that Schillebeeckx distanced himself from the language of "apologetics" in order to avoid the connotations of theoretical foundationalism that often accompany the term. See also, *Jesus*, 33.

97. See *Jesus*, 403–38. In the spring of 1971, as he began his research for this project, Schillebeeckx held the Erasmus Chair at Harvard University and frequently lectured at the Divinity School, where Koester served as professor of New Testament. Francis Schüssler Fiorenza examines the influence of Koester on Schillebeeckx in *Modern Christian Thought*, vol. 2, *The Twentieth Century*, ed. James Livingston and Francis Schüssler Fiorenza (Upper Saddle River, NJ: Prentice Hall, 2000), 221–27. For an introduction to Koester's work utilized by Schillebeeckx, see James M. Robinson and Helmut Koester, eds., *Trajectories through Early Christianity* (Philadelphia: Fortress Press, 1971).

argued, revealed a unique christological perspective and privileged certain historical aspects of Jesus' life. Throughout this argumentation, he followed Koester's exegesis closely. What is especially notable for our purposes, however, is the point at which Schillebeeckx departed Koester's company. Whereas Koester ultimately gave priority to the Easter creed, Schillebeeckx believed he could move even further through the text. He proceeded to argue that in front of these four basic creedal formulas existed a more fundamental confession, a pre-Easter interpretive matrix of Jesus that gave rise to and supported all later creedal strands: Jesus as the eschatological prophet.[98] This concept would take center stage in Schillebeeckx's project. It was the image of Jesus as the eschatological prophet that provided a unified thread to his historical narrative, tactical limitations notwithstanding. The image of Jesus as the latter-day prophet framed the way Schillebeeckx spoke of Christian hope. It placed his story of Jesus in a particular relief and, by doing so, determined the theological character of that story. It also, of course, provided thematic continuity between his christological writings from this period and his earlier work in eschatology.

By speaking of Jesus as the eschatological prophet, Schillebeeckx was well positioned to develop the theological significance of his historical reconstruction. Certainly, it allowed him to prioritize the biblical theme of the kingdom of God and to affirm that Jesus announced an eschatological message. "The kingdom of God is Jesus' central message," he wrote, "with the emphasis at once on its coming and on its coming close. In other words, 'expectation of the end'

---

98. In making this argument, Schillebeeckx characterized the concept of "eschatological prophet" as an intertestamental theme itself informed by Deuteronomic accounts of Moses and Mosaic messianism. See *Jesus*, 475–99; *Christ*, 309–21; and *Interim Report*, 64–74. Although we are concerned with the theological import of his exegetical conclusion, it is outside the purview of this study to evaluate Schillebeeckx's use of biblical scholarship and the subsequent decision to prioritize the image of eschatological prophet in his historical reconstruction. For references to a number of pertinent reviews offered by exegetes, see the pages in *Interim* cited here.

here is an expectation of the approaching rule of God."[99] According
to Schillebeeckx, by proclaiming the imminent coming of God's
kingdom, "Jesus intends . . . a process, a course of events, whereby
God begins to govern or to act as king or Lord, an action, therefore,
by which God manifests his being God in the world."[100] Jesus' own
preaching, then, centered primarily on the present immediacy of
God's reign in history. Nonetheless, Schillebeeckx argued, Jesus was
witnessing to a God as the Lord of all history, a God who both
acts for human salvation within world history and guarantees final,
eschatological salvation. Thus, Schillebeeckx believed that it was
subsequently possible to identify two interrelated though
distinguishable aspects in Jesus' single announcement of God's
approaching kingdom: God's saving activity unfolding in the
historical present, and the definitive salvation toward which that
activity is directed. God's sovereignty over history is complete, and as
such, "present" and "future" are inextricably interconnected in Jesus'
proclamation of a kingdom close at hand.

The theological significance of identifying Jesus as the
eschatological prophet lay more specifically, however, in the question
of Jesus' own relationship to the coming kingdom of God. It is
here that the theological value of Schillebeeckx's decision for the
eschatological image is most clearly revealed. "It is plain from the
life of Jesus," he wrote, "that 'present' and 'future,' although
distinguished, are essentially bound up together; Jesus proclaims the
salvation to come, and at the same time by his conduct he makes it
present, thereby at once suggesting a link between his person and
the coming lordship of God."[101] His proclamation of an imminently
approaching kingdom, a merciful reign close at hand, was realized

99. *Jesus*, 140.
100. Ibid., 141.
101. Ibid., 152.

in his own praxis of the kingdom. In and through Jesus' word and praxis, the kingdom was enacted and promised as an already available yet excessive reality. His was a practical proclamation of the approaching kingdom:

> As an interpreter of God and one who acted in accordance with the life-style of the kingdom of God, Jesus did not act on the basis of a blue-print or a well-defined concept of eschatological and definitive salvation. Rather, he saw in and through his own historical and thus geographically limited practice of "going around doing good," of healing, liberating from the demonic powers then thought to be at large in the world, and of reconciliation, the dawn of a distant vision of definitive, perfect and universal salvation.[102]

Jesus' life praxis revealed God to be a God who is committed to the healing and freedom of human beings, a God who stands against every evil in solidarity with a wounded humanity. At the same time, Schillebeeckx revealed that it is in God, as the One who is committed to the wholeness and emancipation of the human, that men and women find genuine freedom and final fulfillment. In words frequently recited by Schillebeeckx, Jesus revealed that "God's cause is the human cause and the human cause is God's cause."[103] The full content of human salvation remains in the future, he insisted, but it is no longer a vague or totally indefinable reality.

Over hundreds of pages, Schillebeeckx narrated the story of Jesus as the inbreaking in history of God's kingdom, and he persistently argued that Jesus' death and resurrection could not be separated from his life's eschatological praxis.[104] Jesus' death on the cross, he averred, does not bespeak God's conditioned healing of the world through God's own satisfaction. Rather, it reveals in human history the gratuitous and radically unconditional nature of God's

---

102. *Interim Report*, 124. See also *Christ*, 791.
103. See, for example, *Church*, 122.
104. See especially *Jesus*, 115–397; *Interim Report*, 125–39; and *Church*, 102–32.

commitment to the healing and freedom of men and women: "The death of Jesus was a suffering through and for others as the unconditional endorsement of a practice of doing good and opposing evil and suffering."[105] In developing this position, however, Schillebeeckx carefully cautioned his reader against trivializing or passing over the catastrophe of Jesus' death. The crucifixion concentrates and was a consequence of Jesus' praxis and proclamation of the kingdom, yet in themselves his suffering and death were a disaster within history perpetrated by those who sought a kingdom of domination rather than reconciliation. "In Jesus' death," Schillebeeckx wrote, "in and of itself, i.e., in terms of what human beings did to him, there is only negativity."[106]

It is only in the light of Jesus' life and tragic death, warned Schillebeeckx, that Christians can turn to the resurrection without making an ideology of Easter, without passing over the subversive praxis of his ministry or the catastrophe of his death on a cross.[107] Indeed, he would speak of the resurrection as divine judgment on what men and women did to Jesus. At the same time, Schillebeeckx also argued that it is only in the light of the resurrection that the eschatological significance of Jesus' life and death are fully revealed: "In the resurrection from the dead, God's eschatological action with reference to Jesus the crucified one becomes God's own verdict on Jesus, and only in this way does God's evaluation of Jesus and his message, career and death also become clear to believers."[108] We should note that, here, Jesus' life and death do not receive eschatological significance only following the resurrection. Rather, it is through the resurrection that God authenticated or sealed the whole career of Jesus. Schillebeeckx also warned, however, against

105. *Interim Report*, 133.
106. *Church*, 127.
107. Ibid.
108. Ibid., 129.

interpreting Jesus' resurrection in this manner exclusively. The resurrection is simultaneously connected to the Christian's "belief in the permanent and essential significance of the person of Jesus himself in the coming of the kingdom of God."[109] It is the resurrection that affirms the Christian's eschatological hope for history; in it, God's promise of salvation is sealed.

Thus, it was through the life, death, and resurrection of Jesus that God's reign came near as men and women discovered in him renewed life and the promise of final salvation. "The approaching salvation-imparted-by-God which Jesus preached and for which he lived and met his death," Schillebeeckx wrote, "proves in the end to be the person of Jesus Christ himself, the eschatological man, Jesus of Nazareth."[110] As the "firstborn" of God's kingdom, Jesus communicated God's saving activity and the inbreaking of the kingdom through his ministry, death, and resurrection. Through him, "the coming of God's kingdom is mediated by a human being. Man's caring for his fellow-men is the visible form and aspect in which the coming of God's kingdom is manifested; it is the way that God's lordship takes."[111] Identifying Jesus as the eschatological prophet attested, therefore, to Jesus' own unique role in the inauguration of the kingdom and the advent of salvation. It acknowledged his essential significance for the whole of world history, for salvation is salvation only when it is universal and complete. "Jesus has a permanent and constitutive significance in the imminent approach of the kingdom of God," Schillebeeckx wrote.[112] Jesus himself was the eschatological presence of salvation, and his resurrection was the irrevocable promise that a history of definitive and universal meaning is indeed possible and on the way. His story,

109. *Interim Report*, 135,
110. *Jesus*, 669.
111. Ibid., 153.
112. *Interim Report*, 131.

in turn, becomes the promise of a meaningful future, offering the "critical and productive, liberating force" required for stimulating and determining the Christian's eschatological praxis.[113]

113. Ibid.

4

Schillebeeckx's Prophetic Eschatology

Contrast Experiences and Creative Fragments

In chapter 3, we watched as Schillebeeckx worked to identify a critical and productive orientation for the Christian's hope. It was out of this interest that his massive christological project, the story of the eschatological prophet, emerged. It was also within the context of this project that Schillebeeckx once again engaged the Christian claim that Jesus has universal significance for all of human history, considered in chapter 2. In returning to this claim in the 1970s, however, Schillebeeckx would directly confront the questions of whether and how we can speak of the universal significance of any human person and whether it is possible to make any claims about the future of history as a whole. These distinctively modern questions were deepened for Schillebeeckx by the realization that the challenges facing Christian theology arise not only, or even primarily, from the modern process of secularization but from the horrifying reality of human suffering. While still attending to the openness of history that characterized his writings in the mid-1960s, he now placed a heightened emphasis on the ambiguity of history marked by sorrow and subjugation. The first section of this chapter will turn to Schillebeeckx's response to the question of whether Christians can confess total or universal meaning in a history marked by such ambiguity and, if so, how.

As we shall see in the second section of the chapter, although Schillebeeckx has made a significant turn in his eschatological claims from metaphysical participation to anticipatory hope realized in Christian praxis, a theology of creation continues to undergird his efforts. There is, he insisted, a positive ontological relationship between human activity and God's saving activity. The ongoing praxis of the kingdom in world history substantively contributes to the history of salvation. Where evil and suffering are protested and human liberation is achieved, God's promise slowly but progressively comes to be realized within history. The breakthrough of the kingdom in history certainly remains vague, realized as imperfect fragments of a definitive end promised though not yet here. Nonetheless, if salvation is to be human salvation, it will need to be made manifest in human history. Schillebeeckx had returned to the protological faith so prevalent in his earlier writings.

Because an aim of this book is to highlight the differences in the later eschatologies of Metz and Schillebeeckx, the final section of this chapter will focus on Schillebeeckx's rejection of an apocalyptic eschatology in favor of what he viewed as a less dualistic understanding of God at work in human history. Drawing on his positions explored in the previous sections, we will see that Schillebeeckx insisted that salvation does not materialize apocalyptically into the terrestrial event but must be mediated in history through human praxis. Although the significance of this position will be considered in this chapter, it will be only after considering Metz's later eschatological thought in the following two chapters that the relative advantages and limitations of Schillebeeckx's approach ultimately are assessed.

Making Universal Claims in the Ambiguities of History

Reengaging the Dilemma through Negative Contrast Experiences

It was in the final section of his book *Jesus* that Schillebeeckx would reengage the Christian claim that Jesus has universal significance for all of human history, examined in chapter 2. Tracing his writings from the late 1950s through the mid-1960s, we watched as Schillebeeckx gradually placed greater emphasis on the indeterminacy and openness of history. Although the eschatological hope of the Christian affirmed the meaningfulness of history gratuitously established in Christ, that meaning was a task for the future and a project to be fashioned in grace. This was an important development in his thought and allowed him to attend to the practical character of eschatological hope. We saw in chapter 3, however, that his understanding of history continued to evolve. Following his encounter with the work of critical theorists, his attention was turned toward what hitherto had been the systematically overlooked underside of history. Meaninglessness and suffering, he recognized, are inexplicably interwoven in the very fabric of history; "history is an insane complex of sense and nonsense."[1] The challenges facing contemporary Christian theology arise not only, or even primarily, from the modern process of secularization but from the horrifying reality of human suffering. Although still attentive to the openness of history, Schillebeeckx

---

1. "The New Critical Theory and Theological Hermeneutics," in *The Understanding of Faith: Interpretation and Criticism*, trans. N. D. Smith (New York: Seabury, 1974), 128.

placed a heightened emphasis on the ambiguity of a history marked by sorrow and subjugation. It would be from this vantage point, then, that Schillebeeckx now sought to give an account of the Christian's definitive, eschatological hope: "The Christian believes, in and through Jesus, that despite everything the kingdom of God, as salvation for mankind, is still coming and will come; what has been achieved in Jesus Christ is the guarantee of this. Therefore the promise of total meaning is not simply a verbal promise; it is a promised lived reality in the 'firstborn.'"[2] But what can it mean, he now would ask, to make this claim within the ambiguity of a history deeply inscribed with suffering? How are we to proclaim the promise of total or universal historical meaning without reverting to an idealist concept of history, without trivializing or whitewashing the evils of past and present?

Once again, these are the questions of an apologist. In chapter 2, you will remember, Schillebeeckx asked, how can we speak of eschatological hope in a secular society no longer able to speak of God? He responded to the challenge of secularization by identifying within the prevailing experience of hope in the future an existential basis by which, he believed, the Christian's hope for history could be confessed meaningfully. The self-transcending hope for a better future, he argued, presented a universal horizon of understanding and even a new "natural theology." While neither proving nor guaranteeing the claims of Christianity, it offered the transcendental structure needed to confess the faith. Conversely, as we have seen, this line of argumentation uncritically affirmed and authenticated the course of secularization, inadvertently legitimating the destructive excesses of modernity. Needless to say, in his looking for a way to speak of Christian hope, such a path was no longer available to

---

2. *Interim Report on the Books "Jesus" and "Christ,"* trans. John Bowden (New York: Crossroad, 1981), 101.

Schillebeeckx. But even if this danger were left to the side, we can be sure that for those situated on the underside of an ambiguous history, the progressive optimism of modernity never truly offered a sufficient horizon of understanding.

The hope-filled human "yes" to the future must not be construed, then, as a transcendental basis for speaking of the Christian's eschatological hope. Pluriform understandings of what is "humanly desirable," what Schillebeeckx now referred to as the *humanum*,[3] and the dangerous implications of such positively defined conceptualizations make such a strategy both ineffective and irresponsible. Nonetheless, Schillebeeckx continued to maintain that within the quest of men and women for a meaningful future there exists "something . . . common to all of them and therefore universal."[4] It now was the pervasive experience of suffering, however, that he identified as common to all. The sting of contingency and worldly disorder, if not oppression and injustice, is universally experienced. Moreover, and more precisely, he believed that the prereligious experience of resistance and protest against this suffering, an experience of contrast, is equally common.[5] Despite it all, despite persistent evidence that history holds no meaning, the

---

3. Schillebeeckx appropriated the term *humanum* from Ernst Bloch. Intentionally unfamiliar, it was intended to function as a warning against positively conceptualizing in the present what human life should be, while simultaneously affirming that it is nonetheless possible to know what it should not be. Ultimately, for Schillebeeckx, it is anthropology in an eschatological key: the fullness of the human person cannot be defined positively in advance of the eschaton. For one of the earliest appearances of this term, which he used frequently in his later writings, see "Theological Criteria," in *Understanding of Faith*, 65. For an expanded account of this anthropology, see *Christ: The Experience of Christ as Lord,* trans. John Bowden (New York: Seabury, 1980), 731–43. For a brief survey of Schillebeeckx's use of the term *humanum*, see Helen Bergin, "Edward Schillebeeckx and the Suffering Human Being," *International Journal of Public Theology* 4, no. 4 (October 2010): 466–482.

4. "Correlation between Human Question and Christian Answer," in *Understanding of Faith*, 91.

5. By speaking of this experience as prereligious, Schillebeeckx was describing what he earlier had characterized as the "pretheoretical" character of this experience. Ultimately, he believed, experiences of contrast precede and orient the interpretive framework of those who suffer. We will examine his explanation of this universal response in what follows.

human person ceaselessly objects to outbreaks of meaninglessness within history. In this universal experience of resistance, in the protesting "no" against the threatened *humanum*, Schillebeeckx once again located a universal preunderstanding for the story of salvation promised in Jesus.

It is important to emphasize that it is not the experience of suffering itself that makes the proclamation of the Christian story existentially possible, according to Schillebeeckx. Rather, it is the hope-filled protest against suffering that such experiences inherently engender: "The fundamental human 'no' to evil . . . discloses an unfulfilled and thus 'open yes' which is as intractable as the human 'no,' indeed even stronger, because the 'open yes' is the basis of that opposition and makes it possible."[6] It is only the believer, Schillebeeckx recognized, who will interpret in faith God's promise of eschatological salvation on the other side of suffering: "For Christians the fundamental muttering of humanity turns into a well-founded hope. Something of a sigh of mercy, of compassion, is hidden in the deepest depths of reality . . . and in it believers hear the name of God."[7] Yet even the nonbeliever, one whose hope is contained by the bounds of what is deemed humanly possible, responds with a "no" that reveals a tacit "openness to the unknown ground of hope."[8] As such, these experiences establish the very condition for the possibility of communicating the Christian message of hope.

While simultaneously avoiding a positively defined understanding of reality, Schillebeeckx believed contrast experiences unavoidably raise the question of the ultimate significance of human history. They are "the negative and dialectical coming to consciousness of

---

6. *Church: The Human Story of God,* trans. John Bowden (New York: Crossroad, 1994), 6.
7. Ibid.
8. Ibid.

a desideratum, a longing, and of a question about meaning 'on its way' and real freedom, wholeness and happiness to come."[9] Though dialectically revealed, an existential longing for meaning is found in the depths of human existence. Such experiences, he insisted repeatedly, do not offer an a priori guarantee of that meaning: "This logically implied question in no way means that universal history must in reality *per se* have a definitively positive meaning."[10] At issue, however, was the prospect of intelligibility and communicability, not conclusive verification. The Christian faith, Schillebeeckx believed, responds to the extant desires of the human person. Contrast experiences establish the necessary condition from which the offer of salvation tendered in Christ is made fathomable. In the very midst of a history marked by suffering, these experiences provide "a sensitive point of resonance" for the announcement of eschatological hope in a God who promises in Jesus the defeat of even death.[11] The offer of renewed life and decisive salvation finds a potential and, as we will see, attentive audience in those who refuse to dignify evil, though that offer continuously surpasses the upper limits of their most profound longings. Resistance to unjust suffering preconditions men and women for the Christian message of healing and final redemption without positively delineating the inexhaustible contours of that message. As he once did with regard to the self-transcending hope of secularization, he now would describe experiences of contrast as the source of a new "natural theology."[12]

Schillebeeckx was well aware by now of the difficulties surrounding such a claim. He, too, warned against a "purely metaphysically orientated 'natural theology' which tried to attribute meaning to God before he began to speak."[13] As we have seen,

---

9. *Jesus: An Experiment in Christology,* trans. Hubert Hoskins (New York: Crossroad, 1995), 622.
10. *Church,* 174.
11. "Correlation," 99.
12. *Church,* 6. See also "Correlation," 99.

in his writings from the mid-1960s he already was concerned that such an approach presumed a starting point that could no longer be justified existentially. As expressed in chapter 2, it speciously provided a "correct" answer to the "wrong" question. He was equally critical at that time, however, of what he believed to be a pervasive "antimetaphysical" prejudice found in modern theology in which divine revelation is deemed unfathomable and wholly foreign to the human person.[14] By taking such a position, he argued, the universal claim of the Christian faith becomes an unintelligible and alien superstructure unrelated to modern life. At the time, he responded by calling for what he described as a "nonessential" metaphysical account of the Christian faith.[15] Such a project would begin not from theoretical speculation but from an analysis of human existence in the world. It would establish, it might be said, an inductive rather than deductive metaphysics and, in turn, would fashion a natural theology responsive to concrete lived experience. In describing Schillebeeckx's objective, Mark Schoof writes, "Metaphysics therefore can only be a conclusion, not a starting-point, and in any case one will have to rediscover its existential basis."[16] Subsequently, Schillebeeckx located

---

13. "Correlation," 88. See also *Church*, 29, where Schillebeeckx addressed this concern in the context of natural law and ethics.

14. "Towards a Catholic Use of Hermeneutics," in *God the Future of Man*, trans. N. D. Smith (New York: Sheed & Ward, 1968), 40. In this article, Schillebeeckx's criticism appears to be directed toward "dialectical theology" as a whole, though he included only Bultmann by name.

15. Ibid., 47n20.

16. Mark Schoof, "Masters in Israel, 7: The Later Theology of Edward Schillebeeckx," *Clergy Review* 55 (1970): 952. This reevaluation of metaphysics accounts for the significance of Schillebeeckx's oft-cited "clear break" from his mentor Dominicus De Petter, announced in *Jesus*, 817. The "perspectivalist" epistemology Schillebeeckx developed under the tutelage of De Petter posited an implicit intuition of the whole of reality nonconceptually given in every explicit insight. A speculative and theoretical presumption for universal meaning, though always unthematized, precedes every act of knowing, which is precisely the epistemological position he now found inadequate to the task. To understand the precise nature of his concern, however, it is important to note that Schillebeeckx considered his earlier position, which presumed "participation of the total meaning in every particular experience of meaning," appropriate for an age in which Christianity provided the widely agreed-upon plausibility structures of culture. In the contemporary context, he argued, this homogeneous culture no

in the radical trust in the future that was characteristic of the time the existential basis by which to speak of God as the ground of hope.

In Schillebeeckx's later work, his suspicion of metaphysics had become even more pronounced. He now believed that the positivist character and the ideological weight behind traditional metaphysical theories inevitably result in a theology that simply mirrors dominant mores and priorities, legitimating the plausibility structures of those who benefit the most from the status quo. Having recognized the danger in such a move, however, he still maintained the need for a nonessential metaphysics. Once again, he criticized an "antimetaphysical" tendency within modern theology in which "the basic concept of creation withered away and theology became pure eschatology—a variety of theologies of hope flourished without any foundation of creation."[17] If the eschatological hope promised in Jesus is itself to be more than an ideological creed, he argued, theology must discover a sensitive point of resonance in human existence. Contrast experiences, then, provide this necessary universal horizon of understanding but without affirming a positively defined understanding of reality. Though he did not use the expression, his modified position now could be described more accurately as a "nonessential negative metaphysics."[18]

Having noted his intent, however, we should acknowledge that it was in the process of taking this position that the protological

longer exists, and only thus, is there the need for a repositioning of the metaphysical project. This would suggest that his attempted break from his earlier work was of an epistemological rather than a metaphysical kind. This will become clearer in what follows. Though the language of a "clear break" is not found until 1974, in the article cited here, Schoof recounts proceedings from a "talk" given by Schillebeeckx in 1968 in which he expressed this same criticism.

17. "The Crisis in the Language of Faith as a Hermeneutical Problem," in *The Language of Faith: Essays on Jesus, Theology, and the Church* (Maryknoll, NY: Orbis, 1995), 88. See also, "Correlation," 97.
18. In "Edward Schillebeeckx as Critical Theorist: The Impact of Neo-Marxist Social Thought on His Recent Theology," *Thomist* 48 (1984): 362, William Portier described this position as "a minimal, negative realistic metaphysics."

faith of the tradition once again appeared in Schillebeeckx's writing. If a contrast experience was to provide a universally accessible touchstone, it could no longer be accounted for via the eschatological understanding of history particular to Christianity. Schillebeeckx surely could have ascribed a corresponding transcendental structure to history itself, but we will see soon that he was unwilling to concede just such a theorization of history. Thus, he now argued that the human person's resistance to evil is universally experienced, because all men and women are sustained by the gratuitous goodness of creation. It is the essential goodness of creation itself that arouses within religious and nonreligious alike the trust "that goodness and not evil *must have* the last word."[19] It is Christ who changes this "must have" to "will have"; through him we receive the promise that evil will not have the last word and that our protestations against evil are not made in vain. Protology, Christology, and eschatology continue to be essentially linked. Without the "must have" powered by creation, however, the "will have" revealed in Christ would be hopelessly unintelligible. Thus, Schillebeeckx secured the universality of human resistance to evil by affirming the human's statusas created and continuously sustained by God's sheer act of existence. Whether such a move betrays an inadvertent return to the speculative and idealist metaphysics that Schillebeeckx was seeking to overcome is an important question that will need to be addressed. We will return to this question in the conclusion of this study, better positioned to offer a response.

19. "Correlation," 98. See also *Church*, 99 (emphasis mine).

From Participatory Meaning to a Practical Anticipation of Total Meaning

Although a contrast experience dialectically keeps open the possibility of ultimate meaning for history, it also draws our gaze upon the suffering and injustice embedded in human life. The possibility that, in the end, history might be only a surd simultaneously remains open. The indeterminacy of ongoing human history is uncompromising from such a perspective. Ultimately frustrating every attempt to speak prematurely of definitive significance or insignificance, a contrast experience spontaneously brings to light the vicious commingling of sense and nonsense in history. It resists every coherent explanation or abstract reconciliation, repudiating both defeatist interpretations of history in which potential meaning is definitively denied and totalizing interpretations in which absolute unity is prescribed in advance. With his attention now drawn to the ambiguity of history, Schillebeeckx believed it all the more necessary for theology to begin from an analysis of this human experience rather than theoretical speculation. Lest it function ideologically and be found utterly incredible, the Christian claim to the eschatological salvation promised in Jesus cannot be formulated idealistically: "To speak theoretically of a definitive total meaning of history implies, in reality, an insensitivity to the world-historical and personal dramas and catastrophes in our history."[20] This explains, then, Schillebeeckx's unwillingness to ascribe theoretically a transcendental structure to history that would account for experiences of contrast. At the price of credibility and critical vigor, positing an idealistic account of history ignores the suffering and injustice of present and past.

---

20. "Erfahrung und Glaube," in *Christlicher Glaube in moderner Gesellschaft 25* (Freiburg, Ger.: Herder, 1980): 23–116; unpublished translation by Robert J. Schreiter.

Attempting to overcome this impasse, Schillebeeckx now argued that for the theologian, the Christian's hope must first serve as a "hypothesis."[21] The operative and existentially justifiable presumption is not that constant progress is assured but "that it is not impossible to give meaning to history, however ambiguous it may be, and therefore that the attempt to do so should never be abandoned."[22] The Christian claim of universality remains outstanding and provisional in the midst of ongoing suffering. A theoretical pretension of present participation in the total meaning of history is not viable in such a context. Rather, what is required is the practical anticipation of total meaning through eschatological praxis, even if this can be done in only an essentially incomplete and fragmented manner. Though now purposefully directed toward resisting and transforming what is meaningless, once again, meaning must be made in history. The Christian "hypothesis" of eschatological hope promised in Jesus must be tested against concrete historical experience, substantiated practically in a suffering world, if it is to be found at all trustworthy.

By speaking of Christian hope as a "hypothesis," Schillebeeckx did not intend to deny the definitive eschatological significance of Jesus. "Of course," he wrote, "the Christian believes, in and through Jesus, that despite everything the kingdom of God, as salvation for mankind, is still coming and will come. . . . [S]alvation cannot be eschatologized in a one-sided way; in other words, ultimate salvation is no longer undecided."[23] The Christian makes a real claim to the meaning of history; suffering will not have the last word. But precisely because what was decisively accomplished in Jesus occurred within the ambiguity of history, this claim made in faith defies both mediation by theoretical argumentation and unambiguous historical

---

21. *Jesus*, 617–19.
22. "New Critical Theory and Theological Hermeneutics," 153.
23. *Interim Report*, 101.

verification. Consequently, Schillebeeckx argued, "[t]he redemption which has been achieved in Jesus needs to be presented in such a way that our history in fact remains ongoing human history. As long as history is still in the process of developing, it does not have any totality in itself and can only have its total meaning in an anticipatory factor."[24] There is no vantage point from within history, even that of faith, from which history can be seen as a whole. We cannot know from history itself its final meaning and last word: "Only by the living witness of Christians over the course of time can it be shown—and then only to some degree—that the liberating and reconciling activity of the churches . . . is not a chance event, but the realization in history of the message of Jesus, which in this way shows something of its truth in history."[25] Thus the significance of Schillebeeckx's deployment of quotation marks when using the term "hypothesis." In faith, the Christian wholly affirms that the ultimate meaning of history is no longer undecided, but this claim resists conclusive rationalization in the present. Salvation is not provisional, yet Christians face "a theoretical inability to reconcile the redemption already accomplished with our actual human history of suffering."[26] Thus, to some degree, Christians will need to garner support for their hope in lived historical reality if it is to be found credible. Although direct verification remains impossible, the ongoing anticipation of the kingdom indirectly attests to the claim that in Christ an ever-greater hope for history has been made possible. Schillebeeckx once more had placed eschatological praxis at the forefront of Christian apologetics.

Christians are thus enjoined to continue to make manifest the coming of God's kingdom through their own praxis of healing and

---

24. Ibid.
25. Ibid., 68.
26. *Christ*, 819.

solidarity; they are called to take up God's cause as their own cause: "The factor mediating between the historical person, Jesus, and his significance for us now is in concrete terms the practice of Christian living within our continuing human history."[27] Remembering the story of Jesus is a practical affair in which one continues to anticipate a history of meaning and freedom, albeit in a new historical context:

> Jesus' conviction that there is an essential link between the coming of the kingdom of God which he proclaimed and his praxis of the kingdom of God, and the consequent faith conviction of his followers that the mission of Jesus has a definitive, eschatological and universal significance (as is clearly confessed by the New Testament) necessitates a continuation of Jesus' earthly mission by his disciples beyond the limited time of his earthly life—if time has any ordinary continuation after the death of Jesus (which is unmistakably the case). It is as simple as that.[28]

As we have now seen, Schillebeeckx was concerned that unless the meaningless in world history is resisted and the meaning continues to be made visibly manifest, the promise tendered in Jesus will remain simply incredible. If our eschatological hope cannot find support in historical reality, in both the kingdom praxis of Jesus and the ongoing liberating praxis of his disciples, it will remain ideologically suspect, unintelligible, and therefore fruitless. The epistemological priority of praxis championed by Habermas and cautiously but already present in Schillebeeckx's earlier writings on eschatology now was plainly evident.

27. *Jesus*, 623.
28. *Church*, 155.

The Ongoing Mediation of Christian Hope in History

Creative Fragments of Salvation as Anticipation of Total Meaning

The positive content of Christian hope is found not only in the life, death, and resurrection of Jesus but also in the ongoing mediation of the story of Jesus in the history of discipleship, the concrete historical praxis of the followers of Jesus. Schillebeeckx's concern for epistemic efficacy, then, does not yet bring us to a comprehensive understanding of the relationship between anticipatory praxis and the promise of eschatological salvation in his thought. There is, he further insisted, a positive ontological relationship between human activity and God's saving activity. The ongoing praxis of the kingdom in world history is intimately connected and substantively contributes to the history of salvation: "Universal resistance to alienation, inhumanity and the absence of freedom assumes, in Christianity, the form of a redemption by God which can be realized in and through the faith of people in history."[29] Elsewhere, he claimed, "Where good things are achieved to man's advantage . . . the believer sees salvation from God realized through man and the world. . . . Eschatological or final salvation—let us call it heaven—takes shape (heavenly shape) from what men on earth achieve as salvation for their fellow man."[30] Where evil and suffering are protested and human liberation is achieved, Schillebeeckx argued, God's promise slowly but progressively comes to be realized within history. Kingdom praxis is "the material or medium of God's salvific activity, without which

---

29. "Correlation," 93.
30. *Christ*, 791–92. According to Schillebeeckx, although only the believer will "see" or interpret worldly healing and liberation as salvation from God, as the unfolding history of revelation, even the nonbeliever shares in and contributes to the unfolding of salvation history whenever goodness is advanced and evil resisted. For Schillebeeckx's thought on the distinction between the history of revelation and the history of salvation, see *Church*, 9–13. See also Mary Catherine Hilkert, "Experience and Revelation," in *The Praxis of the Reign of God*, ed. Mary Catherine Hilkert and Robert J. Schreiter, 2nd ed. (New York: Fordham University Press, 2002), 69–78.

God is 'powerless'"; it is "an inner constitutive element of the redemption which is God's reign."[31] The breakthrough of the kingdom in history certainly remains vague and imperfect, for the end promised is not yet here. Indeed, he would describe each fragmented but real anticipation of meaning in history as a mere "drop of water on a hot stone."[32] Nonetheless, if salvation is to be human salvation, it will need to be made manifest in human history. Through the process of emancipative praxis informed by and oriented toward the kingdom revealed in the eschatological prophet, Jesus of Nazareth, world history little by little can begin to mediate and embody human salvation.

Here again, Schillebeeckx would return to the protological faith so prevalent in his earlier writings.[33] As created, the human person is essentially incarnate and of this world. God's gift of creation—and it is a gift, for creation need not exist (that is, it is contingent)—is the gift of finitude. The God of creation, therefore, does not save humans from finitude and contingency gratuitously given but rather saves humans precisely as finite and contingent beings. There is "no salvation outside the world," he insisted, and as such, salvation must be mediated in world history; there is no pure and undiluted mediation of God's saving activity available on its own.[34] This is what Schillebeeckx had underscored when speaking of the "powerlessness" of God. Creation is a "risky venture," for it is only through the course of world-historical events that God's saving activity is made manifest in the world.[35] Indeed, if humans fail to confront injustice and to

31. "Theologie als bevrijdingskunde," *Tijdschrift voor Theologie* 24 (1984): 401; translated by Derek Simon in "Salvation and Liberation in the Practical-Critical Soteriology of Schillebeeckx," *Theological Studies* 63 (2002): 509. See also *Church*, 6–9.

32. *Christ*, 821.

33. See especially "I Believe in God, Creator of Heaven and Earth," in *God among Us: The Gospel Proclaimed* (New York: Crossroad, 1983), and "Kingdom of God: Creation and Salvation," in *Interim Report*,105–24.

34. *Church*, 5.

seek the healing of the threatened *humanum*, "history as such can come to grief."[36] History itself offers no guarantee of final success. Nonetheless, through the liberating praxis of free men and women, God's gift of salvation can be gradually realized in history. As we have seen, as early as 1958, Schillebeeckx could write, "Our ordering of life within this world . . . is thus a participation in the eschatology of mankind."[37] Though he now would speak of the fragmented "anticipation" of the eschaton rather than "participation" in the eschaton, the same nondualistic understanding of the divine–human relationship established in creation supported his position. The language of anticipation represents an epistemic-apologetic development; his metaphysics has remained fundamentally the same.

God as Universal Subject of Human History

This becomes even clearer when Schillebeeckx takes up the question of the subject of history. Without doubt, many individuals and whole societies have enormous resources at their disposal to work toward healing and liberation in the world. Without compromise, however, history repeatedly confronts human beings with ongoing suffering and failure. No technological advancement or political program can definitively address the suffering indelibly embedded in history. Definitive salvation means perfect and universal salvation, and no number of food programs or health initiatives can remove the suffering of love lost because of our finitude and mortality, or the guilt that accompanies an honest look into the injustices of the past. Furthermore, the countless men and women who have already died

---

35. "Christian Identity and Human Integrity," in *Language of Faith*, 192.
36. *Church*, 5.
37. "The Intellectual's Responsibility for the Future," in *World and Church,* trans. N. D. Smith (New York: Sheed & Ward, 1971), 275.

find no comfort in the limited emancipative progress of today. And ultimately, Schillebeeckx again reminded the reader, death puts a stop to every partially emancipated life. Given the fragility of our liberating actions and the limitations placed on their ends, it is clear that humans cannot achieve universal salvation by their own accord.[38] Human history again and again has shown this to be the case. There is simply no secular universal subject in history that can bring about total and decisive meaning. Failure to recognize this is precisely the conceit of technocratic society. The "omnipotence" of technical reason, for all its ambition and promise, has failed to alleviate the world's misery while leaving a death-dealing tyranny in its wake. Now using the language introduced by Metz, which we will consider more fully in the following chapter, Schillebeeckx thus would speak of an eschatological "proviso" on history.[39] No individual, program, or even history itself can lay claim to determining total and universal meaning.

Thus, although the history of human emancipation may be coextensive with the history of salvation, the two cannot be identified. The Christian hope, grounded in Christ, clearly exceeds the potential of emancipative praxis. Although eschatological salvation includes sociopolitical and interpersonal liberation, it cannot be reduced to it. Humans are unable to find in themselves the means for their final salvation: "The alienation in man's life cannot be completely overcome in the personal or the social plane; 'liberated freedom' or true well-being transcends both person and society."[40] If the final reconciliation of a history intractably marked by suffering is to be accomplished, then, it can only be by the One who creatively transcends history yet desires to see it come to good. This is precisely

---

38. *Christ*, 764–65; *Jesus*, 624.
39. See *Christ*, 767; and *Interim Report*, 119.
40. *Jesus*, 624.

the God proclaimed and revealed in Christ: the God who is universal subject and Lord of history.[41] "A final healing of the division in our existence in the world can only be the consequence of an active reality which embraces both person and society, i.e., the whole of reality, without doing violence to it; and this is the definition of God, of the one who transcends all things through interiorness, who goes beyond all things from within."[42] Ultimate meaning and the reconciliation of history, Schillebeeckx maintained, come through God alone. Not surprisingly, however, he warned the reader against concluding from this that God's saving activity is limited to a restricted sphere that entails only that which cannot be achieved by the emancipative processes of human liberation.[43] His nondualistic understanding of the divine–human relationship established in creation rejects a dualistic interpretation of history and God's saving activity in it.

As we saw in chapter 2, the infinite and transcendent God of creation is not one among many finite and tangible beings in the world. In his later writings, Schillebeeckx reaffirmed this position: "God does not act in history as men conduct their affairs in it. . . . God's acting in history is not some 'interventionist activity.'"[44] Again, the peculiarity of divine transcendent activity allows for a gratuitous and saving immanence that comes to expression through the free and autonomous human person's right ordering of history. He explained:

> God is the Lord of history and by proxy, as it were, presents salvation
> to human beings as a gift. This is the gist of the biblical notion, to us
> rather strange, of the "kingdom of God." God's lordship, therefore, is
> the exercise of his peculiar and divine function as sovereign Creator: as

41. "Erfahrung und Glaube," 15; *Church*, 175; "Christian Identity and Human Integrity," 192; Correlation," 93.
42. *Christ*, 815.
43. Ibid., 765.
44. *Jesus*, 626–27.

"king" he is purveyor of salvation to that which he endowed with life. That this kingdom comes means that God looks to us men and women to make his "ruling" operational in our world.[45]

There is a distinction but no rivalry between what God does in history for us and what we who have our foundation in God do ourselves. Divine agency and human agency are not competing within a closed ontological economy; they do not play by the rules of a zero-sum game. Because God's immediate saving presence is mediated in and through creation, the autonomy of the world "does not rule out the possibility that what is done here in human terms . . . can also in fact be a historical communication of grace, a foretaste of salvation: the possibility of experiencing human salvation in the making."[46] Thus, Schillebeeckx could write, "'humanity' is not the universal subject of history in general, but human history is made by men, and so they themselves must be the people, the subjects of their own history."[47] God alone is the universal subject of history, but this does not preclude men and women from being the active subjects of history as they gradually bring about God's free gift of salvation in the world.

Schillebeeckx's Rejection of Apocalyptic Eschatology

Rejecting Dualism:
Human Liberation and Eschatological Salvation

In light of this understanding of the human's constitutive role in the unfolding of salvation history, it will be helpful to return to Schillebeeckx's criticism of an apocalyptic understanding of history.

---

45. Ibid., 141–42.
46. *Christ*, 812–13.
47. Ibid., 788. See also *Jesus*, 626.

In 1969, you will remember, he warned that apocalypticism severs the future from the present and past, disrupting the hermeneutic context needed for hope in a transcendent eschatology. Schillebeeckx revisited this topic in greater detail early in the book *Jesus*. In reviewing secondary literature from the 1960s and early 1970s, he attempted to characterize the historical context of Jesus in relation to the apocalyptic commitments prevalent in first-century Palestine.[48] It was through this process that Schillebeeckx further clarified what he understood by the term *apocalypticism* and ultimately identified, though still in rather broad strokes, important themes running through an apocalyptic eschatology. "The basic substance of apocalypticism," he wrote, "bears the stamp of a long experience of human life, an experience which has ceased to look to man's history for any improvement. Suffering and every kind of misfortune . . . are so persistent that . . . it is no longer possible . . . to hope for any final good from our human history."[49] Apocalypticism, he recognized, is itself a mode of hope-filled expectation in the future from the midst of a history of suffering. Within it resides the deep-seated hope that evil and human suffering cannot have the last word. Contrasting it with what he believed to be an authentic Christian eschatology, however, Schillebeeckx argued that in apocalyptic thought, "all hope is founded on the 'turn of the ages,' that is, a sudden intervention on God's part, which just does away altogether with 'this course of events' or 'this aeon.'"[50] Apocalyptic hope is oriented toward a new historical "epoch" in which the present period of suffering and subjugation will be decisively routed. As such, hope-filled expectation is directed toward an abrupt act of God coming from the future, a divine

48. *Jesus*, 116–54.
49. Ibid., 119–20.
50. Ibid., 120.

intervention in history, by which the evils of the present and past will be left behind in lieu of a radically new age.

Interestingly, Schillebeeckx acknowledged that apocalyptic hope creates a certain tension or agitation that encourages a vigilant attentiveness or "watchfulness" for God's saving activity in history. This is acutely needed, he believed, in a modern, secular world devoted to the promises of technological advancement but negligent of the transcendent hope promised in Christ.[51] He also was not concerned with what is frequently perceived as apocalypticism's inherently dualistic understanding of history, suggested by the characteristic language of two "aeons" or "epochs." Apocalypticism, he argued, does not necessarily place the present over against a coming future in a definitive manner. From an apocalyptic perspective, it is possible for God's salvific activity to operate clandestinely in the present world, though this will be brought out into the open only when God's power over history has been established irrevocably in the future. Schillebeeckx's concern, however, was that in this "bringing into the open . . . no consideration is given to the element of continuity."[52] Apocalyptic salvation coming from God interrupts history, untethering the future from the events of the past. Again, maintaining historical continuity was of foremost concern for Schillebeeckx. "The post-terrestrial eschaton," he wrote, "is but a question of the manner in which what is already growing in the history of this world will receive its final fulfillment."[53] Apocalypticism disorders the fundamental relationship between creation and the eschaton; it breaks off the nonidentical but continuous relationship between the history of human liberation and the history of salvation.

51. "Apocalypse Now," in *For the Sake of the Gospel*, trans John Bowden (New York: Crossroad, 1990), 34.
52. *Jesus*, 150.
53. "Interpretation of the Future," 10.

As we have seen, according to Schillebeeckx's reading of the New Testament, the promise offered in Jesus of an imminently approaching kingdom was realized as an already available yet excessive reality in and through his praxis of the kingdom. Though always oriented toward God's gift of definitive salvation still on the way, the present immediacy of God in history was at the center of his preaching and ministry. Apocalypticism, Schillebeeckx believed, locates the realization of this promise in the future alone.[54] It empties the human struggle for good and resistance to evil of all but a temporary and fleeting significance. Emancipative praxis plays no positive and constructive role in the coming of God's kingdom, deflating the salvific value of both Christ's kingdom praxis and the praxis of those who follow after him. Schillebeeckx refused, writes Daniel Speed Thompson, "to separate God's action from human action in the process of salvation. Salvation does not just happen through some divine fiat; salvation comes from God only in and through human activity."[55] The Christian's eschatologically charged hope looks not toward an extrinsic and foreign intervention by God in history but toward the gradual unfolding of God's promise in and through graced human freedom only to be brought to completion at the end of time. A vigilant watchfulness for God's saving activity in history, indeed, stands at the center of the Christian's hope, Schillebeeckx agreed with the apocalypticist, but "true expectation

54. Schillebeeckx also criticized an apocalyptic understanding of history for merely transposing at the end of time the master–slave relationship presently inscribed in the ambiguity of history rather than establishing a kingdom in which there are master and slave no more. The salvation of a broken world hoped for by Christians looks not to God's vengeance and the reversal of oppression, he argued, but to God's gratuitous love and the very end of oppression as revealed in the praxis of Christ: "Jesus will have nothing of the apocalyptic reversal of power-relationships, whereby the poor become top dog and those who are now rich, bottom dog. Jesus sees in the kingdom only an end to all overweening relations based on power" (*Jesus*, 145). Though this is a significant element in Schillebeeckx's critique of apocalypticism and important to note, it will not play a role in the arguments of this study. See also *Church*, 134–35.

55. Daniel Speed Thompson, *The Language of Dissent: Edward Schillebeeckx on the Crisis of Authority in the Catholic Church* (Notre Dame, IN: University of Notre Dame Press, 2003), 57.

of the end in faith is doing the works of the kingdom of God."[56] Salvation does not fall "vertically into the terrestrial event," Schillebeeckx wrote as early as 1968. "Eschatological hope implies faith that the Christian, by God's justification, is responsible for the terrestrial event itself becoming a history of salvation."[57] He was concerned to compromise neither the subjectivity of the human person established in creation nor the transcendence and freedom peculiar to the Creator God when speaking of God's saving activity in history.

Radical Expectation:
The Surplus of God's Eschatological Plan

In spite of his rejection of apocalypticism and his emphasis on the continuity between human liberation and eschatological salvation, Schillebeeckx did insist on preserving the surprising and unpredictable character of God's saving activity. Thus, Schillebeeckx agreed with those who took a more apocalyptic stance that the indefinable horizon of eschatological salvation must radicalize Christian expectation.[58] But he located that discontinuity in the "superabundance" of God's promise, which inexhaustibly extends that for which we might hope.[59] If the "surplus" of the eschatological promise were neglected, he argued, "we would be confronted with a utopian liberation which might perhaps stimulate some chances of life and salvation for people who appear on the far horizon of

---

56. "Apocalypse Now," 35.
57. "The New Image of God, Secularization, and Man's Future on Earth," epilogue to *God the Future of Man,* 185.
58. *Christ,* 791.
59. "Terugblik vanuit de tijd na Vaticanum II: De gebroken idelogieën van de moderniteit," in *Tussen openheid en isolement: Het voorbeeld van de katholische theologie in de negentiende eeuw,* ed. E. Borgman and A. van Harskamp (Kampen, Neth.: Kok, 1992), 170–71; translated by Simon in "Salvation and Liberation," 517.

our history but which has written off the rest of mankind from this prehistory for the benefit of a dreamed-of utopia to be realized one day."[60] Schillebeeckx's concern, here, was not that, detached from the eschatological hope of Christianity, men and women no longer would resist injustice and seek to heal and make right the world. The ongoing possibility of human hope was not at issue. The essential goodness of creation, he believed, arouses within all people the trust "that goodness and not evil must have the last word." Like the martyrs of the Christian tradition, history tells the story of people from many creeds, religious and nonreligious alike, who have risked everything, including life itself, for the cause of justice and another human's emancipation.[61]

It is not hope itself, then, that Christ's promise uniquely engenders but rather a hope with a uniquely inexhaustible range and reach. Again, Schillebeeckx's concern was that without an expectation oriented toward the excessive love of a saving God, the rigid "court" of modern reason would define far too narrowly the contours of that for which we might hope. Jesus brought "the message of a hope which cannot be derived from our world history."[62] Too much of what requires healing in the long story of human history gets covered over when the human person alone is seen as the means by which salvation can be achieved. As we have seen, human failure, guilt, and death itself are intractably immune to fragmented and incomplete acts of human emancipation. If there is to be a radical hope for a truly universal healing of history, that hope must be placed in the hands of the saving God: "Salvation in the full sense of the word is possible only where man can entrust himself to the ground of the possibility of his existence, that is, to the renewal of life through the holy."[63] Only

---

60. *Interim Report*, 123.
61. *Church*, 94–97; and "Doubt in God's Omnipotence: 'When Bad Things Happen to Good People,'" in *For the Sake of the Gospel*, 98–99.
62. *Christ*, 844.

the God who transcends history but who is bent toward humanity can bring about definitive salvation.

It is this surplus of hope found in the Christian story of Jesus, Schillebeeckx once again argued, that possesses the unique capacity to invigorate and reorient an ever-greater hope for history. In his writings from the late 1970s through the early 1990s, however, he would develop the distinctive character of this surplus with much greater clarity, reflecting on its practical significance for the human person's failed efforts in hope of the eschaton, the person's "guilty" failures to respond to this hope, and the critical meaning of a surplus of hope that extends even to the dead.

First, Schillebeeckx now insisted that an eschatological expectation provides the Christian with a unique confidence that protesting suffering and struggling for the good are never done in vain. The promise tendered in Jesus offers credible assurance that acts of resistance and liberation that achieve only partial success, and even those which end in total failure, have redemptive significance nonetheless: "We are shown the true face of both God and man in the 'vain' love of Jesus which knows that its criterion does not lie in success, but in its very being as radical love."[64] That which culminates in utter disaster within history, such as Christ's ministry and message, which end in execution on a cross, is revealed through the resurrection as genuinely having made manifest in history God's saving love. In Christ's self-sacrificing death, then, the very meaning of success has been amended. That which is "experienced as human impotence appear[s] in the *religious* experience . . . as a manifestation of the power of God . . . a love that is disarmed but at the same time disarming."[65] Pragmatic efficacy and assessable productivity are

63. Ibid., 777.
64. Ibid., 837.
65. Ibid., 830.

not the Christian's measures of emancipative value. In light of the resurrection, "the crucifixion of Jesus shows that any attempt at liberating redemption which is concerned with humanity is valid *in and of itself* and not subsequently as a result of any success which may follow."[66] The Christian's hope affirms that every act for the cause of love, no matter how compromised and inadequate when measured in terms of modern rationality, takes its place in the unfolding history of salvation. In turn, this hope engenders an unconditioned courage to love without fear, trusting that by the peculiar power of God, this is not done in vain.

Yet Schillebeeckx believed that even this is not God's last word regarding emancipatory praxis. In both the fragmented and failed historical mediations of God's saving activity, "the believer experiences that redemption is not within our power and that God nevertheless *gives a future* to all our actions towards liberation and reconciliation, a future which is greater than the volume of our finite history."[67] Elsewhere, he wrote, "[P]ractical mediation is taken up in trust in God, whose future for us is greater than our historical future."[68] The good that is realized in history, then, has eternal as well as historical value in God's plan for salvation. The fulfillment of history transcends history itself. Christ's resurrection tendered the promise that acts of resistance and liberation have a permanent redemptive significance both within history and beyond as they are taken up and brought to completion in God; even a historical fiasco is not an ultimate disaster in light of God's transforming power: "Human history—with its successes, failures, illusions and disillusions—is transcended by the living God, who has the last word and wills man's salvation."[69] But having argued so meticulously that

66. Ibid., 837.
67. Ibid., 838.
68. *Church*, 99.

the promise of an eschatological future orients and animates emancipatory praxis in history, Schillebeeckx would leave open the question of how this history is brought into the eschatological future. That God gratuitously affirms and extends history beyond history is clear, but Schillebeeckx resisted speculating on how this will come to fruition.[70] "What final possibilities are contained in the eschatological consummation of this saving presence of God," he simply wrote, "is God's mystery."[71] Indeed, it is difficult to envision how he would account for such a "consummation" without ascribing a direct and unmediated act of God in history, if only at the end of history. He was clear, nonetheless, that "in our history the future of God is at stake."[72] That which is realized in history as true and good, even through failure, receives a constitutive and irrevocable place in God's gift of eschatological salvation. "Only the form of this present world passes," he wrote in 1967 and now reconfirmed, "nothing of what has been achieved in the world by man's radical love."[73] The Christian's hope will not abandon history, then, but neither is it exhausted by history. Although everything is decided in human history, the last word is not with history itself but with the God who is Lord of history.[74]

The Christian's expectation for universal salvation, Schillebeeckx further argued, also extends a unique hope to a world marked by sin. Alongside those failures in history to bring about liberation because of the inevitable limits of human finitude and contingency, which in faith reveal God's special saving power, there also exist what Schillebeeckx described as "guilty" failures: "Just as the good which

69. *Christ*, 845. See also *Jesus*, 639.
70. Simon makes the same observation in "Salvation and Liberation," 519.
71. *Christ*, 837.
72. "God, Society, and Human Salvation," in *Faith and Society* (Gembloux, Belg.: Duculot, 1978), 99.
73. "Christian Faith," 89.
74. *Christ*, 831.

is done for the sake of our fellow men has definitive validity in and of itself, so there is something irrevocable in evil actions which men perform of their own free will. These are not only irrevocably part of the past history of man; in addition this human guilt is a free action against the living God."[75] Though always mediated in and through the world, particularly in the failure to care for the suffering other, the personal failings of the culpable human are an affront to God. Sin, Schillebeeckx reminded the reader, is a theological as well as an ethical concept: "By violating humanity, the sinner is personally guilty before God, the source of all furthering of the good and opposition to evil."[76] Where attentiveness to God's gratuitous love is no longer maintained, attentiveness to guilt fades away. When confronted by this guilt, though, humans discover that the inability to find in themselves the means for their own salvation is accompanied by an inability to find within themselves the means for their own forgiveness. In this experience, it becomes clear that all hope must be "handed over" to God: "Guilt has a dialogical structure and can never be removed one-sidedly; it calls for the creative word of God's forgiveness, which transcends our act of penitence from within."[77] Though always mediated in and through the worldly "material" of penitence, the hope in a genuinely universal salvation, a hope revealed in the conciliatory praxis of Jesus, trusts that release from the shackles of guilt is indeed possible through the gratuitous saving activity of the merciful God.

Finally, Schillebeeckx argued, the peculiar breadth and range of the Christian's hope-filled expectation cannot be confined to the present and that which is yet to come. Hope in universal salvation refuses to abandon even the past: "Jesus is the hope not only of the

75. Ibid., 833.
76. Ibid.
77. Ibid.

living and the generations to come, but even for those who have been written out of our history: for those who are already dead, people who no longer have any future in terms of our earthly order; those who are completely excluded."[78] Though greatly respecting those who struggle against injustice without religious commitment, those who at times even give their lives in hope of bettering the world for coming generations, Schillebeeckx warned that such a hope inevitably turns its back on precisely those men and women from the past who have done the same. It "forgets the many sacrifices which have been made and the countless victims who will still fall. The fallen themselves then experience no liberation or redemption."[79] Without an expectation that extends into the broken past, the dead are excluded from the future that is sought. The unique expectation of the Christian trusts that the Lord of life and history gives a future even to those who know no more future. Christians possess a radical hope that what is impossible for humanity, overcoming death itself, has indeed been made possible through the peculiar and gratuitous power of God.

Conclusion

In the beginning of chapter 3, when tracing the transitions in Schillebeeckx's thought in the late 1960s, I argued that he became increasingly unsure whether the experience of hope or fear most urgently marked the modern situation. As we have seen, he was persuaded by warnings of an emerging one-dimensional society and the subsequent loss of freedom that accompanied the "dialectic of secularization." He grew sensitive to the idealist concept of history inadvertently endorsed by theologies of secularization. Most

---

78. *Interim Report*, 138. See also "New Critical Theory and Theological Hermeneutics," 133–34.
79. "Doubt in God's Omnipotence," 100. See also *Church*, 96.

significantly, he identified the critical negativity of eschatological faith as a powerful theological resource capable of resisting the death-dealing excesses of a myopic commitment to technological progress. Given these developments, it is surprising that Schillebeeckx remained undecided whether hope or fear was the contextual challenge confronting Christian theology. The incontestable logic of technical reason appeared to be choking off the freedom achieved through the process of secularization. An optimistic and well-polished vision of the future had given way to an understanding of history as genuinely ambiguous and inexplicably stained by human suffering. How, then, could Schillebeeckx still speak of hope, still believe that a pervasive longing for a better future marked the human experience? As we have seen in this chapter, his cultural analysis that so strongly suggested the pending demise of the modern person's expectations for the future was ultimately coupled with a creation faith that championed a universal, metaphysical guarantee of enduring human hope. In the midst of a history of suffering, the goodness of creation underwrites practical resistance to human suffering. Despite persistent evidence that history holds no meaning, the human person ceaselessly objects to outbreaks of meaninglessness within history. Hope can be too narrowly circumscribed, its ambition and optimism misdirected, but it will not acquiesce to the meaningless in history.

Contrast experiences, then, became the foundation for Schillebeeckx's apologetic project, providing the universal pre-understanding necessary for the proclamation of the Christian's eschatological hope. His eschatology remained anchored in protology. As we have seen, though, it still needed to find its center of gravity in the eschatological prophet, Jesus Christ, if this dialectical resistance to suffering was to overcome the practical impotence of a theoretical negativity. The life, death, and resurrection of Jesus Christ reveal in human history the "surplus of hope" and positive content needed to orient a genuinely subversive praxis of hope. In 1968, Schillebeeckx had argued that the Christian has "as little positive idea as the non-Christian of what is worthy of man, either ultimately or here and now."[80] His extensive christological studies would amend this claim, revealing an important development in his thought. The full content of human salvation remains in the future, he continued to insist, but it is no longer a vague or totally indefinable reality.

Yet, once again, this claim depended upon Schillebeeckx's continuing commitment to the creation faith of his earlier work. It was his metaphysics of creation that allowed him to speak of the kingdom praxis of Christ and those who disciple after him as substantively realizing in history the beginnings of the salvation for which we hope. These "beginnings" are fundamentally imperfect and fragmented; sociopolitical progress will not bring about the definitive and total salvation gratuitously promised. In this way, Schillebeeckx's prophetic eschatology stubbornly refused to reconcile the ambiguity of history. Consequently, he now spoke of the "anticipation" of the eschaton rather than "participation" in the eschaton. Without the traces of God's saving activity revealed in history in and through graced human praxis, however, Schillebeeckx feared that the eschatological expectations of the Christian would be unintelligible, incommunicable, and ideologically suspect. Thus, his apologetic interests were served by the ontological realism of his nondualistic creation faith. If eschatological salvation is to be human salvation, it needs to be realized and made manifest in history. God alone is the universal subject of history, Schillebeeckx insisted, but God's saving activity must be mediated in and through the praxis of those men and women who might gradually bring about God's free gift of salvation in the world.

80. "New Image of God," 191.

5

———

Metz Contends with a History Marked by Suffering

Sensitivity to Suffering Under the Pressures of Evolutionary Time

In the preceding two chapters, when tracing the developments in Schillebeeckx's thought from the late 1960s through the early 1990s, we observed in his writings his increasing unease with the historical processes of secularization and the distinct form of progressive optimism underlying European and North American technocratic societies. In search of a theological response to what critical theorists called the "dialectic of Enlightenment," Schillebeeckx turned to the critical negativity of Christianity's eschatological hope. He saw in that hope a powerful resource capable of resisting the dangerous excesses of the period's myopic commitment to technological progress while concurrently animating the Christian's constitutive interest in the establishment of a more humane future. From Schillebeeckx's perspective, that hope is sustained by the absolute saving presence of the Creator God. Metz shared Schillebeeckx's concern about the false optimism of modern technocratic societies. But as we shall see in this and the following chapter, in Metz's later eschatological writings the Christian's subversive hope is grounded and sustained by an apocalyptic view of time rather than the doctrine of creation. These chapters examine the development in Metz's eschatological writings from 1967 through the 1990s with particular attention given to the turn to apocalypticism that is characteristic of his mature eschatology and that distinguishes his thought from that of his Belgian colleague.

Following a brief review of Metz's earlier writings (1962–66), discussed in chapter 1, the first section of this chapter will turn to several key essays Metz wrote in 1967 in which he further extended his appreciation of the critical character of eschatology and began championing his well-known notion of an "eschatological proviso," an apologetic strategy shared by Schillebeeckx. In developing the theological implications of the proviso, Metz also began to emphasize the church's role as an institution of social criticism. As we shall see, this decision would anticipate a significant shift in his thought, investigated in the second section of the chapter.

It is in the second section that we will begin to see the origins of Metz's and Schillebeeckx's appreciably distinctive mature eschatologies. After examining the fuller appreciation of a postidealist epistemology that heightened Metz's attention to the social conditioning of the human subject, we will survey his substantially modified analysis of the modern historical context and his subsequent diagnosis of the cultural dynamics that emerged out of the Enlightenment. Far from an optimistic era of expectations and confidence characterized by a generation keenly committed to establishing an ever-greater freedom in history, modernity, in Metz's judgment, had fostered a crisis of hope in an age of evolutionary and fatalistic apathy. Although still affirming its interests in human emancipation, he would argue that the aporias of the Enlightenment had established the historical conditions in which the modern subject was no longer capable of remaining sensitive to the sufferings of others and, consequently, no longer capable of sustaining a hope for the future. This reality moved Metz to argue that if Christian theology seeks to validate and contribute to an unfolding history of human freedom, it must first locate the theological resources needed to maintain a sensitivity to the horrifying reality of a history ever marked by suffering

The final section of this chapter will discuss how Metz's earlier interest in presenting a practical-critical defense of the Christian's eschatological hope found new expression in a practical fundamental theology directed toward destabilizing the current sociopolitical conditions endangering the Christian's hope and forming that subject for whom hope is once again possible. His heightened commitment to the social differentiation of human subjectivity made it impossible for him to accept an already-operative universal consciousness of freedom, even negatively construed. In searching for theological resources that could establish the historical conditions in which an alternative consciousness of freedom could be achieved, Metz turned to his well-known category of dangerous memories. As we will see, it is through this category and the interrelated categories of narrative and solidarity that he believed the conditions begin to be established through which a subversive expectation for the future can withstand the pressures of evolutionary time.

An Eschatological Resistance to the Distortion of Hope

A Review of Metz's Eschatological Response
to the Process of Secularization

Over the preceding three chapters, we traced the lines of Schillebeeckx's theological project as he steadily reconsidered the Christian's eschatological hope in light of the realities and challenges of modern culture. In analyzing this development, I deliberately proceeded under the assumption that a close chronological reading of Schillebeeckx's writings provides the most effective approach to his thought. Though his individual works often reveal a theologian who formulated and revised his positions by way of the writing process, the synthetic and even linear progression of his corpus as a whole lent itself to such a strategy. This same method, you will remember, also was employed in the first chapter of this study, in which we examined many of Metz's early writings. I believe a diachronic advance through the first two parts of *Theology of the World,* read alongside other essays written in the early and mid-1960s, most effectively elucidates the precise contours of Metz's evolving response to secularization and his privileging of eschatology. Indeed, given the transitional nature of that book, any other approach could easily lead to misunderstanding.

Following this procedure, this chapter begins with an examination of the third part of *Theology of the World,* which contains essays dating from 1967. As we advance further into Metz's maturing project, however, we then will depart from this strategy. Like *Theology of the World,* most of Metz's later publications were collections of articles written over a number of years for a variety of academic and ecclesial occasions. Even his most influential work, *Faith in History and Society,* was a collection of essays written over a considerable period of time (1968–77), and many of the chapters were published previously under a variety of auspices.[1] It is not insignificant, though, that, unlike the earlier collection, the chapters in this work were not arranged chronologically for publication. As we have seen, Metz had grown increasingly uneasy with the prospects of modernity by the mid-1960s. At that time, however, his precise concerns had not yet found well-defined conceptualization. Over the ensuing years, Metz would work to identify more clearly both the specific challenges modernity presented Christianity and the theological strategies and resources available to the Christian in fashioning a response. These interrelated objectives unfolded organically in his writings during the late 1960s and 1970s, primarily through succinct and tightly focused essays that precluded extensive contextualization. Approached diachronically, then, his decisions for particular theological themes and categories could seem idiosyncratic and even bewildering, removed from the sociocultural diagnosis from which they arose.[2]

Certainly, Metz's promotion of an apocalyptic eschatology could yield to just such misunderstanding. It is for this reason that this chapter begins by first seeking to orient the reader to Metz's evolving understanding of a postidealist theology, his increasingly critical analysis of modern society, and the revisioning of his political theology as a practical fundamental theology. We then will be

---

1. *Glaube in Geschichte und Gesellschaft: Studien zu einer praktischen Fundamentaltheologie* (Mainz, Ger.: Matthias-Grünewald, 1977), trans. from the 5th ed. as *Faith in History and Society: Toward a Practical Fundamental Theology*, ed. and trans. J. Matthew Ashley (New York: Crossroad, 2007). This title will be abbreviated as *FHS*.

2. The nonlinear development of Metz's writings during this period is well illustrated by comparing the organizational plan of *Faith in History and Society* with the publication dates of the eight previously published chapters included in the collection. Metz structured this book in three parts. In the first part, he presented the sociocultural and historical analysis of modern society that necessitates the critical retrieval of repressed theological categories. Those categories are identified in the third part, whereas their function and efficacy are tested in the second part. Thus, part 1 provides the impetus and context for parts 2 and 3. Interestingly, part 1 was written after the majority of parts 2 and 3, suggesting that his assessment of the pressures facing theology and his effort to respond to those pressures developed in tandem during this period.

positioned properly to evaluate his unique characterization of the Christian eschatological message deliberately formulated and oriented toward the concrete historical conditions unearthed through his increasingly sophisticated cultural analysis.

Before proceeding to that task, which already begins with the examination of the later essays of *Theology of the World*, it will help to revisit briefly the terrain covered in chapter 1. Two fundamental interests informed Metz's early apologetic engagement with the phenomenon of secularization in a way that was not unlike that of Schillebeeckx. First, Metz was concerned with addressing the perceived opposition between Christianity and the modern world and rejecting any standpoint that presumed their essential incompatibility. Second, he hoped to legitimate and stimulate the Christian's participation in the secular task of building up the world. He advanced both of these interests by affirming and determining the historical consciousness of freedom that arose with modernity as essentially Christian in provenance. Moreover, it was precisely this historical consciousness that made possible a genuine and sustained hope for the future. In the earlier writings, Metz contended that creation and the incarnation transcendentally determined this freedom. In the later writings, he proposed instead that it was the eschatological hope in God's promise mediated in history by which this freedom was secured. Far from incompatible, the "primacy of the future" characteristic of an increasingly secularized society was historically determined by the biblical promise of a radically new future. Detached from this genesis, Metz feared, the modern person's interest in freedom risked becoming a dehumanizing dynamic.

Though deliberately striking out in a new direction, Metz's effort to construct a political theology in the mid-1960s was immediately related to the positions he had advanced through his engagement with secularization. In 1967, he provided an entry for "political theology" in a theological encyclopedia in which he outlined two central features of this theological project.[3] We will be familiar with both. First, political theology presents a critical correction to the privatizing tendencies inherent in the prevailing transcendental and existential theologies of the day. It resists abstracting the human person from concrete historical existence, which inevitably compromises the freedom and hope made possible by a genuinely open future. Second, political theology seeks to formulate the eschatological message of Christianity under the conditions of modern society. In doing this, political theology looks to overcome a theoretical correlation with existing cultural structures and to emerge as a practical and critical theology, relating Christian hope to sociohistorical praxis by identifying political society as the essential medium for the historical establishment of eschatological truth. It was evident that Metz's early attempt to formulate a political theology, characterized accordingly, extended his concern with securing theologically the historical consciousness of freedom attributable to secularization and determined by Christianity. He remained confident that the future-oriented hope embraced with modernity could be critically correlated with the creative and militant hope of Christianity.

Metz's corresponding emphasis in the mid-1960s on the critical distance between the existing conditions of the present and the eschatological future in which Christians hope did not undermine this position. Certainly, it revealed a growing concern with the ambiguous direction and prospects of modernity. As Metz argued at that time, eschatology determines the freedom realized through the process of secularization, but it also qualifies it. The critical reserve of Christianity resists the reduction of freedom and hope to the

3. "Political Theology," in *Sacramentum Mundi: An Encyclopedia of Theology*, ed. Karl Rahner et al. (New York: Herder & Herder, 1970), 5:34–38.

potentialities of the human person alone. Metz insisted that the hope of Christianity and the hope of modern culture cannot be identified. Only by attending to this nonidentity, he argued, could the freedom discovered in faith extend and secure the historical freedom realized with the rise of secularization. On the one hand, then, Metz had located eschatology at the center of his theological project by attending to the modern experience of a people committed to the primacy of the future. On the other hand, it was precisely by doing this that he came to recognize more clearly that within Christian eschatology dwells an inherent reserve that staunchly resists an identification of eschatological hope with the confident and optimistic hope of modern European or any culture. Nevertheless, Metz remained confident that the future-oriented hope of contemporary society could be critically correlated with the eschatological hope of Christianity. Although signs of an even more fundamental suspicion were beginning to emerge, he largely believed that the historical consciousness of freedom and a pervasive hope for the future continued to characterize and animate the times. If the Christian's eschatological hope was critically related to this historical consciousness, offering a corrective "thorn" of resistance, Metz maintained a presumption for the extant freedom of the modern person and, thus, believed that the peculiar hope of Christianity could orient the proper realization of that consciousness.

An Eschatological Response to the Dialectic of Enlightenment: Articulating the "Eschatological Proviso"

Although Metz substantially modified his earlier optimism about modernity in his writings from the mid-1960s, as discussed at the end of chapter 1, it was in the later essays of *Theology of the World*, to be considered presently, that his concerns began to find more rigorously defined conceptualization. Having followed the parallel developments in Schillebeeckx's and Metz's early writings, it is hardly surprising that in this maturing work Metz turned to the critical analysis of modernity associated with influential members of the Frankfurt school. Already championing the critical function of eschatology in his decision for a political theology, his commitment to a *theologia negativa* of the future would provide a sensitive point of resonance for a dialogue with these thinkers. It was in the later essays of *Theology of the World* that Metz first cited the writings of Adorno and Habermas, as well as those of Walter Benjamin, whose influence on Metz will be examined later in this chapter as well as in the following chapter.[4] That same year, in the encyclopedia entry on "political theology" from 1967 referenced above, Metz also referenced Marcuse's *One-Dimensional Society* for the first time. Although each of these men developed distinctive projects, we saw in a previous chapter that a common interest in the paralyzing consequences of a culturally concealed epistemological positivism and a corresponding fear of entrenched social hegemony connected Adorno's, Marcuse's, and Habermas's writings. Not formally affiliated with the Institut für Sozialforschung, Benjamin shared their concern, although in his own distinct fashion. The historical truncation and distortion of freedom were at issue, and the unrestricted rise and

---

4. The early reference to Habermas, in fact, is found in the 1966 essay "On the Hiddenness of the Problem of the Future of Metaphysics," examined in chapter 1. Critical of the quasi-transcendental claim of his "ideal speech situation," however, Metz would not make frequent use of Habermas's work. It was in 1969 that Metz first cited Max Horkheimer, with whom Adorno published the landmark text *Dialectic of Enlightenment*, trans. John Cumming (New York: Continuum, 1976). See Metz, "'Politische Theologie' in der Diskussion," in *Diskussion zur "Politischen Theologie,"* ed. Helmut Peukert (Mainz, Ger.: Matthias-Grünewald, 1969), 278n28. Though Metz routinely cites Horkheimer alongside Adorno, in later writing he admits that his "involvement with Horkheimer was not all that deep." See *Hope against Hope: Johann Baptist Metz and Elie Wiesel Speak Out on the Holocaust*, by Ekkehard Schuster and Reinhold Boschert-Kimmig, trans. J. Matthew Ashley (New York: Paulist, 1999), 23. For a helpful study of Metz's use of the Frankfurt theorists, see J. A. Colombo, *An Essay on Theology and History: Studies in Pannenberg, Metz, and the Frankfurt School* (Atlanta: Scholars Press, 1990).

dialectical tendency of instrumental rationalization would draw the sting of their criticism.[5]

Although it was not yet his overriding interest, Metz already had warned of a similar danger in the essay published in 1964 discussed in chapter 1. At that time, though, he resisted attributing this danger to the structure of the modern world as such. Moreover, he insisted that only by accepting a modern understanding of history could men and women overcome this danger and realize a genuine humanization.[6] In the years immediately following these remarks, however, Metz had revealed a much-heightened concern that the progressive optimism of society risked distorting its legitimate and genuine capacity to shape the future. He returned to this position in the essays of 1967, where he began to develop more fully both his concerns regarding these historical developments and the appropriate Christian response.

Though still acknowledging that political systems and scientific rationalization present appropriate methods by which to shape the world, a position he would maintain throughout his career, Metz

5. As we saw in chapter 3, this dynamic was frequently abbreviated by critical theorists as the "dialectic of Enlightenment." Unlike Schillebeeckx, Metz quickly began privileging this language when discussing the problematic processes of modern history confronting the contemporary church. We will see that by speaking of the dialectical processes of the Enlightenment, though certainly still concerned with the pastoral challenges presented by the phenomenon of secularization, Metz believed he could occupy a position with greater leverage from which to extend his analysis of modernity and to identify more fundamental challenges confronting Christianity and the modern person.

6. *Theology of the World*, trans. William Glen-Doepel (New York: Herder & Herder, 1969), 76 (hereafter abbreviated as *TW*). In an interview given in 1993, Metz recounted the story of an early encounter with Horkheimer that illustrates well his primary interests during the early 1960s. Preparing to part ways at a train station in Düsseldorf, Horkheimer said to Metz, "Do you see how cruel a train is, Herr Metz, how it moves off so quickly and separates people from one another?" Metz responded, "But after all, Herr Horkheimer, it does not just draw people apart, it also brings them together." In commenting on this conversation, Metz noted that Horkheimer's remark "was probably meant as a practical critique of the excesses of instrumental reason. . . . Obviously, at the time I was defending the promise of technology" (*Hope against Hope*, 23). It was this defense of the promise of technology and the critique of instrumental reason that Metz revisited in the years following this exchange.

insisted that these technological processes are neither self-sufficient nor absolute. In "The Church and the World in the Light of a 'Political Theology,'" Metz warned that if social progress is positioned as sufficient and an end in itself, whether politically or scientifically construed, a dangerous totalitarian ideology inevitably takes hold in which the human person is "considered exclusively as matter and means for the building of a completely rationalized future."[7] Deemed self-sufficient and absolute, detached from the ethical reflection needed to orient its proper ends, instrumental rationalization dialectically distorts the legitimate and genuine capacity of the human person to transform the world and determines a myopic technological progress that advances without regard for the individual. Consequently, the very freedom gained with the rise of secularization dissolves through its own excesses as men and women once again find themselves enslaved to an external force, freed from nature only to serve the unrestrained logic of technical reason.

At the same time, Metz again insisted that history as a whole stands under God's eschatological freedom. According to Metz, Christian expectation fosters what he now would describe as an "eschatological proviso," an oft-cited expression that refers to the permanent, critical dynamic of the transcendent hope peculiar to Christian faith.[8] This concept would function in Metz's writing in three important ways. First, it resisted an all too early satisfaction with the present that would suffocate the freedom to hope in a better future. Second, it unveiled as absurd the assumption that all forms of estrangement can be overcome through social, political, and technological progress. Finally—and here we see Metz extend the critical efficacy of a *theologia negativa* of the future—the proviso challenged the dangerous

---

7. *TW*, 118.
8. Ibid., 114. As we have seen, Schillebeeckx himself began to make use of this expression in the 1970s.

tendency to absolutize an ideological commitment, which inevitably occurs at the expense of those who do not fit neatly into its particular vision of history. Metz insisted that absolutizing any single program within history can only overlook those forms of estrangement that refuse to submit to human planning and leads either to the instrumental manipulation of one person by another or to the manipulation of many by a bureaucratic agenda abstracted from its human referent altogether. "There is no subject of universal history one can point to in this world," Metz warned.[9] The Christian's hope must resist every such claim upon history.

By drawing the reader's attention to the provisional character of the present in these later articles of *Theology of the World*, Metz was not rescinding his claim for the permanent freedom or "worldliness of the world." "This eschatological proviso does not mean that the present condition of society is not valid," he wrote. "It *is* valid, but in the 'eschatological meanwhile.' It does not bring about a negative but a critical attitude to the societal present."[10] As we have seen in reviewing Metz's earlier articles, an eschatological horizon is precisely the condition by which human freedom and the autonomy of the world are secured. Against this eschatological horizon of freedom, though, Christians will resist every claim that seeks to identify the powers of the present with the future in which they hope. They do this not by offering a divergent yet positively defined vision of the future, which would likewise bring the future into the present. The ineffable character of the eschaton, Metz insisted, can provide no direct program for sociopolitical action. Rather, Christians must take up the prophetic task of criticizing the extant conditions of society. The "critical negativity" expounded by Adorno is here grounded by Metz in the eschatological structure of the Christian faith but

9. Ibid., 118.
10. Ibid., 114.

is similarly employed to safeguard the impassable gap between the future and a present prematurely passed over through identity-thought. Asserting a point that would become a centerpiece of Schillebeeckx's approach to critical negativity, Metz maintained that in spite of the intractable inability to conceptualize in the present what human life should be, it is nevertheless possible to know what it should not be.[11] And it is precisely this dialectical awareness of the pending promises of the future that animates the critical force of the Christian's action in the world.

Like Schillebeeckx, then, Metz had discovered that an eschatological hope is best suited for identifying fissures between the present order and God's eschatological order. But, also suggestive of Schillebeeckx's position in the late 1960s, it was no longer clear how Metz could account for the Christian's positive contribution to the historical inbreaking of the eschatological kingdom. Certainly, his eschatological reflections continued to commit the Christian to a constructive role in shaping history, arguing that critically maintaining the nonidentity between the present and the promises of an eschatological future simultaneously stimulates the Christian's efforts in the world. These promises are "a critical liberating imperative for our present times," he wrote. "These promises stimulate and appeal to us to make them a reality in the present historical condition."[12] The particular contours of the Christian's practical eschatological hope, however, were inherently indefinable and therefore purely negative and unavoidably abstract. Despite his stated intentions to the contrary, Metz's robust account of an

11. For example, Metz argued that, on the one hand, the Christian's hope in a peaceable kingdom can function as an ideological trope for hegemonic authority to the extent that it romanticizes peace and fails to recognize conflicts in society. On the other hand, the Christian's eschatological expectations also serve "to criticize war passionately and to prevent it from arising—not because every fight and every conflict could be avoided, but because modern war is seen to be an inhuman and totally inappropriate means of resolving conflicts" (ibid., 139).
12. Ibid.

eschatological proviso now appeared to limit the possibility of just such constructive action in the world, leaving the Christian with a seemingly wholly critical vocation. We will return to this impasse, and Metz's own effort to overcome it, in the following sections.

The Critical Role of the Institutional Church

Before proceeding, however, it will be helpful to note a further development in Metz's project found in these essays of 1967. In a bold extension of his position, he now would extend the critical calling of the Christian to the institutional church as well. Given the extensive privatization of religion in modern society, a process regrettably legitimated by contemporary theology, Metz now argued that the church itself must play a decisive role in the critical task of Christian life. He feared that without concrete institutionalization, the individual could not overcome the "anonymous structures" of modern society required to sustain the constant and permanent inquiry necessitated by the proviso.[13] The critical task of Christianity could not be the work of isolated individuals detached from their supporting social matrix. Indeed, the church, with its peculiar eschatological message, must itself become an "institution of criticism." Turning prevailing understandings of the relationship between individual freedom and social institutions on their head, Metz argued that effective resistance against the hegemonic forces of a one-dimensional society in fact requires sustained institutional support. The pressing concern within such a culture is not "whether and how critical freedom and constant enquiry can maintain itself permanently within the existing institutions, but rather whether and how critical freedom is at all possible without institutionalization."[14]

13. Ibid., 120.
14. Ibid., 133.

The church's immediate task, then, "is not the elaboration of a system of social doctrine, but of social criticism. The Church is a particular institution in society, yet presents a universal claim; if this claim is not to be an ideology, it can only be formulated and urged as criticism."[15] Positivist ideologies of the future presume to know too much. The poverty of knowledge proper to the Christian hope safeguards and leaves the future open and, by so doing, determines the sociocritical power of the church's eschatological message.

Metz's proposal for a critical ecclesiology certainly complemented his more deliberate intensification of an apophatic eschatology and the permanent, critical function of the Christian's eschatological hope. In view of the wholly inexhaustible character of the eschaton, the dangerous distortion of historical freedom and the corresponding truncation of hope fostered by the excesses of a technocratic society require a reframing of the church as an "institution of criticism." At the same time, however, we also find in Metz's warning of individuals unable to overcome the "anonymous structures" of modern society, and in his call for institutional reinforcement through the church, the beginnings of a more fundamental critique of the historical conditions pressuring Christianity and its peculiar hope for the future. This critique would be developed much more fully in the years ahead, and it is to this shift in Metz's thought that we now turn.

15. Ibid., 123.

Rethinking Modernity:
From the Distortion of Hope to an Age of Apathy

The Socially Contextualized Character of Hope:
Extending a Postidealist Theology

Metz's concern with the distortion and truncation of the modern person's hope for greater freedom in the blowback of a one-dimensional society was clearly evident in the essays of 1967. But another concern was emerging at that time as well: the very viability and possibility of critical freedom under existing social and political conditions. If it was not yet Metz's principal concern in the final essays of *Theology of the World*, his warning that eschatological hope required ecclesial stanchion suggests that an alternative line of questions was evolving: Is our hope sustainable under current social conditions? Is a consciousness of freedom still possible in the modern world? If not, how can it be secured? Just as Metz's earlier warning of a systematic absorption or "leveling down" of the modern person's capacity to hope anew in the face of suffering anticipated, in his writings that followed the publication of *Theology of the World*, Metz judged that a sufficiently critical analysis of the culture would require an even stronger remedy than the critical corrective of an eschatological proviso. Certainly, modernity's distortion and narrow circumscription of human freedom correctly require that prophetic resistance animated by the proviso, but what if corruption strikes at the very conditions required for sustaining that resistance? What if the flames that fueled the modern, hope-filled drive toward the future were systematically extinguished? Though these ominous questions were not yet at the front of Metz's project in 1967, they were clearly taking shape.

The fears underlying these questions not only surfaced more clearly in Metz's later writings but also would provide a new orientation to his theological project. One valuable point of entrance into this important transition in his project can be found in the synodal statement *Unsere Hoffnung*, approved by the synod of West German bishops in 1975. Metz had served as consultant to the synod from 1971 to 1975 and was widely recognized as the principal author of this document. Achieving significantly greater exposure for his ideas than was possible with his more technical writings, many of the themes and categories that came to distinguish his work during this period appeared in this pastoral text. We will return to consider many of these later in this chapter. For now, I simply want to point to a telling observation that appeared in the early pages of that pastoral document, which clearly illustrates Metz's maturing understanding of the theological significance of the modern sociopolitical situation. *Our Hope: A Confession of Faith for This Time* opened in what is, at this point in our study, familiar territory. The synod recognized that the contemporary cultural milieu was no longer that of a society defined by religious commitments and traditional institutions. It was the challenge of accounting for the Christian's hope in this new context that confronted the German church. Though the language of "secularization" was used sparingly in the document, the crisis facing the church was plainly framed in the context of modern persons struggling with the suspicion "that religion is an exploded illusion, a vestige of earlier stages in mankind's cultural development."[16] Once more, then, it was the crisis of faith brought on by the process of secularization that required an apologetic response from the church.

---

16. Bischöfliche Ordinariate und das Sekretariat der Deutschen Bischofskonferenz, *Unsere Hoffnung: Ein Beschluß der gemeinsamen Synode der Bistümer in der Bundesrepublik Deutschland*, Synodenbeschlüsse 18 (Bonn, 1975), translated in English as "Our Hope: A Confession of Faith for This Time," Joint Synod of Catholic Dioceses of the Federal Republic of Germany, trans. WCC Language Service, *Study Encounter* 12, nos. 1–2, (1976): 66. Subsequent citations refer to the English translation.

It was what followed this unsurprising diagnosis, however, that suggests that Metz had reevaluated the precise nature of this crisis. "This milieu is no longer that of a society deeply marked by religion," the synod declared. "The 'axioms' which dominate it often operate collectively as a countercurrent to our hope. Consequently, they make it extremely difficult to correlate this message of hope with people's experiences of their milieu."[17] The two observations—that it is "extremely difficult" to correlate the Christian message with present conditions, and that the dominant cultural axioms of modernity operate as a "countercurrent" to Christians' hope—reveal a significant reorientation in Metz's apologetic program. Several factors suggesting the durable influence of critical theory on his thought contributed to this shift, including the critique of his earlier defense of human freedom and his recognition of important differences in the philosophical positions of Kant and Marx. We will consider each in turn.

In his earlier writings, even as he increasingly questioned the direction of modernity as a whole, Metz had continued to defend the freedom of the modern subject. In the years directly following the publication of *Theology of the World*, Metz would be criticized widely for this position.[18] Despite his explicit efforts to overcome the ahistorical trends of contemporary theology, he was accused of extending the idealist tendencies of theology by proffering an abstract notion of the free person coupled with a theoretical, wholly critical theology of the future ultimately derived from eschatological speculation rather than a genuine analysis of historical conditions. "Metz theologizes," Charles Davis wrote, "when he should offer a

---

17. Ibid.
18. For example, see Henri de Lavalette, "La 'theologie politique' de Jean-Baptiste Metz," *Recherches de Sciences Religieuses* 58 (1970): 321–50. The criticism Metz appears to have taken most seriously was that of his student Marcel Xhaufflaire, whose work had so strongly influenced Schillebeeckx as well; see *FHS*, 258–59n3.

concrete analysis."[19] In turn, his account of the emergence of the modern consciousness of freedom remained ideologically suspicious, in that it preemptively validated the subjectivity of the modern person.[20] Seeking to turn theology's attention to history and society by championing a political theology, Metz's critics argued that his interpretation of modernity was still informed most immediately by theological speculation rather than the existing sociohistorical situation.

It was the proponents of critical theory who provided Metz with the conceptual resources needed to respond to these concerns, allowing him to address the still-idealistic character of human freedom in his theological project as well as to identify as underdeveloped his deliberate turn to practical reason fostered by his dialogue with Ernst Bloch and examined in chapter 1 of this study. In "The Concept of a Political Theology as a Practical Fundamental Theology," a chapter written in 1977 for publication in *Faith in History and Society*, Metz linked the limitations of his earlier efforts with his failure to differentiate adequately between the distinct strains of practical philosophy promoted by Kant and Marx. Both men, he argued, recognized correctly the impossibility of realizing reason's critical demands in a purely theoretical way and saw that the emancipatory interest of the Enlightenment necessarily included a sociopolitical dimension. As we have seen, it was this insight that Metz's first forays in political theology looked to advance under the banner of the eschatological structure of history, and he would further develop the practical character of theological concepts, particularly Christology, in this essay of 1977.[21] Kant and Marx's

---

19. Charles Davis, "Theology and Praxis," *Cross Currents* 23 (1973): 165.
20. See, for example, Erik Rupp, "Der deutsche Emanzipationskatholizismus, 1968–69," in *Kritischer Katholizismus*, ed. Ben van Onna and Martin Stankowski (Frankfurt, Ger.: Fischer Bücherei, 1969). For an analysis of Rupp's position, see Roger Dick Johns, *Man in the World: The Political Theology of Johannes Baptist Metz* (Missoula, MT: Scholars Press, 1992), 169–70.

common interest in practical reason notwithstanding, Metz now believed that he had failed in even the later essays of *Theology of the World* to consider sufficiently an important difference in their philosophical positions.[22]

According to Metz, Kant's project was concerned with only those individuals already politically enfranchised. His interest in the practical dimension of critical reason presumed a subject currently capable of controlling the forces of nature and history; he "focuses on what is already in existence: namely, those who—tacitly, and sometimes manifestly—already have the social power to be mature and require only to be exhorted in order to be set free."[23] Thus, Kant limited the sociopolitical dimension of reason to the moral behavior of those "men who had already come of age socially and economically."[24] Inadvertently approximating Kant, then, Metz had directed his early formulation of a political theology toward a people for whom the consciousness of historical freedom was presumptively determined largely irrespective of their relationship to social and political structures. Consequently, and again like Kant, Metz now feared that the practical dimension of his earlier work too "often had a 'purely moralistic,' purely appellative-exhortative character."[25] By promoting the practical character of eschatology and the critical character of his *theologia negativa* of the future, he called the Christian

21. "The Concept of a Political Theology as a Practical Fundamental Theology," in *FHS*. See also *Followers of Christ: The Religious Life and the Church*, trans. Thomas Linton (New York: Paulist, 1978), 39–44; first published as *Zeit der Orden? Zur Mystik und Politik* (Freiburg, Ger.: Herder, 1977). We will return to this important strategy later in the chapter.

22. See *FHS*, 42. For Metz's earlier reading of Kant concerning the primacy of practical reason, see "Prophetic Authority," ed. and trans. David Kelley and Henry Vander Goot, in *Religion and Political Society*, ed. Institute of Christian Thought (New York: Harper Forum, 1974), an edited translation of "Kirchliche Autorität im Anspruch der Freiheitsgeschichte," in *Kirch im Prozess der Aufklärung*, ed. J. B. Metz, J. Moltmann, and W. Oelmüller (Munich: Kaiser, 1970). See also *TW*, 111–12.

23. *FHS*, 55–56.

24. Ibid., 64.

25. Ibid.

218

to historical action, but he failed to offer an adequate account of the historical conditioning that makes such action possible.[26]

Marx, by contrast, had shown that the historical realization of emancipative reason required the establishment of those conditions in which critical reason is possible. Along with providing the medium for the historical concretization of human freedom, which was already central to Metz's argument in *Theology of the World*, social practices and political institutions shape and determine the human person's interest in freedom, whether genuinely liberating or ideologically distorted. "It is not the consciousness of men that determines their existence," Marx insisted, "but their social existence that determines their consciousness."[27] It was precisely this insight, advanced by Marx and further clarified in the writings of later critical theorists, that would draw Metz's attention more acutely to the social and political conditioning of the modern interest in freedom and corresponding hope for the future. Metz's recognition of the limitations in his own earlier work is evident in a remark he made in 1977 in *Faith in History and Society* regarding what was missing from earlier political theologies. There he observed "[t]hat there is an inner dialectic to emancipation, enlightenment, and secularization; that the Enlightenment has thus raised problems above and beyond the ones it itself has ascertained. . . . [A]ll of this is scarcely seen at all. To be sure this is a difficult insight, which has not been present from the outset even in the new political theology."[28]

---

26. In a valuable survey of Metz's reading and critical appropriation of Kant in *Interruptions: Mysticism, Politics, and Theology in the Work of Johann Baptist Metz* (Notre Dame, IN: University of Notre Dame Press, 1998), 37–58, Matthew Ashley has shown that although Metz correctly identified in Kant's work on practical reason an insufficient differentiation between ethical and social praxis, in his writings in the philosophy of history, Kant in fact had recognized the sociohistorical matrix of practical reason, though rather tentatively. Influenced by the work of critical theorists, Metz would identify the significance of this distinction through the work of Marx.

27. Karl Marx, Preface to *A Contribution to the Critique of Political Economy*, trans. S. W. Ryazanskaya (London: Lawrence & Whishart, 1971), 20.

It was this insight that led Metz to extend the task of political theology more explicitly toward social praxis as well as moral praxis, toward practically establishing the historical-political conditions in which an interest in freedom is made possible.[29] As he queried at that time, "Who will deny that Christian praxis must not only be concerned with one's own being a subject before God, but also has to be concerned precisely with how persons can become and live as subjects in situations of misery and oppression?"[30] Section 3 of this chapter examines the methodological significance of this question for his maturing theological project. With this differentiation in the concept of practical reason in mind, however, we must first turn to the more trenchant analysis of modernity that provoked his observations in *Unsere Hoffnung*. As we shall see, Metz's heightened concern for the social conditioning of critical reason carried with it a parallel concern about the precarious status of human hope in the modern world.

The Logic of the Market and the Formation of the Modern Subject

In a chapter written for publication in *Faith in History and Society*, "Political Theology of the Subject as a Theological Critique of

28. *FHS*, 42. It is important to qualify this admission. Metz had certainly attended to the socially contextualized character of critical consciousness in his earlier writings. In the early stages of developing his political theology, Metz had argued that it was God's promise historically offered and mediated within the Jewish and Christian traditions that forms and constitutes the modern person's interest in freedom. As early as 1965, he also had warned that the dynamics of modernity were impinging on the possibility of hope in the face of human suffering. And, as we have just seen, he believed that sustaining the critical character of Christian hope required ecclesial institutionalization. Yet Metz himself could now point to the underdeveloped character of his earlier remarks.

29. Contrasting his position with Kant and Marx, though, Metz argued that a dialectical relationship between social and moral praxis still needs to be maintained, warning that although the social dependence of moral praxis must be secured, the ultimate submission of moral praxis to social praxis would lead to the negation (often violent negation) of the individual; see *FHS*, 66.

30. Ibid., 64.

Bourgeois Religion," Metz structured his renewed analysis of the modern situation around a more rigorous evaluation of the individual deemed in control of her world and future. Now more attentive to the social and political matrix that constitutes the modern subject, and no longer content with an abstract description of this subject as "free" and "autonomous," he would set out to clarify the particular constitution of the modern person who emerges in history through the processes of the Enlightenment. He began by revisiting the widespread phenomenon of religion's privatization already criticized in many of his earlier writings. Noting the legitimate need of European political states to distance themselves from the ecclesial conflicts that violently marked the late Middle Ages and the Reformation and Counter-Reformation, Metz affirmed in this essay that a valid historical concern for human emancipation underwrote the modern social distinction between the public and private. He simultaneously warned, however, that in the name of ongoing emancipation from the tutelage of authoritarian religion, this important distinction ultimately expelled religion from public life. Although a safe domain for religion continued to exist, it was only in the capricious and sheltered domain of private whim. "Religion became a 'private matter,'" he noted, "which one 'makes use of' following criteria of cultural needs and sobriety, but which one really does not need (anymore) in order just to be a subject at all."[31] Gradually removed from the "public" sphere, this subject's religious commitments were considered less and less suitable for informing social existence. Christianity subsequently became little more than a "sort of ornamentation," appropriately useful for emotional consolation or ritualistic celebration but no longer formative of one's identity.[32]

31. Ibid., 49.
32. Ibid., 47.

This process of privatization, Metz believed, ultimately left the foundations of European society unoccupied, resulting in a cultural vacuum that needed to be filled with a new, publicly acceptable value system by which to mediate social life. According to Metz, this vacuum was gradually filled by a value system he described as the principle of exchange. It was upon this principle, he acknowledged, that men and women had legitimately overcome the oppressive economic structures of feudal society. The problem that Metz highlighted, however, was that with the market's efficiency validated, the same principle was then allowed to reoccupy the space left open by the privatization of religion. At the same time, the myriad of other important cultural customs, stories, and traditions that had shaped and mediated social life were also evacuated of public significance. Rather than determining only economic transactions, the principle of exchange now would determine the whole of social existence without qualification, establishing a social system in which all goods, without distinction, were commodified and ascribed convertible value. Describing such a system, Rebecca Chopp writes, "The marketplace—the primary location for the principle of exchange—adjudicates all norms and values of human life by supply and demand, by replacement and substitution. In modernity anything can be bought or sold; nothing—including values, traditions, and relationships—can stand in the way of the . . . market."[33] It should be clear that Metz was not merely describing the birth of modern capitalistic economies. He was arguing that the cultural framework of the modern subject became one in which all of life was organized and evaluated in terms of exchange.

Metz described the resultant individual, this subject of modern history, as the "bourgeois individual." The bourgeois subject, if only

---

33. Rebecca S. Chopp, *The Praxis of Suffering: An Interpretation of Liberation and Political Theologies* (Maryknoll, NY: Orbis, 1986), 71.

tacitly, understands her identity and agency almost exclusively as the freedom to participate according to this principle: "All the other values that had heretofore shaped social existence, and that did not contribute directly to the function of this bourgeois exchange society, retreated more and more into the sphere of the private."[34] The traditions and values of the past possess little worth in the market system. Metz observed that these values may entertain the individual or reinforce the individual's existing plausibility assumptions, but they are denied any legitimate role in the formation of that individual.[35] Metz's fear that the modern subject was being systematically deformed by the principle of exchange is well summarized in his own words: "The social crippling and devaluation of those traditional attitudes—friendship, gratitude, and attentiveness for the dead—for which no corresponding value can be set, for which you literally get nothing in exchange, proceeds apace."[36] If neither celebration nor mourning could contribute to an efficient marketplace, their worth could no longer be affirmed. The consequences for a religious worldview—and hence the critical vitality of the Christian's eschatological hope—were significant for Metz. To the extent that religion is valued at all, it, too, must become a commodity, put to service as a useful instrument for the private gratification of the bourgeois individual.[37]

---

34. *FHS*, 49.

35. Metz further warned that if these traditions are remembered at all, they are cheapened into the objects of historical knowledge; the religion of the bourgeois offers a mere warehouse of information with no authoritative claim on the present. Herein lay Metz's concerns regarding historical-critical reading of Scripture; see ibid., 106, 196–98.

36. Ibid., 51.

37. We can note that the principle of exchange closely corresponds with the ascent of instrumental reason in modernity. In its drive to control nature and society, technical reason ascribes value based solely on a good's utility in the market and structures society in such a way that it is impossible to recognize the value of the human person beyond her ability to contribute to the marketplace. Thus, the freedom of the bourgeois subject is sold at the price of productivity. Or, more accurately, the peculiar subjectivity of the bourgeoisie is effectively achieved only in productivity; human freedom is construed as the ability to control or dominate production.

The Logic of Evolutionary Time and a Crisis of Hope

Metz's more rigorous analysis of modernity uncovered, then, a distressed modern subject inadvertently passed over by his earlier theological reflections. Adorno's and Marcuse's warnings of an entrenched cultural hegemony governed by instrumental rationality had given finer shape to Metz's account of the pressures facing modern men and women. The unqualified logic of technical reason, he recognized, shapes a social existence determined by the principle of exchange, tightly circumscribing the very character of freedom and human identity achievable in modernity. Clearly, the social and political matrix of subjectivity was now in Metz's sights. It would be the related work of Walter Benjamin, however, that most distinctly influenced Metz's investigation of modernity, further extending his analysis of the modern subject by identifying the often tacit understanding of temporality that orients and shapes that subject while heightening his attention to those individuals who are denied the historical freedom promised by the Enlightenment. This critical reevaluation of temporality was a central factor in Metz's shift to an apocalyptic eschatology.

Though Benjamin was never affiliated formally with the Institut für Sozialforschung, his wide-ranging interests were closely associated with the work of the Frankfurt theorists, and it was Adorno who arranged for the posthumous publication of his final essay, "On the Concept of History."[38] In this essay, as well as in a number of other evocative texts, Benjamin developed an uncompromising

Those who do not contribute to or lack the means to participate in the market of exchange, by contrast, are systematically denied this freedom; see ibid., 56.

38. Walter Benjamin, "Theses on the Philosophy of History" (an alternative title frequently ascribed to this essay), in *German 20th Century Philosophy: The Frankfurt School*, ed. Wolfgang Schirmacher (New York: Continuum, 2000), 71–80. For an introduction to this work, see Rolf

critique of what he believed was modernity's prevailing historical consciousness. He feared that the idea of progress, a unilinear and homogeneous notion of history that advances relentlessly without reference to the human subject, had come to dominate modern thought. And it was just this characterization of history, he further argued, that "recognizes only the progress in the mastery of nature, not the retrogression of society."[39] Though certainly related to the critique of technical reason with which we are now familiar, for Benjamin it was this modern philosophy of history, the particular image of time guiding the modern subject, that ultimately suppresses the contingent character of social reality by overwhelming and erasing the human subject in lieu of an absolute yet anonymous subject of history. He warned that time envisioned accordingly, as undialectical progress, effectively blinds the modern person to precisely those events in history no longer deemed productive and to those individuals who fail to contribute to that progress. The failures that accompany history's advance and the victims who suffer in its wake grow increasingly invisible as the steamroller of history sweeps over the human person.

The distorted consciousness of history Benjamin ascribed to the concept of progress found powerful expression in his interpretation of Paul Klee's painting *Angelus Novus* in "On the Concept of History":

> *Angelus Novus* shows an angel looking as though he is about to move away from something he is fixedly contemplating. His eyes are staring, his mouth is open, his wings are spread. This is how one pictures the angel of history. His face is turned toward the past. Where we perceive a chain of events, he sees one single catastrophe which keeps piling wreckage upon wreckage and hurls it in front of his feet. The angel

Tiedemann, "Historical Materialism or Political Messianism? An Interpretation of the Theses 'On the Concept of History,'" *Philosophical Forum* 15, nos. 1–2 (Fall–Winter 1983–84): 71–104.
39. Benjamin, "Theses on the Philosophy of History," 76.

would like to stay, awaken the dead, and make whole what has been smashed. But a storm is blowing from Paradise; it has got caught in his wings with such violence that the angel can no longer close them. This storm irresistibly propels him into the future to which his back is turned, while the pile of debris before him grows skyward. This storm is what we call progress.[40]

It is the angel of history, Benjamin suggests in his fragmented remarks, who correctly perceives the contours of human history. Looking to the past, the angel sees that history is not a chain of logical events progressing with reasonable and predictable explanation. Indeed, seemingly with a countenance of horror, the angel sees that history is anything but reasonable, and is instead marked by senseless tragedy and suffering. It is this history of the suffering and oppressed, Benjamin argued, that can teach "us that the 'state of emergency' in which we live is not the exception but the rule."[41] Incessantly pushing history forward, however, is the dominant commitment to the idea of progress, a commitment that makes it impossible for men and women to attend to the shattered lives left in the wake of history's advance while it obfuscates the urgency of the present.

The critical analysis performed by Benjamin presented Metz an important vantage point from which to further appraise the terrain of modernity. In "Hope as Imminent Expectation—or, The Struggle for Lost Time: Untimely Theses on Apocalyptic," a collection of thirty-five theses published in 1977, which closely follows, both in structure and content, Benjamin's "On the Concept of History," Metz, too, would locate within the dialectical dynamic of technical reason a concealed master theory or myth of history distorting the modern subject's consciousness of freedom.[42] "The understanding of reality

40. Ibid., 74–75.
41. Ibid., 74.
42. It is important to note that the genre or structure of this text deftly complemented the ideas under development by Metz. As with Benjamin, Metz's suggestive and fragmented theses self-consciously resist systematization and, thus, can be seen to reinforce his criticism of that

that guides the scientific-technological domination of nature," he wrote, "is shaped by a particular image of time: an image of time as an empty continuum, expanding evolutionarily into infinitude."[43] Metz described the underlying assumption supporting this ontology of history as the logic of evolution, a now-governing paradigm of temporality with far-reaching consequences for modernity's subject: "In this logic the leveling out of time, which makes all time the same, has come to systematically dominate our common awareness. On its basis everything is 'reconstructed' in terms of a timeless continuum."[44] The bourgeois subject construes time as an endless march forward through a history without end. This subject's compulsion toward production and repetition reveals not only the pressure imposed by the principle of exchange, then, but also an operative understanding of temporality. An ever more efficient and productive society is predetermined by the logic of evolution, yet history itself, rather than the human person, determines this progress.

Metz charged this peculiar historical consciousness of the bourgeoisie with fostering a "cult of the possible." Anything is possible, the bourgeoisie believe, in an endless time continuum. Not now, not immediately, maybe, but certainly someday; the cult of the possible passes over the urgency of the present by deferring every historical possibility for another tomorrow. Yet if the weight of the present has lost consequence and time is envisioned as unfolding endlessly without reference to the human subject, with the events and people of the past no longer possessing value because they have ceased to be "productive" or "profitable," Metz warned, in the end

totalizing and homogeneous account of time diagnosed by Benjamin that underwrites modern existence.
43. *FHS*, 157.
44. Ibid., 158. Here, Metz is not challenging the theory of evolution proposed by the natural sciences. Rather, he is challenging the uncritical application of that theory to society and history, precisely the positivistic confusion of scientific and social analyses diagnosed by critical theorists which effectively suppresses the contingent character of social existence.

all people and every historical event are eventually evacuated of significance: "The understanding of reality . . . from which the cult of the possible draws its reserves is shaped by a particular image of time: an image of time as an empty continuum, expanding evolutionarily into infinitude, mercilessly encompassing everything."[45] The cult of the possible inevitably self-destructs as it makes impossible a valuation of the past, the meaningfulness of the present, and a genuinely new future. The traditions, values, and even people that do not aid in history's advancement are ultimately expendable; the catastrophic events and human misery that repeatedly rupture the seemingly smooth progression of history are systematically disregarded. Nothing can interrupt the progress of evolutionary time. Evolutionary logic prescribes a paradigm of temporality with devastating consequences. The cult of the possible devolves into a listless "cult of fate." Time's endless advance forward endangers the human subject by compromising the very possibility of acting responsibly in history.

Of course, Metz already had begun to hone his counterattack on the particular logic underwriting this inadequate understanding of history under the tutelage of Bloch, and he appropriately dedicated "Hope as Imminent Expectation" to the philosopher. As you will remember, Bloch also feared that the very hope of historical transformation had disappeared from the men and women of late modernity, because of the sedation of an entrenched cultural hegemony and the corresponding inability to imagine even the possibility of an alternative future. Time construed as wholly contiguous and self-fulfilling suffocates the radical hope for a genuinely new future. If there is "nothing new under the sun," the very possibility of the substantively novel in history inevitably dissolves. Benjamin's analysis offered a valuable complement to

45. Ibid., 157.

Bloch's work, yet it is important to note that, for Bloch, it was the repression of utopian expectations that had pacified men and women's expectations for history and prematurely determined future possibilities. For Benjamin, it was modernity's dominant temporal framework that drains expectations, making it impossible for men and women to remember the suffering persons of the past and thus masking the "emergency" of the present and the possibilities of the future.

We will return to Benjamin's position and his influence on Metz's writings in the following pages. We can already note, however, that it was in light of Benjamin's insights that Metz grew increasingly attentive to the deleterious effects of this modern understanding of temporality on the human person. Consequently, a well-defined question began to control his investigation: What becomes of the subject and a society that reflectively or, much more likely, unreflectively exists under the spell of evolutionary logic? "With this experience of a more fragile identity a new culture is in the offing," Metz responded. "[I]ts first name is apathy, the absence of feeling."[46] The cult of the possible finds itself mired in a deadening culture void of genuine expectation. With the historical conditioning of the human subject now in Metz's sights, the acute vulnerability of human hope had been exposed. An evolutionary view of time was fostering a modern crisis of hope.

Metz's writings in the 1970s reveal that modernity's prevailing fundamental temporal framework had ushered in not an era marked by confidence and optimism but "a golden age of apathy."[47] Infected by the logic of evolution, the palpable hope for the future that marked the rise of modernity morphs into an overwhelming weariness. The ongoing suffering and absence of freedom experienced in history,

46. Ibid., 26.
47. Ibid., 81.

first Benjamin and now Metz warned, are allowed to continue unnoticed and without redress. The reports of urban warfare coming from all over the world today, to offer just one example, so often identify the "unfortunate" victims of battle as "collateral damage"; their deaths are the regrettable but necessary consequence of securing freedom. Such a fatalistic indifference to the suffering of others in the name of history's advance, Metz might warn, betrays the logic of evolutionary time. The never-ending progression of history corrupts critical freedom, drains men and women of both expectation and complaint, and thus prepares the way for the disintegration of history and the corresponding "death" of the free subject.

Of particular significance for Metz's eschatology, this modern crisis of subjectivity cultivates a crisis of hope, and the origins of both can be found in a culturally concealed yet dominant myth of time. The logic of evolution corrupts or "flattens out" the hope-filled expectations of the modern person. As Metz remarked,

> Whose identity would be more fragile than that of the so-called "modern man"? Fitted into complex systems that already function virtually without reference to their subjects, he stands in danger of becoming increasingly faceless and (to speak biblically) nameless. His dreams and fantasies cannot keep up anymore; they are flattened out. In the name of evolution and progress he is being bred back more and more into a cleverly adaptable animal, into a smoothly functioning machine.[48]

---

48. Ibid., 80. According to Metz, the death-dealing effects of this condition would spare neither pole of the late-20th-century sociopolitical situation. Neither the subject of liberal capitalism nor the subject of Marxist historical materialism, he argued, avoids being sucked into the waves of an anonymous evolution. In the West, the logic of evolutionary history overwhelms the individual caught up in the drive for techno-economic progress and merely inscribes the modern compulsion toward production and repetition. In the East, with religion dismissed as a legitimate ground for an emancipatory interest, the state appropriates this interest only to "secularize" it upon an evolutionary interpretation of matter and history, thus passing over, and often brutally, the human subject. In both cases, Metz warned, the hopes of men and women are deeply compromised.

As we have seen, Metz drew much of this ominous analysis from the perceptive insights of Benjamin. In seeking to respond to the situation, he also would draw from Benjamin, and in the process Metz discovered powerful resources deeply embedded in the Jewish and Christian traditions. Before we turn to this work, however, it will be important to survey briefly Metz's corresponding evaluation of the state of theology at that time and his call for a countercultural theological sensitivity to the history of suffering.

The Complicity of Contemporary Theology

As a theologian, Metz was particularly concerned about what he viewed as theology's complicity in offering religious legitimacy—even unwittingly—for modern bourgeois ideology. In his critique of the transcendental and existential theologies that dominated the theological scene through the 1970s, Metz focused on the precise limitations we have just outlined: an idealistic view of history that abstracted from the concrete historical situation, a view of the modern subject as bourgeois individual, and the implicit assumption of an evolutionary view of time. Here we will view each briefly, with particular emphasis on Metz's critique of his own earlier writings as well as the work of his theological mentor, Karl Rahner.

Metz warned his readers against interpreting his more trenchant analysis of the modern subject as an unqualified rejection of modernity itself. To the contrary, he believed that the positive historical developments of the Enlightenment, its underlying interests in human emancipation from repressive structures—political, economic, and even religious—require vigilant preservation. But if the positive dynamics of the Enlightenment are to be preserved, he further argued, theologians will need to confront modernity's unqualified excesses by taking up a "theological enlightenment of the

Enlightenment."[49] And in doing this, the complicity of contemporary theology, the ongoing theological legitimation of modernity's aporias, will need to be unveiled.

Theology's Idealistic View of History

For Metz, this required a reevaluation of his own earlier theology of secularization. He returned to this topic in "Roundabout Ways to a Fundamental Theology," a chapter written in 1977 for publication in *Faith in History and Society*. As we saw in chapter 1 of this study, in his early writings Metz had argued that Christianity was the originator rather than the victim of the processes of secularization. More specifically, creation and the incarnation were construed as the transcendental conditions for the "autonomy" of the world. In his reassessment of that apologetic strategy in 1977, Metz again would distance himself from that view, noting that any attempt to bridge transhistorically the divide between the world and faith risked overlegitimating the conditions of the historical present.[50] Moreover, by his taking up this strategy, his theology of secularization had uncritically released the world to itself at the price of the faith's disarmament. Commenting on this danger, Metz wrote, "When the worldlessness of faith is virtually a presupposition of secularization, then the specific critical-liberating power of Christianity in relation to history and society inevitably is forgotten or at least obscured."[51] Abstracted from concrete history and withdrawn to a transcendental

---

49. Ibid., 48.
50. See ibid., 41, where Metz writes, "One cannot avoid the suspicion that a faith that is conceptualized in a radically worldless way can (due to its privatized isolation) be turned into the ideological superstructure or symbolic paraphrase of *any* historical-social process in the world *whatsoever*."
51. Ibid.

vantage point, theology surrendered the location from which it could critically engage the modern world.

Theology's Bourgeois Subject

Yet it was not just the sociohistorical processes of secularization that theology had prematurely assumed as its own in responding to the period's pastoral challenges by seeking to reestablish the significance of Christianity for a modern world. As we saw earlier in this chapter, Metz was also concerned that theologians must carefully avoid tacitly accepting the subject who emerges through those processes as the religious subject envisioned by the Christian tradition. "Theology must not uncritically take over 'the subject,' 'existence,' 'person' as the result of modernity and its privatization process," he warned. "The bourgeois-private, insofar as it is the outcome of the modern Enlightenment process, is simply not identical with the subject (existence, person) in a religiously and theologically relevant sense."[52] But the failure to honor this distinction, he believed, was precisely the consequence of strategies employed by much of contemporary theology.

On this point, Metz was particularly critical of the subject developed by his mentor, Karl Rahner. Metz argued that a transcendental anthropology in which the human person "always already" (*nolens volens*) exists as an anticipatory grasp of God, intrinsically longing for transcendence that is always within yet still fundamentally unconstrained by concrete historical conditions, inadvertently endorses the compromised subject of modernity while providing cover for those conditions liable for the distortion of that subject's freedom. Metz praised Rahner's benchmark effort to

52. Ibid., 58.

introduce human subjectivity into his reflections on the Christian faith, and even dedicated *Faith in History and Society* to his friend and teacher. He carefully acknowledged that Rahner inductively worked from the concrete experiences of the human person to the universal anthropological structure according to which the person is always already with God. The historical experiences of the individual were explicitly the starting point of Rahner's project, and Metz's mentor was undoubtedly concerned with the precarious status of that individual in the wake of modernity.[53] Nevertheless, Metz feared that by seeking a transhistorical, universal foundation from which to correlate the faith with the experiences of the modern subject, the transcendental method exacts an unacceptable price: "Those social contradictions and antagonisms that are the stuff of painfully lived historical experience, and within which historical subjects constitute themselves, disappear with transcendental theology's concept of experience, in the abstractness of a preconceived 'transcendental experience' in which these contradictions are already undialectically reconciled."[54] Metz worried that by transcendentally determining a universal anthropological structure, Rahner's project, along with much of contemporary theology, prematurely enthrones the modern subject as the religious subject before the precise historical pressures shaping subjectivity are taken into account. Consequently, such a project concedes the surest ground from which to combat the disintegration of Christianity into bourgeois religion as well as the capacity to rescue the subject from the crisis of hope fostered by the paralyzing conditions of modernity.

53. Ibid., 203.
54. Ibid., 74.

Theology's Acceptance of Evolutionary Time

In an essay from 1977 entitled "Transcendental-Idealist or Narrative-Practical Christianity? Theology and Christianity's Contemporary Identity Crisis," Metz would extend his critique of transcendental theology's strategy for dealing with the challenges of secularization by arguing that such a tack inevitably reinforces the paralyzing notion of time governing modernity. Here, he again asked, in moving from the historical to the universal by way of speculative-transcendental theory, does theology not still circumvent the concrete historical situations in which human hope is continuously being given shape? Does theology make an end run around history, proclaiming "I'm already here" without resolutely contending with a still-unfolding human history that, as we have seen, conditions (and endangers) the very character of the Christian's hope?[55]

Metz believed that despite Rahner's intention, his theology overrides the risky and indeterminate venture that is human history. If the individual's hope is always already transcendentally determined, then history itself is envisioned as only actualizing and confirming more of the same. Christianity is envisioned as merely corroborating rather than instilling the transcendent longings of the human person. Subsequently, by theoretically determining the human person's openness to the transcendent, a transcendental theology effectively affirms timeless time: "The beginning is like the end; paradise like the end of time; creation like the fulfillment. History itself—with its ever threatened, vulnerable, and at any rate endangered forms of identity—barely intervenes at all. The transcendental spell is complete."[56]

---

55. Ibid., 152.
56. Ibid.

Metz warned that a transcendental theology prematurely leaves behind the ambiguities of human history, emptying temporality of genuine value. Of particular significance for this study is Metz's concern for the eschatological consequences of this position. Hope is immunized from the risks of history, yet time is stripped of significance. As a result, he feared, the historical vulnerability of hope is overlooked as the catastrophes of history and the suffering that endangers human expectations within history recede from view.

It is here that we can begin identifying an important development in Metz's maturing thought. Early on, Metz voiced his critique of Rahner's theology and of any form of transcendental theology for compromising the genuinely new in history and obfuscating the indeterminate possibilities of the future. Metz feared that the indefinable potential of history was circumscribed in advance; theological reflection performed with its back to history veils the future in a merely presentist and privatized eschatology. Consequently, the inability of a transcendental theology to account for the openness of the future was the target of his criticism. It was in response, you will remember, that he began to advance a political theology characterized by a practical eschatology and a utopic theology of history. In his later evaluation of Rahner's work, these concerns were undoubtedly still present. Having extended his appreciation of the primacy of praxis, however, the specific manner in which Metz now framed this danger had taken a decisive turn.

The insights of critical theorists, particularly the work of Benjamin, had linked the distortion of temporality with the veiling of human suffering, systematically neglecting an anguished underside of world history that radically conditions and endangers the freedom and expectations of modern men and women. Subsequently, Metz came to recognize this dynamic in his mentor's methodological strategy. His later criticism of a transcendental theology here was cast in terms of its inability to face up to the catastrophes of human history that continuously endanger the hope of the human person and, in turn, its inability to recognize a burgeoning "age of apathy." With the transcendent longings of the human person transcendentally determined, the historical conditioning of hope remained largely undetectable.

In addressing the pressures of the Enlightenment, then, Metz now was insisting that the particular challenge facing contemporary Christianity requires locating not only the theological resources needed to validate and contribute to an unfolding history of human freedom, the controlling interest underwriting his response to the process of secularization, but also the resources needed to meet head-on the horrifying reality of a history ever marked by human suffering. Indeed, he was convinced that these two tasks were fundamentally related. As we now will see, Metz believed that a viable history of emancipation simply cannot be sustained without simultaneously maintaining a heightened awareness of the human tragedies that repeatedly interrupt the seemingly smooth advance of history and jeopardize the vitality of the human person's hope for the future.

The turn to human suffering that Metz called theologians to embrace was the challenge that ultimately resulted in his own turn to an eschatology characterized by an apocalyptic hope. But this turn to the temporality of suffering initiated a corresponding shift in theological method as well. Before turning to Metz's apocalyptic eschatology in the following chapter, the final section of this chapter will consider his modified articulation of political theology as a practical fundamental theology. This methodological approach would provide the resources that Metz judged to be essential for the formation of a subject for whom hope would be possible.

Christian Hope in a History of Suffering

Redemption and Emancipation:
A Theological Enlightenment of the Enlightenment

In his critique of modernity, Metz called for a theological enlightenment of the Enlightenment. In an important essay dating from 1972, "Redemption and Emancipation," Metz argued that fundamental to theology's contribution to fostering hope amid the widespread apathy of modernity was critically distinguishing between the Christian hope for "redemption" and the Enlightenment expectation of "emancipation." By underscoring this distinction, Metz would scrutinize the Enlightenment's own inability to acknowledge the comprehensive breadth of the history of human suffering despite the pronounced and still-mounting dialectical failures of the modern project of freedom.

Turning a critical eye to the normative conceptualization of emancipation that emerges with modernity, Metz argued in this essay that prevailing philosophical paradigms have established a "totalizing" and uncompromising understanding of the history of freedom in which emancipation is categorically defined as *self*-liberation, essentially excluding the possibility of "gratuitously given, liberated, or redeemed freedom, whose mere appearance keeps men and women from winning their real freedom."[57] Reiterating his earlier warning that a wholly inner-historical and self-fulfilling account of emancipation would inevitably delimit the character of the future freedom for which one hopes, Metz claimed in this essay that modernity had "halved" the theme of freedom by limiting the history of suffering to a sociopolitical history of oppression and violence while refusing to provide a word of hope that might speak to the

---

57. Ibid., 116.

human experiences of guilt and finitude that resolutely resist inner-worldly redress.

Metz would not be satisfied in this essay, however, with critically resisting the abstract and overly circumscribed account of freedom that characterizes modern thought, or with placing an eschatological reserve on the work of human emancipation. In advocating this change in strategy, Metz clearly was not dismissing the theological claim on history that he had articulated in an abbreviated fashion as the "eschatological proviso." Nonetheless, this expression and the apologetic strategy it encapsulated noticeably began to disappear from his writings during this period. In Metz's judgment, the freedom required to sustain this critical task was no longer available.

Moreover, he now warned that the totalizing understanding of emancipation operative in the Enlightenment refuses any correlation with the Christian understanding of redemption, even a critical one. It is important to make clear that in seeking to disassociate the promise of emancipation from the promise of redemption in this essay, Metz was not abandoning Christianity's constitutive interest in the establishment of historical freedom. What we see, rather, is a now-heightened and even controlling concern that this interest cannot be facilitated by means of reconciling these two promises, even if critically, for such a resolution could come only at the price of theologically legitimating existing plausibility assumptions and, ultimately, faith's capitulation.

Metz's fear of Christianity's superficial and thus debilitating accommodation with modern culture was perhaps most clearly evidenced in his warning that not even the "dialectic of emancipation" diagnosed by critical theory, which itself firmly insists on the ever-pending gap between present and future, provides an adequate opening for appeasement. Metz argued in this essay that by locating the origins of both the interest in historical freedom and the dialectical distortion of that freedom within the inner-historical dynamic of reason itself, the negative dialectics of the Frankfurt school decisively corroborates the totalizing character of self-emancipation: "This dialectic in no way blunts the total and uncompromising character of the concept of emancipation; on the contrary, it makes it even more unassailable, more opaque, more immune from being contested from without, by trying yet again to absorb the social contradictions that surface in the process of emancipation back into it."[58] Metz believed that it was in seeking to absorb the entirety of the history of freedom into the process of emancipation, locating every hope and expectation for the future in the promises of policy engineering from the political left or right, that modernity had ultimately run aground, compromising the very freedom it sought to secure.

One of Metz's primary concerns in this essay was to expose the connection between the modern effort to restrict the history of freedom to self-emancipation and the truncation or even denial of the history of human suffering. The catastrophic failings of the Enlightenment project, having taken up sole responsibility for history as *Homo emancipator*, could fall only on the shoulders of the modern subject. Yet guilt itself was resistant to inner-historical redress and thus deemed outside the purview of the modern interest in freedom. The effect of this incongruous situation, Metz warned, would be an obstinate refusal by *Homo emancipator* to face up to the oppression and violence that continued to mark world history. Rather than humanity's accepting the burden of guilt for history's mounting sufferings, he argued, competing "exculpation mechanisms" constructed in terms of the philosophy of history emerged with

58. Ibid.

modernity by which the modern subject could safely defer her responsibility.

Various strands of idealist theory, for example, posited a universal subject progressively coming to be in history. Whether construed by way of Hegel's *Geist* or the romantic's "nature," culpability for the necessary, if unfortunate, tragedies of history was ascribed to a transcendental subject rather than the human subject. The Marxist account of history likewise declined responsibility for the failings of emancipation by projecting sole liability upon the bourgeoisie. The proletariat, the rightful subject of history, was immunized from the sufferings of history by restricting blame to a specific and isolated enemy of freedom. Finally, Metz would turn to the technocratic conception of history dominant in modern market economies, finding that in such societies the interest in establishing a responsible subject of history had been dismissed altogether in lieu of unqualified technological and economic progress determined by nothing but the invisible hand of the market. The presumption for ever-greater productivity establishes a subjectless conception of historical progress that simply has no need to offer an account of the history of suffering.

According to Metz, the modern project of emancipation had turned its back on its own interest in liberation in exchange for exoneration from the guilt it could not admit. As a result, that project had become a false ideology of evolutionary progress that benefits only the few while excluding too much, and too many, from the promise of freedom. Here, as Matthew Ashley has written, "Metz's criticism of the Enlightenment is now framed in terms of its unwillingness or inability to face up to and cope with the suffering that continually erupts within it."[59] Clearly, contemporary theology was not alone in passing over a history marked by tragedy. Using

---

59. J. Matthew Ashley, "The Path to *Faith in History and Society*," introduction to *FHS*, 19.

language suggestive of Benjamin's "On the Concept of History," Metz argued that the history of emancipation had unwittingly become a history of victors, a history of progress that systematically abandons without hope the countless victims of history who suffer and die in its wake.[60]

But it was also here, Metz believed, that Christianity could counter these self-serving conceptualizations of history, and the death-dealing sociopolitical practices they foster and legitimate, with a theological enlightenment of the Enlightenment. It is the promise of redemption, he would insist, that makes possible a genuine history of freedom:

> A universal theory of emancipation without a soteriology is continually subject to irrational mechanisms for making excuses or repressing guilt. A history of emancipation without a history of redemption subjects the historical subject to new irrational compulsions in the face of concrete histories of suffering. . . . Refusing to accept guilt does not promote a specific, concrete freedom, but rather a laboriously concealed heteronomy.[61]

The Christian promise of redemption, the promise of a gratuitously given freedom that includes the possibility of forgiveness, offers a culturally subversive account of history that can resist the construction of exculpation mechanisms. "Christian soteriology," Metz argued, "relentlessly directs our attention to the history of suffering as a history of guilt."[62] Holding open the possibility of forgiveness, Christianity invites the human person to face up to the reality of guilt and, thus, makes possible the ongoing struggle for

60. See *FHS*, 123.
61. Ibid., 121–22.
62. Ibid., 122. Revealing his ongoing respect for Rahner's work, Metz credits Rahner with deliberately keeping the concept of guilt in theological play despite frequent accusations, often legitimate, that the very concept functions as an oppressive ideological trope. Interestingly, in his earlier effort to reintroduce the question of guilt in his 1965 address to the Paulusgesellschaft, considered in chapter 1 of this study, Metz also had cited the influence of his mentor.

historical freedom. Only when they are self-consciously responsible for their actions in history can men and women take responsibility for the plight of others. Refusing to halve the theme of freedom, inscribing the hope for a liberation that outstrips what humans themselves can secure, the promise of redemption uniquely enables all people to remain the subjects of their history by refusing to bury their responsibility for the history of human suffering. It possesses the peculiar resources required to keep the tragedies of human existence in play, deliberately taking the side of history's victims without excuse.

This peculiar capacity to attend to the human sufferings that resist inner-worldly redress finds its most subversive expression, according to Metz, in Christianity's unyielding hope for the dead, an eschatological expectation that excludes no one from the promise of redeemed freedom. The sheer incredibility of a claim for the future freedom of history's defeated and forgotten, it can be noted, only reveals the degree to which the plausibility assumptions of the present have been determined by the totalizing notion of emancipation operative in modernity. Nevertheless, Metz insisted that the ideologically repressed sufferings of the past manifestly characterize a real and all-embracing history of human suffering. Otherwise, he warned, "[a] second order Darwinism rules, an objective cynicism with respect to the suffering of the past and the freedom of the dead and vanquished."[63] A genuine and all-embracing history of freedom will need to overcome this treacherous halving of the history of suffering if the freedom and hopes of all people are to have a future: "If we submit too long to the meaninglessness of death, and to indifference toward the dead, then in the end we will have only banal promises to offer the living."[64] The Christian's confession of a God

63. Ibid., 123–24.
64. Ibid., 83. See also "Our Hope," 70.

who "is God of the living and of the dead, God of universal justice and of resurrection of the dead," underwrites an account of history that refuses to forget the past.[65] The history of redemption predicated upon this God purposefully broadens the promise of freedom even to the vanquished of history.

Once more, though, Metz warned against seeking a superficial accommodation with contemporary culture, merely inserting the Christian's hope for the dead into the modern project of emancipation. Again, such a facile reconciliation would overlook the precise character of freedom championed by the Enlightenment. This freedom does not simply exclude the dead from the future, he argued, but rather "multiplies and advances over the backs of the *massa damnata* of the dead."[66] Social and technological progress has been achieved through the exploitation and often bloody sacrifices of history's victims. "There is no document of civilization," Benjamin famously insisted, "which is not at the same time a document of barbarism."[67] The lavish and highly profitable plantations of the American South, to offer just one instance from the modern era, document not only the rise of a productive agrarian civilization in the new world but also the barbarous enslavement of those men and women whose very lives were all too callously expended for its erection.

Undoubtedly, this reading of human history "against the grain," rather than modernity's reading of history as evolutionary progress, was now at the center of Metz's project as well. It is the vanquished of history who have made possible the particular subjectivity of history's victors, as the travails and dreams of men and women are consumed in the name of progress only to be discarded in the receptacle of the

65. *FHS*, 82.
66. Ibid., 123.
67. Benjamin, "Theses on the Philosophy of History," 74.

past. Rather than introducing the Christian's eschatological hope into existing social conditions, then, Metz was convinced that Christianity needed to disrupt these conditions and establish the historical conditions that make this inexhaustible hope genuinely possible. In his judgment, that required a political theology that was a practical fundamental theology, the focus of his methodological interests in his *Faith in History and Society*.

Political Theology as a Practical Fundamental Theology: Refining the Apologetic Strategy

We noted earlier Metz's concern that much of contemporary theology veils the concrete sufferings of men and women in history through the transcendental and idealist strategies it frequently employs. In his later writings, Metz encountered the pressing apologetic challenge that arises when human tragedy moves to the fore of theological reflection. In his essay "Redemption and Emancipation," he argued that the history of redemption offers a culturally subversive and desperately needed message of hope that uniquely refuses to cut short the promise of freedom. But how can the Christian confess this hope in the midst of a history so deeply inscribed with misery? The questions Metz would confront at this point in his writings were markedly similar to those faced by Schillebeeckx:

> Can theological talk about salvation and redemption stand up in a genuine and honest way to this history of suffering, with the painful nonidentity of historical life that is manifest therein? Does it evade the risk and the suffering of nonidentity in historical existence from the very outset by talking about salvation that is sealed by Jesus Christ and the redemption and reconciliation of human beings that has irrevocably happened in Christ? . . . Is there any theological "mediation" between

redemption and a history that, as a history of suffering, is really taken seriously in its specifically historical character?[68]

Though important differences between the theologians exist that will need to be identified, it will not be a surprise that Metz also responded to these questions in a fashion similar to that of Schillebeeckx, although Metz would orient his response by way of theological method and the construction of a practical fundamental theology, whereas Schillebeeckx turned to his christological project.

We have already seen Metz's criticism of a transcendental theology. He was equally critical of those theologies which construed the salvation established in Christ as provisional and still indefinite.[69] He feared that in taking such a tack, the promise of redemption would function only as a "cipher for a sought-after self-liberation and self-redemption on the part of humanity, which once again falls victim to the aporias" of the modern condition.[70] Nor would he accept those sundry efforts to convey suffering into the very life of the Triune God by way of the incarnation, a strategy prominently advanced by Moltmann and Hans Urs von Balthasar, among others. Metz warned that these speculative projects, though correctly seeking an explicitly theological point of mediation, achieve a precarious reconciliation by metaphysically eternalizing suffering, which still fails to account for the nonsensical and destructive character of human suffering that "is not the same thing as that negativity that belongs to a dialectically understood historical process, be it even that of the Trinitarian history of God."[71]

---

68. *FHS*, 125.

69. Such an approach would lend theological legitimacy, for example, to the "transcending without transcendence" championed by Bloch. Here, we are reminded of Schillebeeckx's own concern to qualify the meaning of salvation as a "hypothesis," and he explicitly affirmed Metz's position in *Interim Report on the Books "Jesus" and "Christ,"* trans. John Bowden (New York: Crossroad, 1981), 150n80.

70. *FHS*, 125; see also 153.

Of course, Metz's dissatisfaction with each of these projects only confirmed the position his already-established commitment to a postidealist theology anticipated. While affirming the concerns that animate their various theological projects, Metz resisted his contemporaries' efforts to resolve theoretically the nonidentity of human history. Every purely argumentative "mediation" of salvation and human history ultimately passes over and whitewashes the concrete sufferings of men and women within history. In the midst of a history in which suffering persists unabated, only a Christian praxis as a social praxis can credibly, though always controvertibly, mediate the Christian's hope in a redeemed or indebted freedom.

When first advancing a political theology, in the 1960s, Metz already had argued that the defense of the Christian's hope in response to the processes of secularization requires a practical apologetics in which human history is the essential medium by which hope is realized. In doing this, eschatology itself emerged as a practical theological category. The future cannot be devised as an object of speculative contemplation, nor can it be envisioned as a private and individualistic affair; the future qua future must be mediated practically in history and society. As we have seen, however, in advocating this practical mediation, Metz had failed to differentiate adequately between distinct strains of practical philosophy, and he consequently presumed that the historical conditions required for this "creative and militant" task were already present. Moreover, his apophatic eschatology had left the contours of the Christian's practical hope largely indefinable and therefore unavoidably abstract. Having now attended more carefully to the socially contextualized character of the human subject and the tragic

71. Ibid., 126–27. Metz would develop this critique further in "Theology as Theodicy?," in *A Passion for God: The Mystical-Political Dimension of Christianity*, ed. and trans. J. Matthew Ashley (New York: Paulist, 1998), 69–71; *Hope against Hope*, 47–48; and "Suffering unto God," trans. J. Matthew Ashley, *Critical Inquiry* 20, no. 4 (Summer 1994): 618–20.

history of suffering that profoundly shapes and endangers that subject, Metz recognized that this earlier effort at mediating the Christian's hope in history, though firmly critical of a purely theoretical mediation, could not stand up to the entrenched and paralyzing social conditions of modernity.

It was with his heightened sensitivity to the particular dangers of this situation that Metz further honed his political theology as a practical fundamental theology. As previously suggested, in doing this he would continue to develop the practical character of theological categories, particularly Christology. "No matter what the Christology," he argued, "Christ must always be thought in such a way that he is not just thought. For the sake of the truth that is proper to it, every Christology is nourished by praxis: the praxis of discipleship. It expresses a knowledge that is essentially practical."[72] Even the very idea of God, he insisted, is a practical idea: "God simply cannot be thought without this idea irritating and disrupting the immediate interests of the one who is trying to think it. Thinking-God happens as a revision of those interests and needs that are directly organized around one's self."[73] By repositioning traditional theological categories in this way, Metz not only clarified further the significance of speaking of political theology as a *practical* theology but also assumed a more effective position from which to champion the practical character of all Christian theology.

It was his unique approach to a fundamental theology that Metz now advocated, however, which reveals most clearly significant development in his apologetic and eschatological project. In offering a defense of the Christian's hope in *Theology of the World*, Metz had sought to reassure those who experienced the process of secularization as a crisis of faith by affirming the reasonableness and

72. *FHS*, 62.
73. Ibid.

relevance of Christianity, first by way of the transcendental method and then through the practical mediation or passing down of the Christian tradition's eschatological expectations. Despite strident claims to the contrary, he argued, secularization does not liquidate the validity of the Christian's faith. In both cases, he attempted to secure the meaningfulness and even historical necessity of Christianity by identifying a sensitive point of resonance, if critically, between the faith and extant conditions.

Though he never abandoned his claim for the Christian provenance of modernity's liberating interest, we have seen that it was precisely this apologetic strategy that Metz later found impossible to support in his writings from the 1970s. The critical-liberating power of the faith, at least under present conditions, would not be found primarily in its ongoing adaptation to culture, no matter how progressive or "contemporaneous" the modification. Thus, it was during this period that Metz began to argue that it was precisely in those moments when Christianity appears strangely out of step with the times, noncontemporaneous and even antediluvian, that the faith can emerge as a productive and creative dynamic for freedom.[74] As we have already seen in his reclamation of a hope for an indebted freedom in the midst of modernity's unqualified commitment to self-emancipation, Metz now believed that it was primarily through its uniquely unfamiliar and disruptive character that the Christian faith can avoid offering a banal duplication of the modern consensus and attain its contemporary significance and genuine historical force.

The rationale for Metz's alternative strategy will by now be evident. The principle of exchange has construed freedom as the ability to control production and has domesticated religion in such a

---

74. See "Productive Noncontemporaneity," in *Observations on "The Spiritual Situation of the Age,"* ed. Jürgen Habermas and trans. Andrew Buchwalter (Cambridge: MIT Press, 1984), 169–77, first published in *Unterbrechungen: Theologische-politische Perspektiven und Profile* (Gütersloh, Ger.: Gütersloher, 1981), 11–19.

manner that it is finally little more than an instrument for the private gratification of the bourgeois subject. The logic of evolution has engendered an experience of time that sedates the modern person's hope, fostering an age of apathy that deadens every expectation for the future. The Enlightenment's interest in enthroning the human subject as the subject of history has been whittled down to an exercise in exoneration, abandoning those whose freedom and hope are most radically vulnerable in history. With the identity and agency of the modern subject so profoundly compromised, Metz was convinced that the current historical situation simply could not provide a foothold or foundation by which to mediate, even critically, the Christian's hope for history. The unqualified excesses of modernity were such that the conditions required for a sustained protest had been extinguished.

Far from advocating a theological disengagement or withdrawal, however, Metz proceeded to reenvision his apologetic tack. He now argued that a practical fundamental theology, a political theology that seeks to defend and animate in history the Christian's hope for the future, will need to identify and employ a body of practical theological resources capable of "irritating and disrupting" rather than critically resonating with the identity of the modern subject and the current historical situation. Only then, Metz was convinced, can this message of hope be confessed, be heard, and begin to transform a world so profoundly marked by suffering and tragedy.

As noted earlier, Schillebeeckx believed that experiences of negative contrast provided an existentially universal phenomenon that disrupts and contests the hegemonic trajectory of a one-dimensional society and the tragedies and injustices that continuously touch human life. Contrast experiences draw the person's gaze to the mounting sufferings in history, making possible the confession of the Christian's hope by dialectically keeping open the possibility of ultimate meaning for history. Metz, too, was in search of a resource that could awaken the human to alternative possibilities for history by disrupting those plausibility assumptions established in the Enlightenment that suppress the sufferings of both past and present. For reasons now clear, however, he would resist locating that subversive vantage point within the experience of the modern subject. Indeed, it was precisely the failure of modern men and women to stand up and give an account of suffering that Metz's analysis of modernity had unveiled. Whereas Schillebeeckx believed a defiant "no" arises from human persons, religious and nonreligious alike, in the face of ongoing oppression and injustice, Metz warned, "Catastrophes are reported on the radio in between pieces of music. The music plays on, like the 'passage of time' rendered audible, rolling over everything mercilessly, impossible to interrupt. 'When atrocities happen it's like when the rain falls. No one shouts "stop it" anymore.'"[75] An age of apathy had swept over modernity, Metz believed, making it impossible under current conditions for men and women to recognize, let alone resist, evil. We will return to this important difference in Metz's and Schillebeeckx's projects in the conclusion of this study. What is important to recognize here, though, is that, for Metz, the very task of a practical fundamental theology would be directed toward the destabilization and reformation rather than the identification of that subject for whom hope is possible.

A Narrative-Practical Hope

Metz was convinced that the formation of a subject capable of Christian hope amid a culture of widespread apathy required

---

75. *FHS*, 156. The concluding quotation comes from Bertolt Brecht.

theological resources that could make possible a new consciousness by destabilizing the historical conditions in which identity is achieved.[76] Christian formation, for Metz, needed to interrupt and determine, rather than corroborate and extend, the longings of the human person. In Metz's judgment, three fundamental and interrelated categories were necessary for this project: memory, narrative, and the praxis of solidarity. These categories, he argued, would establish the historical conditions that make possible an alternative subjectivity in which a hope for all people, including the vanquished and those still suffering in history, might withstand the evolutionary pressures of the day.

Memory

Important traces of the first category, that of memory, were already present in Metz's early formulation of a political theology. Emerging out of his encounter with Bloch, Metz began to apply a messianic hermeneutic to the reading of Scripture. He recognized that history itself must be the basis of Christian theology, and he argued that it was the power of promises offered and mediated within history, rather than the transcendental structure of history itself, that grounded the modern person's expectations for the future. In the aftermath of the Enlightenment's critique of tradition, however, Metz now feared that these promises passed down in history through the Jewish and Christian traditions were being denied a role in the formation of the subject's identity. Human consciousness, including the very interest in historical freedom, is entwined with memories of the past, and the repression of these memories inevitably circumvents the capacity to envision a better future.[77] As we saw in chapter 3, it

76. Ibid., 74–75.

was precisely this dynamic that led a number of critical theorists to advocate the practice of "critically remembering," a practice in which select memories culled from history are retrieved as destabilizing alternatives to the hegemonic conditions of the present, in which a technological consciousness alone determines what is deemed objectively possible for the future.

As early as 1967, Metz recognized the need to bring these allied insights together under the category of memory, and he explicitly took up this task in an essay published in 1969 entitled "'Politische Theologie' in der Diskussion," in which he defined Christian faith as that "stance in which a person remembers the promises of the past and the hopes out of which people lived because of those promises, and binds herself or himself to those memories in a life-determining way."[78] Confirming his earlier position, then, yet now evincing more clearly the influence of Benjamin's insights into the "revolutionary chance in the fight for the oppressed past," Metz would argue that remembering the past provides the very foundation for the human person's interest in freedom.[79] Memories underwrite and stimulate a hope for the future. And, for the Christian, a specific historical memory vivifies this hope, the *memoria passionis, mortis, et resurrectionis Jesu Christi*, which uniquely introduces a dangerous promise of a sovereign God who takes the side of history's invisible and oppressed.[80] This is the memory that has sustained Christians'

---

77. It is not by accident, Metz warned, "that the destruction of memory is a typical measure taken by totalitarian governments. People's subjugation begins when their memories are taken away" (ibid., 105–6).

78. "'Politische Theologie' in der Diskussion," 286. See also *FHS*, 182, from which the translation is taken. For Metz's earlier reference to memory, see *TW*, 148n12.

79. Benjamin, "Theses on the Philosophy of History," 79. Along with Benjamin, the influence of many of the critical theorists who informed Schillebeeckx's reflections on the subversive character of memory cited in chapter 3, perhaps mostly notably Marcuse, was also evident in "'Politische Theologie' in der Diskussion."

80. "'Politische Theologie' in der Diskussion," 286. Though Metz had already anticipated the need to extend his account of the Christian's hope for the future with the memory of the past, in this essay he positioned this turn to memory, in part, as a response to critics of his project who

unrequited hopes down through the centuries, supporting expectations that refused to be determined by existing powers and possibilities. Remembering this promise in the present, Metz argued, can break through the dominant consciousness of modern existence, counter the idea of progress inscribed in a one-dimensional society, and reclaim past hopes for a future that is still outstanding.

Throughout the early 1970s, Metz seized upon the dangerous character of the *memoria Jesu Christi* to counter that consciousness of temporality which no longer has time for suffering and, thus, can no longer call into question the identity of the modern subject or even history itself. And in doing this, he would sharply cast this memory in light of the history of suffering. "Christian faith articulates itself as a *memoria passionis, mortis, et resurrectionis Jesu Christi*," he wrote. "The memory of the crucified Lord stands at the heart of this faith, a specific *memoria passionis*."[81] Further evincing the influence of Benjamin, Metz argued that, to the extent the repression of past suffering deceptively stabilizes the identity of both subject and history, the remembrance of suffering conversely reveals the nonidentity of the bourgeois subject and the lie of an ever-unfolding history of freedom: "It holds a particular anticipation of the future as a future for the hopeless, the shattered and oppressed. In this way it is a dangerous and liberating memory, which badgers the present and calls it into question, since it does not hold just any open future, but precisely this future, and because it compels believers to be in a continual state of transformation in order to take this future into account."[82] To remember suffering is to recall a dangerous memory of an anticipatory freedom that can withstand the hegemonic forces

feared his political theology lacked a genuinely theological character. Roger Dick Johns offers a helpful survey of these criticisms, which included challenges from Joseph Ratzinger, in *Man in the World*, 158–64.

81. *FHS*, 107.
82. Ibid., 89.

of modern life. Paradigmatic of all painful memories of past suffering, the *memoria passionis* possesses a critical, eschatological reserve of hope that disrupts the banal contentment of the modern subject and the seemingly smooth progress of history; it does not submit to the past but introduces the concrete leverage needed to crack open the dull apathy of the modern age and offers an alternative vantage point from which to envision the unrealized possibilities of history.

Metz's effort to cast the *memoria Jesu Christi* in the dangerous light of the history of suffering was immediately related to his warning of the superficial accommodation of Christianity to the bourgeoisie, as well as to the evolutionary account of history that underwrites bourgeois society. He feared that the resurrection of Christ risks becoming an ideological trope detached from "the darkness and threats found in humanity's history of suffering. A *memoria resurrectionis* which was not understood as a *memoria passionis* would be sheer mythology."[83] When reduced to the *memoria resurrectionis*, even inadvertently, the promises of Christianity too easily fall into the hands of those who reap the benefits of a history construed as success. For this reason, he argued, the memory of the resurrection must always pass through and remain permanently informed by the memory of Christ's suffering. The *memoria passionis, mortis, et resurrectionis Jesu Christi* provides a dangerous promise of future freedom for all, a freedom for history's vanquished and destroyed and not just history's victors. But only by passing through the memory of suffering can the *memoria resurrectionis* acquire this genuinely critical-liberating power. "Resurrection mediated by the memory of

---

83. Ibid., 109. In *Hope against Hope*, 45–46, Metz warned, "In Christology we have lost the way between Good Friday and Easter Sunday. We have too much pure Easter Sunday Christology. . . . What is called for is the experience of Holy Saturday and precisely the kind of Holy Saturday language in our Christology which is not, as in mythology, simply the language of victors." J. Matthew Ashley notes in the translation of this text that "Holy Saturday" in the German (*Karsamstag*) is more closely tied etymologically to "Good Friday" (*Karfreitag*).

suffering," Metz wrote, "means that there is a meaning for the dead, for those already defeated and forgotten, that has not yet been made good on. History's potential for meaning does not depend only on those who have survived."[84] Carefully united to the passion, the memory of Christ's resurrection permits a hope for precisely those men and women who have been abandoned by the modern history of freedom. In turn, it frees the Christian to pay attention to, and carry forward, the sufferings and hopes of all people, even the dead, in a world in which just such a hope has been deemed foolish.

In the face of criticism that his writings did not offer sufficient account of Christ's resurrection, including criticism from Schillebeeckx,[85] Metz persistently advocated for a one-sided *memoria* that asks his reader to tarry longer on Christ's passion before offering an account of the resurrection. In considering a response to this criticism, it can be tempting to suggest that in taking up a corrective task, Metz was merely introducing a critical or therapeutic moment in the larger and more genuinely systematic work of Christian theology.[86] And, certainly, he did not undertake a comprehensive

84. *FHS*, 109.
85. *Christ*, 755. See also R. R. Reno, "Christology in Political and Liberation Theology," *Thomist* 56, no. 2 (April 1992): 291–332.
86. Though we will have an opportunity to return to the topic at the beginning of chapter 6, here it will be helpful to consider briefly what Metz described as the "corrective" character of his theology. Throughout his writings, Metz often represented his unique employment of the category of memory, as well as his larger theological project, as a corrective enterprise. Although this characterization of his work is never entirely clarified, and it is not clear whether this function should be understood in a uniform manner as it emerges in different contexts, when making this claim we unfailingly find Metz encouraging the reader to pause and consider just a little longer that which might otherwise appear so obviously incontrovertible. He cited Søren Kierkegaard in explanation: "Now whoever shall present a 'corrective' must study the weak sides of what exists carefully and fundamentally—and then bring the contrary one-sidedly into play: thoroughly one-sidedly." Kierkegaard's comments offer a valuable entrance into Metz's understanding of the corrective character of his theology, yet, to the extent that they may suggest either a purely provisional or a wholly unqualified task, they can also be misleading. That is to say, Metz's employment of the memory of suffering is a genuinely constructive project, yet it is self-consciously "one-sided" and not comprehensive. See "Theology as Theodicy?," 63.

christological project of his own. As we have just seen, though, in offering this corrective, he was not simply introducing a provisional step that finds its value only in the later formulation of a more fully integrated Christology. To the contrary, he argued that the memory of Christ's resurrection can offer a dangerous and liberating promise only when it passes through and remains permanently informed by his suffering. On the one hand, by privileging the *memoria passionis*, Metz did not forsake the hope of the *memoria resurrectionis* but sought to reframe it. Only in this way, he warned, can Christians wrest the hope of the resurrection away from history's victors and preserve a hope for those already defeated and forgotten. This is a constructive, if intentionally one-sided, position. On the other hand, and with precisely this in mind, we also see that his one-sided *memoria* was not without underlying qualification. Again, although Metz did not relinquish the *memoria resurrectionis*, its powerful word of hope is undeniably mediated almost exclusively in and through the *memoria passionis*. If this qualification is deliberately made explicit only rarely, which perhaps can account for the criticism noted, the censure offered through the corrective task is not absolute. His corrective project seeks clarification by way of amplification. Indeed, it was only by amplifying the memory of Christ's suffering that Metz believed one could arrive at an account of the resurrection that might withstand the ideological pressures of modern life.

As we now could expect, for Metz, this weighted retrieval of the memory of suffering does not ascribe positive meaning to human suffering or death itself, which would once more rationalize that which is inherently senseless.[87] Nor does it provide positive content to the hope it bespeaks. The *memoria passionis* is an eschatological

---

87. *FHS*, 124. Schillebeeckx responded to the same concern by emphasizing that it is not the experience of suffering itself but rather the hope-filled protest against suffering that makes possible the proclamation of the Christian's hope.

memory, an anticipatory memory that builds up an "antiknowledge" of historical freedom and, thus, conveys the "future content" of a hope not yet realized.[88] It does, however, overcome the abstract and limited account of freedom established in the Enlightenment by shaping a negative yet distinct consciousness of a future freedom: "Memory of suffering is an anticipatory remembering; it holds the anticipation of a specific future for humankind as a future for the suffering, for those without hope, for the oppressed, the disabled, and the useless of the earth."[89] It will be clear that the work performed by Schillebeeckx's category of a contrast experience is here being performed in a similar fashion by Metz's employment of the memory of suffering. The following excerpt from "The Future Seen from the Memory of Suffering" is particularly revealing:

> This *memoria* shows its determinative power in the question about what direction transformation should take. It is not a total leap into the eschatological existence of the "new human being," but a reflection on human suffering in its concreteness that forms the starting point for proclaiming the new form of life worthy of human beings heralded by the resurrection of Jesus. A knowledge of the future grows from the soil of the memory of suffering, a knowledge that does not at all mean a formless anticipating, but rather takes up the quest for a more human way of life.[90]

For each theologian, his respective category disrupts the plausibility assumptions of the present and the ideological resolution of the nonidentity of history that always comes at the expense of those most vulnerable in the world. It resists a complete positive accounting of the possibilities of human existence in advance of the eschaton, and thus keeps open the possibility of a gratuitously given future. In both cases, a negative consciousness of future freedom is revealed and a

88. Ibid., 105–6.
89. Ibid., 112.
90. Ibid., 108.

powerful stimulus to overcome injustice in history is found. And, in the end, the practical confession of the Christian's hope within a history of suffering begins to be possible.

Narrative

But can memories avoid warping into private ruminations or mythological tales under the privatizing processes of the Enlightenment? It was with this question that Metz turned to the second theological category under consideration: narrative. Influenced by the work of Benjamin and Harald Weinrich, among others, Metz seized on the capacity of narrative, or storytelling, to keep alive the dangerous memories of suffering that convey the repressed hopes of history's vanquished.[91] Narratives publicly stage a plotting of events that explicitly unfold within history and society and thus uniquely avoid the dangers of privatization and dehistoricization. Moreover, this essentially temporal and contingent character of narrative allows for the communication of the Christian promise of redemption within a history of suffering without offering that exhaustive and therefore reductive response to suffering that accompanies every purely argumentative "mediation" of salvation and human history.[92] Indeed, Metz identified the narrative as that medium by which the history of salvation and world history intersect and find an anticipatory continuity without premature reconciliation or superficial identification.[93] In his words, "Salvation history is the world's history in which space is made for defeated and repressed

---

91. Metz referenced Benjamin's "The Storyteller: Reflections on the Works of Nikolai Leskov," in *Illuminations*, ed. Hannah Arendt, trans. Harry Zohn (New York: Schocken, 1968); and Harald Weinrich's "Narrative Theology," in *The Crisis of Religious Language*, ed. Johann Baptist Metz and Jean-Pierre Jossua (New York: Herder & Herder, 1973), 46–56.
92. *FHS*, 154.
93. Ibid., 192–95.

hopes and suffering to have meaning. Salvation history is that history of the world in which meaning is promised to the vanquished and forgotten possibilities of human existence."[94] It is the narration of a dangerous memory, Metz believed, that begins to create this space: "This memory thus resists the triumphalism of what has come into existence and remains in existence. This is a dangerous memory, which, precisely as such, saves the 'Christian continuum.'"[95]

We will return to this dialectical understanding of the Christian continuum in chapter 6. The vital role performed by the narrative in Metz's larger project, however, is already evident. In recounting the stories of others' sufferings as well as one's own, the storyteller wrests away authorship of human history from those who have managed to narrate history as a one-sided story of progress and success. These stories engage both the narrator and the hearer in the sufferings of others, allowing them to pay attention to and carry forward those memories of past sufferings through which expectations for a future freedom arise.

It is important to keep in mind, though, that the narratives Metz sought to introduce into the theological task were the remembered stories of those whose hopes had gone down in history in defeat. The cognitive knowledge attained in the narrated memories of suffering, above all in the *memoria passionis*, is primarily a negative consciousness with a dangerous and destabilizing interest. Narratives carve out a space where defeated and repressed hopes may have future meaning. In describing Metz's distinct employment of narrative, Matthew Ashley argues,

> The authentic function of narrative is not to build up identity; [narratives] do not only or primarily help us to interpret and reflexively secure our present experience. Rather, it is to break down, interrupt,

94. Ibid., 109–10.
95. Ibid., 158.

and upset our present self-interpretation, to open us to an eschatological meaning of our present existence, that, if not encompassing the meaninglessness and suffering of the past, at least allows it to exist, to have its (counter) voice.[96]

In Metz's hands, narratives guard against the modern propensity to turn one's gaze too quickly from the sufferings of history, the propensity to pass over rather than pass through the *memoria passionis*. What those involved in the recounting of past sufferings discover is a story's unique capacity to animate still-unrequited expectations rather than the affirmation of their present expectations.

Metz's employment of the narrative affirmed the practical depth structure of the story, particularly the story of Jesus. That is to say, for Metz, the recounting of the story of *Jesu Christi* has a practical bent. "Every attempt to know him, to understand him, is . . . always a journey, a following," he insisted. "It is only by following and imitating him that we know whom we are dealing with."[97] Accordingly, one does not first learn the story of Jesus and only then apply it by way of some subsequent practice. Rather, "to follow Jesus means ultimately not only to admire him, to take him as a model, as can still be said by a moderate bourgeois-liberal theology . . . but something more radical and more dangerous: putting him on, putting Christ on."[98] In this way, the storyteller, the practitioner of Christology, enters into a genuinely radical solidarity with Christ. Yet Metz persistently insisted we remember this story as the *memoria passionis*. Only then can Christians protect their subversive story against ideological distortion from both within and outside the church. In recounting the story of Christ's passion, Metz wrote, "His cry from the cross is the cry of that God-forsaken man who for his

---

96. Ashley, *Interruptions*, 121. In the context of dangerous memories, Metz develops this point in *Hope against Hope*, 33–34.

97. *Followers of Christ*, 39.

98. Ibid., 34; Cf. Rom. 13:14.

part has never forsaken God. It is this kind of suffering that provides the point of reference for his obedience, his obedience 'unto death, even death on a cross.' In the situation of radical hopelessness and contradictoriness there stands his yes, his assent."[99] It is this dangerous memory, Metz believed, that determines the unique character of Christian discipleship. Putting on Christ ultimately demands taking up his cross. Solidarity with the suffering and conquered Christ requires making his cry one's own. It means refusing to abandon or even to reconcile prematurely his painful obedience and assent, his obstinate "yes" to the future despite the overwhelming contradictoriness of his crucifixion. This is a mystical and practical solidarity. It is fastened to an unrelieved hope from the past, a hope in the midst of hopelessness and death, that stimulates a life of discipleship in the present, a life of solidarity with all of history's suffering and crucified people.

Praxis of Solidarity

We have already turned, then, to the third category through which Metz developed his political theology as a practical fundamental theology: the praxis of solidarity. We will see in what follows that he believed that it is liberating praxis carried out as solidarity that best conveys that hope for history which persistently keeps the history of human suffering in view. Solidarity unearths and offers a practical response to that question systematically repressed in modern existence: "For whom am I responsible?"[100] As suggested earlier, Metz framed memory, narrative, and solidarity as fundamentally

---

99. Ibid., 64.

100. "In the Pluralism of Religious and Cultural Worlds," in *Love's Strategy: The Political Theology of Johann Baptist Metz*, ed. John K. Downey (Harrisburg, PA: Trinity, 1999), 170; translated by John K. Downey and Heiko Wiggers from *Zum Begriff der neuen Politichen Theology, 1967–1997* (Mainz, Ger.: Matthias-Grünewald, 1997), 197–206.

interrelated theological categories, and the interrelationship between memory and narrative was hopefully evidenced in the preceding paragraphs. This mutual dependence is further elucidated in his reflections on the category of solidarity. It is only through solidarity, he argued, that the practical status of a dangerous story achieves sociopolitical weight, and it is only through narrated memory that the praxis of solidarity is evoked and nourished: "Only together are memory, narrative and solidarity the basic categories for a practical fundamental theology. Memory and narrative do not have their practical character without solidarity, and solidarity does not attain its specifically cognitive import without memory and narrative."[101] Here, then, we have arrived at the distinctive manner in which Metz would render the practical epistemological force of the Christian faith. It is in the dangerous *memoria passionis* that Christian praxis finds its stimulus and character, and by further specifying this praxis as mystical-political solidarity, Metz set out to distinguish that unique form of discipleship evoked by this memory.

Maintaining his commitment to the social differentiation of human subjectivity, Metz introduced the category of solidarity, connected with memory and narrative, as the social matrix of an alternative consciousness of freedom. By speaking of Christian praxis as solidarity, he looked to safeguard the political character of human existence as well as the Christian's eschatological hope. The language of solidarity recognizes that subjectivity and salvation are realized not in social isolation but always in relationship with the other. For Metz, then, the praxis of solidarity does not merely connote a political ethic or even a proper religious practice performed by an already free and authentic subject. Rather, it is only as a community-in-solidarity that men and women can hope to become the free subjects of their

---

101. *FHS*, 167.

history. Informed by the *memoria passionis*, however, this praxis of solidarity by which men and women can emerge as subjects takes the form of a practical yet anticipatory hope. It is the formation of that body politic in which a hope for the future freedom and authenticity of all people is preserved: "Solidarity is a category of assistance, of supporting and encouraging the subject in the face of that which threatens him or her most acutely in the face of his or her suffering."[102] Solidarity bears a hope for those whose freedom has been denied; it is the praxis of sensitivity to another's suffering that resists the historical pressures that prevent people from becoming subjects.[103] In doing this, solidarity contests the apathy of the modern age by binding those who still can hope to the victims of history, taking responsibility for and carrying forward the suffering others' unfulfilled expectations and only thus enlivening their own.

The praxis of solidarity, then, begins to establish the concrete historical conditions that can sustain the Christian's hope in the all-embracing promise of redemption revealed by the God of Jesus who is the God of the living and the dead. It resists the halving as well as the abstraction of freedom carried out by the Enlightenment that ultimately corrupts the very possibility of historical freedom. As such, it is both a universal and a particular, mystical and political, category. Solidarity reveals its mystical and universal character above all in its solidaristic hope for the dead: "In the light of this history of redemption there is not only a 'solidarity looking forward' with future generations, but a 'solidarity looking backward,' a practical solidarity of memory with those silenced by death and forgotten."[104] As we have seen, Metz warned that when, in the name of progress,

---

102. Ibid., 208.
103. *The Emergent Church: The Future of Christianity in a Postbourgeois World*, trans. Peter Mann (New York: Crossroad, 1981), 42; originally published as *Jenseits bürgerlicher Religion: Reden über die Zukunft des Christentums* (Mainz, Ger.: Matthias-Grünewald, 1980).
104. *FHS*, 124.

the hope of a future freedom for the dead is forsaken, the freedom of all men and women is jeopardized. An indifference to the vanquished of history leaves nothing but banal promises for those still living. Only a universal solidarity that extends to the past, that makes a space for and accompanies the unrequited hopes of the dead into the future, can sustain and nourish expectations for the future. In this way, Metz envisioned solidarity as anamnetic: anamnetic solidarity or anamnetic hope.[105] The practice of solidarity does not just remember the past as a curious yet distant artifact; it also discovers its own hope in the hope of the past and, thus, re-presents that hope that it may have a future. As a practical remembrance of past suffering, solidarity is an active expectation for the dead. And it is precisely here that a solidaristic hope for the dead becomes more than a pious religious prescription or soothing words in the face of one's own pending death: "Solidarity of memory with the dead is not defined by some abstract interest and not in the first instance by the concern about what death will mean 'for me.' Rather, the concern that defines this solidarity has to do with what death means 'for you,' which is to say, for the other, especially for those who suffer."[106] In the name of a future freedom for all, the universal-mystical character of solidarity keeps a hope alive for those whose hope has been extinguished.

Precisely because a solidarity informed by the *memoria passionis* possesses a universal breadth of scope enlivened by the hopes of history's suffering persons, it will simultaneously take on that particular and political character in the present which actively anticipates a specific future, a future for the world's suffering, for those without hope, for those deemed useless and unproductive. Solidarity achieves this particular character as it is embodied today

---

105. "Theology Today: New Crises and New Visions," in *Love's Strategy*, 80; originally published in *Proceedings of the Catholic Theological Society of America* 40 (1985): 1–14.
106. *FHS*, 211.

in specific actions in defense of those who are most threatened and vulnerable. Living in solidarity requires standing with and accompanying a specific people, the "least among us," protesting and resisting the oppressive structures and ideologies that dehumanize these men and women in the name of progress.

Only in this way, Metz believed, can universal and particular solidarity complement one another and overcome the dangerous internal contradictions inscribed in modern life. Universal solidarity without particular solidarity, on the one hand, has no practical force; it never enters into the fray and, thus, reinforces the listless apathy of the modern subject. Particular solidarity without universal solidarity, on the other hand, risks precisely that danger Metz unveiled in his analysis of the modern history of emancipation. It bifurcates and then corrupts the theme of freedom, frequently at the expense of an isolated historical scapegoat. Here, for example, we might think of Metz's critique of Marxist praxis. Particular solidarity without universal solidarity is too often an alliance of mutual benefit among a faction, a religion, or those deemed suitably "rational."[107] Approximating the principle of exchange, it excludes—and often violently—those outside the faction, those of a different religion, or those who do not productively contribute to the progress of the technocratic society. Universal-particular solidarity, in contrast, is a concrete praxis that remains attentive to and protests the suffering of past and present in order to preserve a hope for the future freedom of all.

107. Ibid., 209.

6

Metz's Apocalyptic Theology of History

Holding Open Hope by Binding History

As we have just seen, Metz turned to a practical fundamental theology developed through the categories of memory, narrative, and solidarity in search of the resources necessary to disrupt the conditions of modernity and to revivify an eschatological hope. It is to that central focus of this chapter—Metz's apocalyptic eschatology—that we now turn. As we shall see, Metz located in the apocalyptic the fundamental temporal framework through which a subversive expectation for the future becomes possible within the historical context of modernity and, ultimately, postmodernity. He became convinced that in the face of persistent and intractable suffering, an apocalyptic hope rightly admits the hopelessness of progressively engineering a history of genuine freedom yet simultaneously refuses to surrender to that hopelessness. By calling history into question, by disclosing the limited nature of time and expecting its disruption, apocalyptic time holds open a hope for those who have no hope other than time's end. This is a practical-critical hope, Metz insisted, that will not allow the promises of God simply to reinforce the expectations and practices of today. Rather, it is a subversive expectation that sustains a sensitivity and solidarity with the suffering persons of history, protesting against injustice and faithfully demanding that God remain faithful to a promise made. In examining the diverse and interrelated aspects of Metz's turn to apocalyptic, we will consider six key elements in his mature eschatological writings: apocalyptic as corrective, the praxis of solidaristic hope, the centrality of *memoria passionis*, the move from utopia to apocalyptic, the emphasis on God as subject of history, and the theodicy question and its implications for a theology of creation.

Apocalyptic as Corrective

In turning to apocalyptic, Metz believed he located that posture toward history, deeply imbedded in the Jewish and Christian traditions, which best corresponds to "an anti-evolutionary consciousness"[1] that might remain sensitive to the history of suffering and self-consciously hold open a future for the redemption of history's unrequited hopes. It is an apocalyptic temporality that creates a space for, or makes time for, history's forgotten. Here, Metz would find a dangerous theological resource by which to counteract the logic of evolution and to interrupt the steamroller of progress that continues to leave countless victims in its wake. The evolutionary account of history underwriting modern life smothers the dreams of men and women by systematically refusing to make time for history's suffering and defeated; an apocalyptic account of history, he argued,

---

1. *Followers of Christ: The Religious Life and the Church,* trans. Thomas Linton (New York: Paulist, 1978), 81.

can sustain these dangerous memories from which arise a solidaristic hope for the future.

From the outset, it is important to recognize that Metz consistently represented his decision for an apocalyptic eschatology as a corrective project.[2] As we have seen, he regularly exploited this strategy by offering a one-sided amplification or "exaggeration" deliberately formulated to provoke the reader to pause and consider again that which currently may appear so obviously established. This interest is immediately clear in his turn to apocalypticism, where the leverage he attributed to this fundamental time structure is found in its ability to put into relief and call into question modernity's dominant yet concealed understanding of history.

In admitting the one-sidedness of his task, though, Metz presented his reader with a distinct challenge. On the one hand, a corrective apocalypticism cannot be approached as a fully comprehensive project. As such, we must carefully avoid offering an overly integrated account of a position that self-consciously eschews extensive systemization; indeed, it is precisely the totalizing account of history presumed by an evolutionary view of history that his turn to the apocalyptic seeks to disrupt. On the other hand, we will fail to recognize the substantive gains Metz believed he achieved by way of this disruptive task if we construe his project as a purely remedial or provisional enterprise. Metz claimed that an apocalyptic eschatology "is to a certain degree the hem of my theological approach, although I have not learned to speak consistently and convincingly about it."[3] Although he explicitly warned against interpreting his position as

---

2. See *Faith in History and Society: Toward a Practical Fundamental Theology*, ed. and trans. J. Matthew Ashley (New York: Crossroad, 2007), 156 (hereafter abbreviated as *FHS*); and "Theology as Theodicy?," in *A Passion for God: The Mystical-Political Dimension of Christianity*, ed. and trans. J. Matthew Ashley (New York: Paulist, 1998), 63.

3. "On the Way to a Post-Idealist Theology," in *Passion for God*, 47; first published as "Unterwegs zu einer nachidealistichen Theologie," in *Entwürfe der Theologie*, ed. Johannes B. Bauer (Cologne, Ger.: Styria, 1985), 209–33.

a decision for apocalyptic time over against eschatological time, he unapologetically challenged contemporary Christian theologians to honor the apocalyptic dimension of eschatology in order to avert the hazards of evolutionary logic.[4] As we will see, it was precisely by way of its disruptive and critical function that Metz makes truly constructive use of the apocalyptic motif, and it is by way of this motif that he believes theologians might speak of salvation history without passing over history's suffering and vanquished.

In what follows, it will be important to keep both facets of this corrective task in view. This is all the more important, of course, in light of Schillebeeckx's pointed opposition to apocalyptic eschatologies in general, examined at the end of chapter 4. Consequently, we will limit our objective in this chapter to identifying the unique role of the apocalyptic in Metz's work.[5] Having done that, we will be better positioned in the conclusion of this study to evaluate both Metz's proposal and Schillebeeckx's criticism.

Early Insight

In tracing the origins of Metz's appeal to the apocalyptic motif, it is rather remarkable that we can first look to one of his earliest professional writings. In a small meditation published in 1959 entitled *The Advent of God*, Metz had already exhibited a nascent willingness to employ the rhetoric of apocalypticism. Though this early work unsurprisingly evidenced the transcendental-linear theology of history that characterized his thought during that period, it is

---

4. *FHS*, 164.
5. For a helpful examination of Metz's use of apocalypticism that situates his work in the broader context of the history of apocalyptic thought and literature, including its relationship to Latin American liberation theology, see J. Matthew Ashley, "Apocalypticism in Political and Liberation Theology: Toward an Historical *Docta Ignorantia*," *Horizons* 27, no. 1 (2000): 22–43.

significant not only for its use of an apocalyptic discourse but also because that discourse was retrieved in order to speak of a God who is the Lord of history, a God who continuously exceeds and thus disrupts the plausibility assumptions of modern men and women. Invoking the language of the book of Revelation, he wrote, "Our hearts and souls awaken to each new day with the possibility that God's advent may dawn. The New Testament does not close simply with an Amen to what has already passed. It also pronounces an Amen to what is yet to come: Maranatha, 'Come, Lord Jesus!'"[6] Although Metz's use of apocalyptic rhetoric in conveying this crucial interest remained principally dormant in the years that immediately followed, we noted in chapter 1 that this disruptive character of God's eschatological promise came to occupy an increasingly decisive role in his theological program.

Influence of Bloch and Benjamin

It was through his encounter with Bloch and, most importantly, through Benjamin's influence in the 1970s that these early suggestive intuitions would gradually reemerge as Metz slowly learned to exercise the critical-liberating potential of an apocalyptic account of history. Bloch markedly influenced Metz with his critical resistance to the prevailing strategies of demythologization as well as his advocacy for a messianic hermeneutic in the reading of biblical stories. Alongside his study of later Jewish and Christian sources, perhaps most notably the fifteenth-century apocalyptic revolutionary Thomas Münster, Bloch's effort to uncover in history traces of a utopian hope for a radically new future had offered Metz an important point of entrance into an apocalyptic sensibility.

---

6. *The Advent of God*, trans. John Drury (Paramus, NJ: Newman, 1970), n.p.

It was with his reading of Benjamin, however, that this apocalyptic sensibility explicitly seized Metz's imagination and permanently came to the fore of his writings. Although Benjamin's own religious commitments remain a matter of debate, in a manner redolent of Bloch the idiosyncratic philosopher interweaved Marxist materialism with a wide range of cultural and religious sources, particularly Jewish Kabbalah, in an attempt to uncover and interrupt the hegemonic notion of progress that had come to dominate the modern historic consciousness. In his collection of theses "On the Concept of History," Benjamin tried to counter that unilinear notion of historical progress in which every expectation for the future is arrested in advance, where the image of time as an empty continuum makes impossible the surprising in history, with evocative reflections on the messianic hope of the Jewish faith tradition. "We know that the Jews were prohibited from investigating the future," he wrote. "This does not imply, however, that for the Jews the future turned into homogeneous, empty time. For every second of time was the strait gate through which the Messiah might enter."[7]

In search of the potent possibilities that might still reside in this long-forgotten temporal deportment, Benjamin's fragmented remarks resist impetuous conclusions and instead skillfully invite his reader into a series of critical questions. Could the hope that at any moment the Messiah might break into time disrupt that undialectical myth of time that threatens to overwhelm and even erase the human subject in lieu of an absolute though anonymous subject of history? Could remembering the apocalyptic expectations of the Jewish people hold open a future that might still offer something new? Could it make time for the forgotten victims of history, even the dead, who have suffered in the wake of history's unrelenting

7. Walter Benjamin, "Theses on the Philosophy of History," in *German 20th Century Philosophy: The Frankfurt School,* ed. Wolfgang Schirmacher (New York: Continuum, 2000), 80.

advance?[8] Benjamin's theses were deliberately provocative, offering little in the way of resolution. Yet it is in his effort to uncover a temporal consciousness that would make time for history's oppressed and vanquished that we can locate the significance of his thought for Metz's turn to the apocalyptic. In retrieving the apocalyptic imagination of the Jewish tradition, Benjamin believed he had discovered a promising vantage point from which to interrupt modernity's nearly imperceptible though death-dealing consciousness of time.

Learning to Speak Apocalyptically: Religion as Interruption

It was in his own collection of theses "Hope as Imminent Expectation—or, The Struggle for Lost Time: Untimely Theses on Apocalyptic" that Metz once again took up the task of "learning to speak" of apocalypticism. As we have already seen, it was in this text that he appropriated Benjamin's analysis of the modern situation and examined the paralyzing consequences of the myth of evolutionary time. It was also here that he, too, would position a retrieval of an apocalyptic hope for history as a subversive hope that might interrupt that myth. "The shortest definition of religion: interruption," Metz suggestively wrote.[9] Yet Christianity can function as a forceful interruption, he further argued, only to the extent that the long-repressed apocalyptic strands of the faith are allowed to reemerge.

It is important to note, however, a crucial way in which Metz's task differed from that of Benjamin. Benjamin enlisted "the services of theology" in an effort to expose the propensity of the idea of progress to underwrite totalitarian structures on both the political left and

8. Ibid., 73.
9. *FHS*, 158.

right.[10] Though Metz was sensitive to this danger, for the theologian, uncovering and correcting the crippling theological consequences of the modern historic consciousness for the Christian's faith was an urgent task. The "logic of evolution is not innocent," he argued. "Neither is it agnostic (in the style of a methodological atheism). God—the God of the living and of the dead, the God for whom even the past and the dead are not left to rest in peace—is absolutely unthinkable within this logic."[11] At the heart of Metz's project, then, lay the pressing desire to reclaim the Christian's eschatological hope in an apocalyptic key, to reclaim a demanding expectation that can endure as an "imminent expectation" and resist the paralyzing pressures of modern existence. "Surely we Christians," he warned, "offer the world a painful spectacle: that of people who talk about hope but really no longer look forward to anything."[12] What has become of that incalculable hope, Metz queried, for which every second of time is a strait gate through which the Messiah might come again? What has become of the hope that the God of Jesus Christ is the Lord of history? What has become of Christianity's apocalyptic inheritance?

With only a hint of qualification, Metz averred, "All the prevalent forms of eschatology today—whether they focus on the present or the future—seem to have been successfully accommodated to an alien, evolutionistic understanding of time."[13] His fear that a transcendental theology ultimately reinforces the paralyzing notion of time governing modernity has already been noted. If the individual's hope is always already transcendentally determined, then history itself is envisioned as only actualizing and confirming more of the same.

10. Benjamin, "Theses on the Philosophy of History," 71. Throughout his essay, Benjamin describes the concept of history supported by the idea of progress as "historicism."
11. *FHS,* 160.
12. *Followers of Christ,* 76.
13. *FHS,* 160.

Though an end of time is correctly posited, its advent holds neither pressing significance nor the possibility of something new. If such an end were to come, would it matter? With history's end transcendentally ascertained in advance, Metz believed, the spell of timelessness would take hold, jeopardizing the historical agency of the human subject. A history construed as marching onward toward an already-determined resolution inadvertently would reinterpret the Christian's imminent expectation as "continual expectation" or "constant readiness." Here, Metz's concern is not with a vigilant attentiveness or "watchfulness" for God's saving activity in history, but with that absence of any sense of historical urgency that accompanies the logic of evolutionary time.

Unsurprisingly, Metz further argued that this profound misinterpretation of the Christian's expectation for the future could not be overcome by way of a detemporalized eschatology. As we observed in chapter 1, an objectivist cosmology in which transcendence and temporality are rent asunder drastically privatizes the Christian's hope in terms of the death of the individual alone, emptying history of value or possibility and betraying the biblical witness itself. Here, Metz extended his criticism of this theological approach, adding that, far from bypassing the logic of evolution, it wholly submits to that image of temporality in which nothing new can be hoped. Tacitly accepting modernity's evolutionistic understanding of time, every expectation is simply directed toward a disembodied other-world positioned somewhere "above" or outside of history, whereas history itself proceeds apace without surprise and without end. Metz warned that this strategy, like much of contemporary theology, too readily offers an anthropological reduction of eschatology that draws the apocalyptic sting from Christianity by reframing the end of time as a private, atemporal, and ultimately barren concern. Once more, this strategy falls victim to the spell of timelessness, making it impossible for men and women to take responsibility for their history.

Metz additionally cautioned, however, that in failing to recognize the underlying pressures of the myth of evolution, contemporary efforts to redirect expectations toward society and history have offered little in the way of avoiding this reduction of hope. Indeed, the degree to which the expectations of men and women have been infected by modernity's myth of time is perhaps most evident in those versions of history "in which the category of fulfillment is calculated in terms of process or evolution. The Kingdom of God becomes nothing but utopia, achieved in the course of 'progress.'"[14] This criticism will increasingly find a theological target in Metz's writings during the 1980s, an important development that we will examine shortly. Here, though, the target of his criticism once more seems to be modernity's sundry accounts of self-emancipation, and particularly Bloch's, in whose honor Metz's theses were dedicated and from whom Christian theologians would "be able to learn . . . only by contradicting him."[15] Metz warned that even as Bloch championed a "transcending without transcendence" with the intent of fostering a revolutionary hope for the future, without a hope in the God who can interrupt history, the hope for history within his project still betrays the logic of evolution. The defeated hopes of history, though deemed rhetorically useful, dwell beyond the purview of historical emancipation and are thus allowed to languish in the past. At the same time, Metz points out that every expectation for the future is exhausted by the limits of what the human person can envisage in terms of advancement. And ultimately, there is no end, as historical processes themselves rather the Lord of history have the final word regarding the realization of freedom. Again, then, the

14. Ibid., 161.
15. Ibid., 156.

debilitating logic of evolution rears its head, for nothing lost can be saved, nothing genuinely surprising or new can be realized, and no end can be expected. As we have seen, Metz feared that it is just such an account of history that inevitably reinforces the entrenched hegemonic forces that the Enlightenment sought to overcome.

Of course, Metz's critique of these theological and philosophical positions was present already in his earlier political theology examined in chapter 1. What was new in his "Untimely Theses," as well as in many of the other texts written in the 1970s and 1980s, was the warning that these various positions ultimately end in paralyzing contradiction, because they have unwittingly fallen under the spell of timeless time and, thus, pass over the crucified and vanquished of history. It was in response that Metz had begun to advocate the liberating potential of the apocalyptic tradition. Yet he would warn that even here, the creeping reach of modernity's dominant myth of time must be discerned. When the apocalyptic has been construed as a temporal framework for calculating or forecasting some future calamity, or when even its most robust biblical expressions have been cheapened to an archaic genre of literature that need only be demythologized, the peculiar hope offered by this framework has already been defeated. Despite the distinctive use of an apocalyptic discourse, these strategies betray the effects of timeless time no less than the projects examined earlier by reducing history to a manageable and predictable extrapolation of the present.

Metz insisted, however, that this need not be apocalypticism's fate, for the very origins of the apocalyptic tradition are to be found in precisely those historically concrete experiences of danger in which time is anything but manageable and predictable. It is in the face of irrepressible suffering, tragedy, and death, as we also noted in Schillebeeckx and examined in chapter 4, that the apocalyptic finds the hope for history's progressive and engineered advance toward greater freedom impossible to sustain. Like Schillebeeckx, then, Metz traced the origins of the apocalyptic tradition to the dangerous experience of unabated and intractable suffering.[16] Unlike Schillebeeckx, however, he identified in this tradition embedded in tragedy a historical witness to a fundamental temporal matrix that, if all too often buried, can both counter timeless time and safeguard apocalypticism from further reinforcing the often-self-serving interests of those who embrace the tradition in the present. In an essay from 1985 entitled "On the Way to a Postidealist Theology," Metz explained:

> Apocalyptic texts talk about the end of time and of history; they bring interruption into proximity. In that regard these texts and images must be scrutinized carefully. They do not contain idle speculation about the exact point in time of some catastrophe, but vivid commentaries on the catastrophic essence of time itself. In the apocalyptic's subversive vision, time itself is full of danger. Time is not just that evolutionary stretched-out, empty and surprise-free endlessness that offers no resistance to our projections of our future.[17]

Although Metz made little use of the vivid symbols and imagery characteristic of apocalyptic literature, what he found in this eidetic tradition was a consciousness of the catastrophic nonidentity of time, an antievolutionary consciousness of temporality that counters that endless continuum that inevitably leads to the disintegration of time and, thus, the defeat of hope: "The awareness of catastrophe present in apocalypticism is fundamentally an awareness of time. And this does not mean an awareness of some point in time of catastrophe, but rather awareness of the catastrophic nature of time itself, the element of discontinuity in it, of the termination and end of time."[18] Metz argued that apocalyptic time makes a claim not just on the future,

16. Ibid., 162.
17. "On the Way," 52.
18. *FHS*, 162.

then, but on all of human history. It challenges the myth of evolution by insisting that the identity of history has been and is repeatedly interrupted by senseless and incalculable catastrophe. History is filled with crisis; it is in a "state of emergency," as Benjamin suggested, and only an apocalyptically charged account of this history can fashion that sensitivity to suffering that saves men and women from the consequent crisis of hope that characterizes modern existence. The spell of evolution radically distorts the human's experience of time, compromising every expectation for history by construing time as an uncomplicated story of progress. Apocalyptic time subverts this story by drawing attention to the painful nonidentity of history and, thus, a temporality of discontinuity.

From Metz's perspective, it is by creating this awareness of time's discontinuity that apocalypticism makes possible not only that hope for a surprising God who exceeds both what already exists and what humans themselves seek to bring into existence, but also the hope that God can interrupt history and bring time to a close, saving those who have suffered and fallen in defeat to this history. "For the apocalyptic, God is the one who has not yet fully appeared, the still outstanding mystery of time," Metz insisted. "God is seen not as that which transcends time, but as the end which is pressing in upon it, its delineation, its saving interruption."[19] Apocalyptic hope, then, admits the utter hopelessness of engineering a history of genuine freedom yet refuses to surrender to this hopelessness. Rather, it holds open a hope for those who would have no other hope by calling history into question, disclosing the limited nature of time, and expecting its disruption and end. With this expectation for time's disruption and end, "time itself gains a temporal structure and ceases to be that timeless infinity into which the present can be arbitrarily projected."[20]

19. "On the Way," 52.
20. *FHS*, 162.

This, Metz argued, is a practical-critical posture toward history, and it is in the life of Christian discipleship that the subversive character of an apocalyptic hope finds practical confirmation. If history is recast as the arena in which it is precisely the surprising and unexpected that can be expected, catastrophe and redemption alike, then men and women can reclaim the freedom to act in history. Moreover, if the end of history is imminent yet equally surprising and incalculable, then men and women are impelled to act now.

Metz emphasized that the apocalyptic sensibility trusts in God's binding of time—it even expects the end of time—and thus fashions the hope that present existence, so acutely stained by suffering and death, need not have the final word. His apocalyptic writings sought to break the spell of timelessness that consumes those people who have fallen to the past or who do not "productively" contribute to progress in the present, those who possess no value under modernity's logic of evolution, by offering the hope that an imminent future, a new and indebted future in which their value will be guaranteed, is just over the horizon. By doing this, apocalypticism counters the apathy and fatalism of the modern subject with a consciousness of freedom through which taking responsibility for history is indeed possible. Christianity's apocalyptic sting frees the past, present, and future from the predictability and inevitability of evolution. It carves out the time in which the forgotten and vanquished of the past can be reclaimed as meaningful and, in turn, frees modern men and women to live that solidaristic hope by which they may become the subjects of their history. Indeed, as we now will see, it is apocalyptic time that makes this solidaristic hope possible.

The Praxis of Solidaristic Hope

The solidaristic hope animated by the *memoria passionis* is a harrowing and risky endeavor. Shouldering the unrequited hopes of history's vanquished and accompanying those who suffer today seem to be nearly impossible undertakings. Is such a radical form of solidarity genuinely sustainable? Following after the suffering and conquered Christ requires taking up his cross and making his cry one's own. Is this life of Christian discipleship simply beyond human endurance? The dangers of discipleship are undeniably terrifying, Metz cautioned, and the praxis of solidarity indeed will be found an impossible task to the degree that Christianity has submitted to the pressures of evolutionary consciousness. It is in reclaiming the apocalyptic dimension of Christology, however, that he located the possibility of sustained discipleship:

> Following Christ when understood radically, that is when grasped at the roots, is not livable—"if the time be not shortened" or, to put it another way, "if the Lord does not come soon." Without the expectation of the speedy coming of the Lord, following Christ cannot be lived; and without the hope of a shortening of the time it cannot be endured. Following Christ and looking forward to the second coming belong together like the two sides of a coin.[21]

Metz lamented that if the hope for Christ's return has been retained at all within Christian theology, it has been detached from its christological context and hidden with at least a hint of awkwardness and embarrassment in the far recesses of theological speculation.[22] Yet it is precisely the imminent expectation of time's end, of Christ's second coming, that he believed provides the temporal matrix in

---

21. *Followers of Christ*, 75. See also *Hope against Hope: Johann Baptist Metz and Elie Wiesel Speak Out on the Holocaust*, by Ekkehard Schuster and Reinhold Boschert-Kimmig, trans. J. Matthew Ashley (New York: Paulist, 1999), 19.
22. *Hope against Hope*, 46.

which the life of discipleship becomes possible. Moreover, it is precisely the unnerving and noncontemporaneous character of this dangerous expectation that can counteract the paralyzing pressure of endless time and sustain the demanding praxis of solidarity.[23] The radical solidarity of "putting on" the suffering Christ and the suffering of history's defeated and vanquished is simply unendurable unless, in taking on their passions, one also takes up the hope for Christ's imminent return; the universal-particular solidarity that bears a hope for those whose hopes and dreams have been denied is unfathomable unless the apocalyptic redemption of history's suffering and vanquished is expected to come soon. Lest it fall victim to the myth of evolutionary time, Metz warned, the life of discipleship requires this apocalyptic dimension.

The Centrality of *Memoria Passionis*

Metz's effort to reclaim the apocalyptic context of Christology was immediately related to his fear that, detached from the *memoria passionis,* the promises of Christianity too easily fall into the hands of those who reap the benefits of a history construed as progress. Apocalyptic time refuses to release this memory to history's victors by refusing to envision history as an unfolding series of successes; it places Christ's anguished cry from the cross, and the cries of all those who suffer, at the very center of history. In light of this, Metz

23. Metz was highly sensitive to the challenges surrounding his effort to advance an apocalyptic theology. In one of his final conversations with Rahner before the Jesuit's death, in 1984, Rahner challenged Metz not to "forget that you can't just talk about it, you have to convince people." Metz took his mentor's warning very seriously, yet it also is important to note that even as he struggled to learn to speak of the apocalyptic tradition more convincingly, it was precisely its noncontemporaneous and unsettling character that Metz believed subsequently makes possible an authentic hearing and performance of the Christian faith under current conditions. See Metz, "Communicating a Dangerous Memory," in *Communicating a Dangerous Memory: Soundings in Political Theology,* ed. Fred Lawrence, Lonergan Workshop 6 (Atlanta: Scholars Press, 1987), 46.

would ask several important questions of contemporary theology's all too easy dismissal of Christology's apocalyptic dimension: Can these projects unwearyingly hear the cries of those who suffer? Can a Christology reframed within an evolutionary eschatology in which Christ initiates the gradual unfolding and realization of the kingdom of God in history remain ever sensitive to the crises of history? In taking up this strategy, the Christian's hope has been correctly situated within history, but does not the operative logic of history underlying such an effort still leave this hope vulnerable to the aporias of modernity?[24]

Metz's weighted use of questions, a rhetorical tactic employed in many of his writings, further serves the disruptive task of a corrective theology that invites the reader to tarry longer on that which has been too quickly passed over while at the same time avoiding unqualified denunciation. He warned that a "bland" or "soft" eschatology infected by timeless time was discernable in contemporary theology, placing Christology in service of the status quo: "Has not this eschatology, in the name of the triumph of Christ, cleansed time of all its contradictions and ironed out all catastrophes?"[25] With its apocalyptic sting drawn, does not the *memoria Jesu Christi* simply reinforce that banal contentment with the present that haunts modern men and women? Can it offer a word of hope to the otherwise hopeless, or only to those whose hopes are already, if only gradually, coming into existence? The difficult, nearly unendurable call of discipleship becomes manageable and even easy to bear, Metz wrote, when it emerges as "the symbolic exaltation of what is going on anyway and of what determines the way of the world."[26] If the memory of Christ no longer awakens a sense of crisis,

---

24. "On the Way," 48–49.
25. "Theology Today: New Crises and New Visions," in *Love's Strategy: The Political Theology of Johann Baptist Metz,* ed. John K. Downey (Harrisburg, PA: Trinity, 1999), 79.
26. "On the Way," 49.

if it evades rather than heightens a sense of danger, it can serve only those who benefit from "what is going on anyway."

It was with this concern in view that Metz cautioned against precipitately employing the biblical image of the kingdom of God, the eschatological image that permeated his earlier writings as well as the work of Schillebeeckx. Only by retrieving Christianity's apocalyptic hope, Metz argued, can "the other images of hope, the images of the Kingdom of God, not collapse like images long ago unveiled as archaic daydreams. Only if we remain faithful to the images of crisis will the images of promise remain faithful to us."[27] The kingdom offers a radical promise of hope, Metz agreed, but Christians should be ever cautious as they turn to this image in speaking of their hope for history. It is a dangerous promise indeed, but only in that it has been offered within the horizon of suffering and crisis. Only within this apocalyptic context can Christians wrest this image from those who would use it to mimic and legitimate the historical processes of the present and reclaim its promise for those men and women of both past and present who would find no hope in such processes.

Here again, though, we must keep in mind the corrective character of Metz's project. In Metz's offering his warning, his interest did not lie in abandoning the dramatic and hope-filled imagery of the kingdom. Rather, he hoped to save it by showing precisely how dangerous and endangered the promise it bespeaks is. He wanted to save it from presenting to modern society just one more category of fulfillment that is surely being achieved, if only gradually, by way of history's evolutionary processes—the same ideological distortion that empties Christian discipleship of its perilous and subversive character. It is important to recognize that what was at issue here for Metz was not to what extent the kingdom is "already" being fulfilled or to

27. Ibid. See also "Communicating a Dangerous Memory," 52–53.

what extent it is "not yet" realized. Indeed, in his estimation, such a paradigm often betrays the unspoken influence of evolutionary logic. At issue, rather, is the central question, to whom does the promise of the kingdom belong? Is it the playground of history's victors, or is it first and foremost a promise of God's sovereignty over time offered to history's suffering and vanquished?[28]

From Utopic to Apocalyptic

Here, we have an instructive point of entrance for examining the relationship between what was described in chapter 1 as a utopic account of history and the apocalyptic view of history that now marked Metz's project. In turning to a utopic understanding of history, Metz believed he had located a resource for understanding history as something more than "the story of the origin of the present."[29] Continuity, he argued, is not the mark of an eschatologically charged history. The eschatological character of history, and thus the Christian's hope, is predicated upon a new and discontinuous future, not an irreversibly emerging past. A utopic theology of history looks to "a future which does not arise from the potentialities of human freedom and action but summons our freedom to its historical possibilities."[30]

Moreover, and in contrast with Metz's earliest work, it was God's promise historically offered and mediated that formed and constituted this hope for a genuinely new future. The tradition passed down by the early Christian community, he wrote in 1965, "was characterized by its immediate expectation of the end of the world and by its universal missionary task."[31] Metz warned that without this

28. *FHS*, 164–65.
29. "The Responsibility of Hope," *Philosophy Today* 10, no. 4 (1966): 282.
30. Ibid., 284.

expectation, the creative longing for a better day so characteristic of modern men and women could not be sustained, and their hopes would be exhausted from the outset by the delimiting possibilities of the past and present. Though he had not yet fully retrieved its distinctive discourse, we undoubtedly see important traces of Metz's interest in the apocalyptic in his earlier work. His utopic theology of history held open a hope for a genuinely novel future by recognizing the discontinuity of the present and the end of time. It critically maintained the gap between present reality and the future possibilities that God alone defines, precisely an interest advanced by an apocalyptic account of time.

Yet if Metz's earlier understanding of history recognized the discontinuity of present and future, that discontinuity was predicated upon an eschatological expectation that, as we have seen, presupposed an already-operative hope for history derived most immediately from theological speculation rather than an analysis of historical conditions. Drawing on Bloch's effort to identify in history the traces of utopian expectations for the future, Metz located in the biblical promises remembered and handed down through the community the historical mediation of the Christian's eschatological hope. Of course, what this position failed to account for fully was the ideological distortions and radical interruptions that mark history, the way in which the oppression and suffering of human history profoundly distort and endanger the historical mediation and very possibility of hope. Here, we might recall his admission that even his early turn to a political theology failed to take full account of the social conditioning of human consciousness. The evolutionary processes of modernity have expelled the traditions and stories of the past and, in the end, have overwhelmed the critical reserve of the

---

31. "The Controversy about the Future of Man: An Answer to Roger Garaudy," *Journal of Ecumenical Studies* 4, no. 2 (1967): 227.

Christian's hope as well as the dreams and expectations of modern men and women. In light of Metz's later work, we can now see that his project was poorly positioned to address that crisis of hope or age of apathy that arises in modernity.

Furthermore, in light of Metz's later writings, we also can see that the peculiar character of eschatological hope within a utopic theology of history risked a still too easy reconciliation with that modern consciousness of freedom determined by the logic of evolution. The contours of the Christian's eschatological hope were inherently indefinable and therefore unavoidably abstract, establishing a *theologia negativa* of the future. Grounded on a speculative and abstract account of the Christian's eschatological hope, its militant "innovating and changing of the world toward the Kingdom of God"[32] risked inadvertently accepting those modern social processes already operative and calculated in terms of progress. Metz's later effort to differentiate more deliberately between the promise of redemption and modernity's promise of emancipation illustrated well his fears of such superficial reconciliation. Of course, grounded in the promises of the God who alone is the Lord of history, Metz's *theologia negativa* of the future persistently and critically qualified the emancipative processes of the present. Yet, again, this position presumed that the conditions required for sustaining that practical-critical hope already existed. .

In turning to apocalypticism, Metz still insisted that an awareness of the discontinuity of history provides the only possibility for a sustainable hope in the future. Bloch's important insights into the practical significance of the gap between current reality and the future continued to inform his thought. In Metz's apocalyptic account of history, however, a new emphasis would land on not

---

32. "The Church and the World," in *The Word in History,* ed. Patrick Burke (New York: Sheed & Ward, 1966), 81.

only the openness of history and the discontinuity of present and future but the painful nonidentity of all of human history. As we have seen, the origins of this development in Metz's project can be traced to his commitment to retrieving dangerous memories of suffering, the *memoria passionis*. Not unlike Benjamin's angel of history, Metz looked to the past and saw a history of senseless suffering and catastrophe. It was this turn to the past that would augment his earlier emphasis on the Christian's expectations for the future and would place in greater relief the interminable breadth of God's promises for history, promises made by a God "before whom not even the past is fixed."[33]

Metz came to recognize that the Christian's hope for history is a specific hope, a particular anticipation of the future as a future for the hopeless and vanquished of history. Describing this development, Alan Revering writes, "No longer is the future understood as that which is simply and radically still ahead of us, and which therefore guarantees the eventual downfall of every present structure; instead the future impinges on the present more concretely, through the living memory of unfulfilled futures."[34] It was in the years immediately following this development that Metz identified in the apocalyptic tradition that posture toward history which best sustains sensitivity to human suffering and holds open a future for the redemption of history's unrequited hopes. No longer founded upon a *theologia negativa* of the future, an apocalyptic hope recognizes that history is in a state of emergency, and thus it inherits and carries forward still-unrequited expectations for a future for all those who have no hope other than time's interruption and finale. An apocalyptic hope maintains not only a hope in the promises of a

---

33. *FHS*, 162.
34. Alan John Revering, "Social Criticism and Eschatology in M. Walzer and J. B. Metz" (PhD diss., Harvard University, 2001), 93.

surprising God who exceeds both what already exists and what humans themselves seek to bring into existence, but also a hope in the promises that God can interrupt history and bring time to a close, saving those who have suffered and fallen in defeat to history. By binding the disruptive and unrequited cries of history's suffering and defeated with a dialectical hope for God's proximate interruption of time, Metz found a subversive and practical temporal framework both responsive to a culture now drained of utopian expectation and resistant to superficial identification with that bifurcated history of emancipation which ultimately determined modernity's deep-seated fatalism and apathy.

Consequently, it was through the temporal framework of apocalypticism that Metz's later interpretation of the inner-relationship between world history and the history of redemption emerged. Maintaining his position examined in chapter 1, he continued to argue, "There is not a history of the world on the one side and a history of salvation on the other side." Amending this earlier position, however, Metz now would add, "[W]hat we call the history of salvation, as I understand it, is that history of the world in which you have an indestructible hope for past sufferings."[35] Paradoxically, for Metz, it was through the temporal matrix of apocalypticism, time envisioned as ruptured and discontinuous, that salvation history impinges on world history, establishing anticipatory continuity without premature or easy reconciliation: "For the apocalyptic, the continuity of time is not the empty continuum of evolution, but rather the trail of suffering."[36] An apocalyptic theology of history remembers suffering and allows it to exist with the expectation that an end is coming soon. In doing this, it dialectically anticipates in world history the promise of God's redeeming action.

---

35. "Communicating a Dangerous Memory," 48.
36. "On the Way," 52.

Again, then, we see that, in turning to the apocalyptic, Metz's interest did not lie in delineating to what extent salvation is "already" being fulfilled or to what extent it is "not yet" realized, with a clichéd presumption for the latter. And, clearly, his position did not entail an unqualified deferral of salvation. Rather, Metz believed that it is an apocalyptic sensibility that allows one to keep faith with the God who has promised to keep faith with history's suffering. Through the temporal framework of apocalypticism, the Christian discovers "a more reliable understanding about the proximity and distance of God, about God's transcendence and God's indwelling, about the 'already' and the 'not yet' of God's salvation—the pairs in each case not somehow pasted together but rather the one in the other and as the other."[37]

Interrupting the Sovereignty of Timeless Time: God as Subject of History

In turning to the apocalyptic, Metz had hoped to put the concord of history in question, to demonstrate that again and again history has shown itself to be tumultuous and unmanageable, and to arouse the suspicion that humans cannot by their own accord bring about the reconciliation of their history. Sustaining this interest was a fundamental theological issue that Metz continually sought to underscore: the question of the subject of history. "The apocalyptic traditions of the end of the world," Metz wrote, "were always combined and connected with questions: Who is the Lord of our time? To whom belong the processes of the world? Who is the subject of history?"[38] Apocalypticism discovers in the cries of history's suffering and defeated the practical wisdom that there is simply no

---

37. "Suffering unto God," trans. J. Matthew Ashley, *Critical Inquiry* 20, no. 4 (Summer 1994): 620.
38. "Communicating a Dangerous Memory," 48.

identifiable subject in history that can bring about its universal and decisive reconciliation. Failure to recognize this was the conceit of those modern projects that in the name of self-liberation halved the history of freedom.

It was in response to this conceit, then, that Metz had developed and honed his apocalyptic reflections on time, and the structure of his mature theology of history was largely determined upon this terrain. If the contours of this project were fundamentally established in the late 1970s and much of the 1980s, however, the same would not be true of his evaluation of the concrete historical situations continuously conditioning and endangering the hopes of the human subject, the context in which he repeatedly sought to offer a defense of the Christian's hope. In his writings from the late 1980s and 1990s, the reader is introduced to Metz's growing fears that even as a heightened awareness of the Enlightenment's dangerous failings had widely and correctly appeared by the end of the twentieth century under the unwieldy appellation of postmodernism, a new unmarked carrier of evolutionary logic was now emerging precisely by way of a temporal framework explicitly sensitive to the chaotic nonidentity and irreconcilability of history. Once again, though, it was not the quasi-apocalyptic fanaticism of the doomsday cult that drew his concern. Rather, it would be Friedrich Nietzsche's madman crying out from the market, "God is dead! God remains dead! And we have killed him! How shall we comfort ourselves?"[39] If those in the market had not yet recognized the wisdom of this cry, Metz found in the madman's warning the prophetic harbinger of modernity's final submission to empty and timeless time.

It had been more than a century since Nietzsche told this famous fable. When doing so, he, too, had taken up the cause of exposing

---

39. Friedrich Nietzsche, *The Gay Science*, trans. Walter Arnold (New York: Vintage, 1974), 181.

the lie of modernity's pretense for the stability of human history, introducing his "perspectival" philosophy in an attempt to reveal for a "myth" the sacred notion that some sort of "real world" underwrites human existence.[40] Though he did not lament the pending demise of Europe's God, which he presciently understood would accompany the processes of the Enlightenment, the profundity of his observations did not reside in drawing attention to the approaching phenomenon of secularization. Rather, what he recognized was that, in the wake of this phenomenon, modernity's rigid account of reason and history had unwittingly surrendered its tacit foundation. "Nietzsche ripped the disguise from the mythical totality standing in modernity's background," Metz observed. "He forced modernity to own up to its consequences."[41] In seeking to show the consequences of this surrender, the iconoclastic philosopher strove to unearth the historically contingent character of men and women's deepest beliefs about the world and the human person. He attacked foundational theories of history, religious and nonreligious alike. The idea that time, or even the human person, has a "real" purpose, goal, or finale is sheer myth, he warned, a myth invented and perpetuated to shield the human person from the unstable, indeterminate, and risky experiment of life. Nietzsche envisioned time as an "open sea" with no beginning, no purpose, and no end; it is the eternal recurrence of the same within which the truly courageous individual, his infamous *Übermensch*, might willfully enact a great life experiment.

40. See Friedrich Nietzsche, *The Twilight of the Idols, with The Antichrist and Ecce Homo*, trans. Antony Ludovici (Ware, UK: Wordsworth, 2007), 22–24.
41. "Theology versus Polymythicism: A Short Apology for Biblical Monotheism," in *Passion for God*, 78; published in the German as "Theologie versus Polymythie oder kleine Apologie des biblischen Monotheismus," in *Einheit und Vielheit: XIV Deutscher Kongreß für Philosophie, Giessen, 21–26 September 1987*, ed. Odo Marquard (Hamburg, Ger.: Meiner, 1990). For a valuable account of Metz's reading of Nietzsche's approach to time, see Matthew T. Eggemeier, "Christianity or Nihilism? The Apocalyptic Discourses of Johann Baptist Metz and Friedrich Nietzsche," *Horizons* 39, no. 1 (Spring 2012): 7–26.

If Nietzsche's assault on the pretenses of modernity was frequently overlooked in the years immediately following his work, or conveniently interpreted as simply one more attack on religion by an Enlightenment thinker, the bloody madness of the twentieth century soon cleared a way for the reemergence of his ideas. The catastrophic and tumultuous nature of time had been exposed, mocking the ideologies of technological and historical progress. Moreover, these hegemonic accounts of reason and history were found guilty of underwriting the violent structures and regimes that had placed a dark shadow over the century. As many have observed, this "postmodern" situation shares much with an apocalyptic sensibility.[42] Yet, although important parallels certainly exist, it was here that Metz believed we can see evolutionary logic's alarming potential for absorbing and distorting the apocalyptic consciousness.

As a nineteenth-century "prophet" of postmodernity, Nietzsche correctly recognized the chaotic and irreconcilable nature of world history, the risks entailed in historical existence, and the contingent character of our expectations and beliefs. Metz cautioned, however, that even as Nietzsche struggled to overcome modernity's dominant myths, he was "still a victim of that time-myth which [he] tried so perceptively to contest."[43] Taking in the disparate voices of late or postmodern philosophy influenced by his work, Metz warned that Nietzsche's view of history was no less immune from the paralyzing pressures of timeless time than those evolutionary philosophies of history which maintained that time has a reflexively determinable purpose and goal: "Nietzsche's message about the death of God is the announcement of the rule of time, the elementary, inexorable, and impenetrable sovereignty of time. God is dead. What now remains in

---

42. See, for example, John D. Caputo, *The Prayers and Tears of Jacques Derrida: Religion without Religion* (Indianapolis: Indiana University Press, 1997).
43. "Theology versus Polymythicism," 79–80.

all passing away is time itself: more eternal than God, more immortal than all gods. This is time without a finale; indeed, as Nietzsche explicitly emphasizes, 'without a finale in nothingness.'"[44]

With Nietzsche's dethroning of a sovereign God, Metz averred, it was time itself that would now reign as the absolute sovereign over all. Time emerged as timeless time, arresting the unlimited life experimentation that Nietzsche had hoped to sanction. Under the dominion of this time, Metz warned, the human person "becomes the 'pilgrim without a goal,' the 'nomad without an itinerary.'"[45] For Metz, then, Nietzsche was the prophet of that age of listless fatalism ushered in by the Enlightenment: "He announced the end of historical time, since once the horizon of God is erased history collapses into an anonymous, temporally unbounded evolution that wills and seeks nothing except evolution."[46] What Metz found in this prophet was confirmation of his fears that the disintegration of history and the corresponding death of the subject would ultimately follow from the failings of modernity, unless Christianity could muster the resources needed to counter its excesses with a theological enlightenment of the Enlightenment.

Despite the widespread interest in his ideal of the *Übermensch*, Nietzsche himself expressed little confidence that men and women could genuinely accept that terrifying fate of a goalless existence on "the open sea" of time. Thus the madman's piteous question "How shall we comfort ourselves?" Metz's reading of the current historical situation belies the prescience of this question. While continuing to

44. "Time without a Finale: The Background to the Debate on 'Resurrection or Reincarnation,'" *Reincarnation or Resurrection?*, Concilium, ed. Hermann Häring and Johann Baptist Metz (Maryknoll, NY: Orbis, 1993), 124.
45. "God: Against the Myth of the Eternity of Time," in *The End of Time? The Provocation of Talking about God*, ed. and trans. J. Matthew Ashley (Mahwah, NJ: Paulist, 2004), 30; German edition published as *Ende der Zeit*, ed. Tiemo Rainer Peters and Claus Urban (Mainz, Ger.: Matthias-Grünewald, 1999).
46. "Theology versus Polymythicism," 78.

affirm the valid interest in overcoming the overarching ideologies of history that had marred so much of modernity, he found in contemporary philosophy as well as in the rapid rise of detraditionalized religious movements a willingness to take flight from the world through the construction of any number of now-self-consciously contingent myths that seek to steady, if only for the "therapeutic" comfort of the individual, that drifting and goalless existence determined by timeless time. Religion had indeed survived the pressures of modernity, Metz noted, but as a godless religion free of modernity's demanding risks and dangers. A new mythology unaccountable to history or God emerged in its place, more amenable to the work of "contingency-management."[47] Nietzsche's own perspectival philosophy, his unearthing of the self-deceptive myths invented to tidy up a chaotic existence, was now being employed to comfort the madman.

The construction of these consoling myths, Metz warned, gives birth to a "'new man' [who] is less and less his own memory and more and more his own experiment, and nothing more. All the exigencies that come to us from our pasts are transformed into continually open options. And now the mystery of redemption no longer finds its roots . . . in remembering, but in forgetting, in a new cult of amnesia."[48] Of course, Metz had spent the preceding twenty years diagnosing the perilous consequences of forgetting. Though now performed in the name of nonidentity and radical fragmentation rather than the progress of history, forgetting the past entails the ultimate submission to the sovereignty of time. Without our memories, our experience of time undergoes that anthropological reduction in which time can no longer be put in question by the cries of those who suffer.

---

47. "Suffering unto God," 613. Metz references Hermann Lübbe when assessing religion's capacity to function as a form of "contingency-management."
48. "God," 30.

No less than the totalizing monomyths of historical progress, the polymythicism of the postmodern situation abandons to time the catastrophes of history; it mythologizes away the question of unmitigated suffering and, in the end, fosters that banal apathy and irresponsible form of existence which inevitably accompanies evolutionary logic.

It is postmodernity's enthusiasm for the myth, then, its willingness to repress through myth that demanding question which emerges in the memory of suffering, that sharply distinguishes its quasi-apocalyptic sensibility from theology's apocalypticism. In Metz's words, "Here lies the distance between theology and mythology. In myth the question is forgotten."[49] And it was precisely here that Metz once again called for a theological enlightenment of the Enlightenment by explicitly raising the apocalyptic question of God as the subject of history. Standing in solidarity with the suffering and vanquished, the apocalyptic will refuses to evade or talk away the crises and dangers of human history. The apocalyptic will find no relief in either therapeutic treatment or the inner-historical processes of emancipation. There has been too much suffering, too much tragedy, too much death. Rather, the urgent and protesting questions that emerge in times of crisis and despair are sustained and directed toward God, through whom "risk and danger enter into, or return to, religion."[50] The apocalyptic rejects the numbing comfort of time's sovereignty, holding on to that hope against hope that God alone is Lord of history, "the one to whom time belongs, as the end that sets its bounds."[51]

Yet even here, the apocalyptic cry of Jesus from the cross, and the cries of all those whose suffering has gone on unrelieved, will not

49. "Suffering unto God," 614.
50. Ibid., 620.
51. "Theology as Theodicy?," 71.

accept premature comfort or reconciliation. Faithfully longing for Christ's return, the apocalyptic also finds no comfort in the promise that a new kingdom is slowly, gradually breaking into history: "To plead with God in order to know God is, at the end of the day, the message which Jesus gives his disciples (see Luke 11:1–13). Correctly understood, he offered no other comfort. In any case, the biblical comforting does not carry us away into a mythical kingdom of a tensionless harmony and of a questionless reconciliation."[52] In mystical solidarity with Jesus on the cross, made possible by the imminent expectation of his second coming, the apocalyptic obstinately redirects the cry for salvation back to God in the expectation that God will fulfill a promise tendered and will soon respond as the Lord and redeemer of history. Only within the temporal framework of the apocalyptic, Metz insisted, could such a dangerous and subversive expectation, a hope that protests suffering even unto God, withstand the hopelessness of evolutionary time and keep faith with history's suffering.[53] Yet he also recognized that raising the question of God in this context inevitably raises the still-pressing question of whether and how one can speak of God in a world of radical suffering.

The Theodicy Question:
A Negative Theology of Creation

Here, Metz's sustained effort to reclaim the apocalyptic dimension of Christian theology finds perhaps its most distinctive expression:

---

52. "Suffering from God: Theology as Theodicy," *Pacifica* 5 (1992): 285.
53. It is beyond the purview of this study to offer a treatment of Metz's inspired analysis of apocalypticism's mystical correlate developed in his writings on the "mysticism of mourning" and the spirituality of "suffering unto God." For important examples of this work, see "Suffering unto God"; and "A Passion for God: Religious Orders Today," in *Passion for God*, 150–74, first published in *Gottespassion: Zur Ordensexistenz heute* (Freiburg, Ger.: Herder, 1991), 7–9 and 13–62.

the temporalization of the theodicy question. Metz believed that the heightened sensitivity to history's intractable suffering nourished by an apocalyptic eschatology forces upon theology precisely that question which by now had animated his work for two decades: "How one can speak of God at all in the face of the abysmal history of suffering in the world, in 'His' world." Indeed, he now argued that theodicy "is 'the' question for theology; theology must not eliminate it or overrespond to it. It is 'the' eschatological question, the question before which theology does not develop its answers reconciling everything, but rather directs its questioning incessantly back towards God."[54]

Overcoming theology's penchant for reconciling or even eliminating this irreconcilable question, however, required that Metz offer a reframing of theodicy from an apocalyptic perspective. In approaching this task, he quickly disavowed those historically pervasive forms of theodicy which looked to exonerate or justify God in the face of the long history of suffering. Augustine, in particular, drew his criticism. Metz argued that, in seeking to counter the theological dualism of Manichaeanism and Gnosticism, Augustine located "the cause as well as the responsibility for evil and suffering in the world exclusively in humanity and the history of guilt that is rooted in its no to God. . . . Not God but humanity become sinful bears sole responsibility for a creation that has been distorted by suffering, shot through with suffering."[55] By absolving the God of creation from responsibility for a creation distorted by evil and suffering, Augustine successfully silenced the theodicy question by extracting God from the question itself. In doing this, however, Metz believed Augustine also had repositioned the biblical promise of

---

54. "Suffering unto God," 612.
55. Ibid., 616.

salvation as redemption from guilt and sin alone, for suffering was the just consequence of human transgression.

Metz's fear was that Augustine's theological strategy too closely approximated the evasive strategies found in modernity's exculpation mechanisms and postmodernity's therapeutic polymythicism, though at issue here was the accountability of God rather than that of the human person. Moreover, Metz feared that Augustine's position had largely determined the Christian theological tradition's response to the theodicy question. In seeking to excuse and even excise God from the theodicy question, Augustine had effectively halved the biblical promise of eschatological salvation. "Invisible from this perspective," Metz warned, "is that suffering and that history of suffering which cannot be traced back, in any clear or obvious way, to guilt or a history of guilt and yet which makes up the major part of the experience of suffering that cries out to heaven."[56] With the theodicy question silenced, suffering steadily departed from theological discourse. In turn, Metz lamented, "the" eschatological question also fell mute. The incessant cry to heaven for redemption from oppression and suffering, the apocalyptic expectation that God would soon intervene and make good on a promise, increasingly receded from Christian theology.

In seeking to retrieve the theodicy question as the eschatological question, Metz insisted that theology will need to resist overburdening its doctrine of creation, forcing it to carry the full weight of the history of suffering. Indeed, he believed that Augustine's project showed that the theology of creation can "answer" the theodicy question only at the price of its own contradiction. If responsibility for evil and suffering in creation lies exclusively with the human person, then the freedom of the human person must be construed as fully autonomous and independent of

56. Ibid., 617.

God, precisely that understanding of freedom which marked the Enlightenment. Yet, as we have seen, and as Augustine himself affirmed, creaturely freedom in the Christian tradition is not autonomous but theonomous. "That is, it is posited, empowered and encompassed by God," Metz wrote. "Because of this, it cannot bear ultimate responsibility for the histories of suffering in the world, and the question rebounds to some degree upon God and God's foreordained sovereignty."[57]

Here, Metz was not discounting this Christian understanding of creaturely freedom which had played such an important role in his earlier writings, nor was he attributing the distortion of creation to God, two strategies that would merely diminish the theodicy question prematurely. Instead, he was pointing out that theonomous freedom invites rather than silences the theodicy question. Nonetheless, it is important to note that although it had once offered him a resource for speaking of men and women as "coworkers" with God in the inbreaking of the kingdom, the Christian doctrine of creation now was being introduced as a warning against too quickly reconciling the irreconcilable history of suffering. "Even Christian theology, drawing on its doctrine of creation," he wrote, "cannot eliminate the apocalyptic cry, 'What is God waiting for?'"[58] Thus, alongside the range of theological loci already examined, Metz cautioned that, without turning its back on those who suffer, Christianity's theology of creation cannot outflank the faith's apocalyptic core.

Metz believed that Augustine, in his attempt to speak of God in the midst of suffering and evil in the world, would have been better served by turning to the apocalyptic witness of the biblical tradition. There, he would have found the strengthening rather than

57. "Theology as Theodicy?," 61.
58. Ibid., 71.

diminishing of the theodicy question, not by way of its answer but by way of an almost inexplicable commitment to asking the question. Why the plight of our widows and orphans? the prophets protested. Why the trial and suffering of an innocent man? Job pleaded. Why have you forsaken me? Christ cried out to his Father from the cross. These apocalyptic voices did not blithely accept God's innocence in the face of human freedom. Nor, as many of Metz's contemporaries would now have it, did they find consolation in a God who suffers with creation. Rather, they demanded that God show God's creative and redeeming power in history; they impudently expected a response that was still forthcoming. In doing so, they temporalized the *Theodizeefrage*, offering witness to the vitality of apocalyptic hope.

But from where does such a subversive hope emerge? Returning to that reading of Scripture that emerged in his earliest writings in political theology, Metz once again located at the heart of the scriptural tradition the heralding of God's "promise": "All the divine predicates in the biblical traditions—from the self-definition in Exodus to the Johannine word "God is love" bear the mark of a promise. . . . 'I will be for you who I will be'; 'I will prove myself to you as love.'"[59] It is the stamp of temporality on God's promise that makes possible a theology responsive to the theodicy question without overresponding in God's defense. "If there is a justification of God, then it is that God will justify Godself, in God's own time," Metz averred. "This is what really the whole of the biblical tradition teaches us."[60] Thus, if Christians dare to speak of God's promise within a world of suffering, or, more accurately, if they dare to remember the promise of God found in the cries of history's suffering, it must be in a demanding and questioning idiom that

59. "Suffering unto God," 620.
60. "God, Sin, and Suffering: A Conversation" (with Joseph Ratzinger), in *End of Time?*, 53.

passionately expects that God indeed will fulfill a promise made, proving God's self as saving love.

What does this mean for God's creative power? Is God powerless in the face of human freedom? in the face of human suffering? In responding to such questions, Metz admitted that the temporalization of theodicy "necessitates theology speaking of creation and the creative power of God in the form of a negative theology."[61] Construed temporally, the theodicy question resists every effort to peer through creation in an attempt to make sense of a history marred by senseless suffering in advance of its end; subsequently, Metz argued that the temporalization of theodicy "prevents the clarity of creation and the power of God as creator."[62] At the same time, however, he also refused to cease speaking of the omnipotence of the Creator God.[63] The cries of the apocalyptic are predicated upon God's sovereignty, and to relinquish hope in God's creative power would only calm the eschatological questioning of God and abandon the suffering and vanquished to the sovereignty of time.

It was in these anguished and protesting cries, then, in the apocalyptic expectations found in the memory of history's suffering, that Metz believed Christian theology can discover a way to speak of God's omnipotence without precipitously quieting the question of theodicy by way of its creation faith, without excising God from theodicy by locating God in "eternal" repose outside of time or by admitting God's powerlessness within time. When approached from this apocalyptic context, he argued, God's creative power is properly "thought of as a power setting bounds, as the end of time coming toward it, in which alone it will be proven what it 'is' and how it sustains us."[64] Understood accordingly, Metz believed, Christianity's

---

61. "Suffering unto God," 620.
62. Ibid., 613.
63. "God, Sin, and Suffering," 52.
64. "Theology as Theodicy?," 71.

creation faith carries the same temporal stamp as its eschatological hope. It, too, bespeaks a hope in God's sovereignty over time. And in doing so, it, too, sustains a hope for all those in history who have no hope other than time's end.

Conclusion

Metz's retrieval of the apocalyptic tradition has taken us a long way from his early efforts to respond to the "dialectic of Enlightenment" and his advocacy of the eschatological proviso examined at the beginning of chapter 5. By tracing this shift, I have attempted to show not only the unique character of his later eschatology but also the various factors that compelled the development in his thought. In introducing the proviso, Metz had sought to address the distortion and truncation of hope that he feared accompanied the excesses of a technocratic society. He insisted that, in defense of historical freedom, Christians must oppose every claim that identifies the powers of the present with the future in which they hope. As we have seen, however, supporting this influential strategy was the presumption that the conditions required for sustaining the critical inquiry necessitated by the proviso currently existed. Although indications of a more fundamental suspicion were already evident, in the 1960s Metz had not yet recognized the full extent of the crisis of hope encircling modernity.

It was with his heightened sensitivity to the social conditioning of human freedom and his more trenchant analysis of the concrete historical conditions endangering the Christian's hope that we found the antecedents of Metz's turn to the apocalyptic. Infected by the logic of evolutionary time, he warned that European culture had been drained of its utopian expectations; an age of apathy had settled over modernity, sedating every expectation for the future and obscuring the sufferings and catastrophes of history. It was from this context that Metz called Christians to stand in anamnetic solidarity with Christ on the cross and all the suffering of history. Unlike his proviso, however, this strategy was not primarily an ethical religious prescription determined by the Christian's eschatological hope. At issue, rather, was Metz's interest in establishing the historical conditions in which the Christian's eschatological hope might emerge and withstand the pressures of evolutionary time. He insisted that only by making time for the anguished cries that arise from the past can we rediscover for today that unrequited hope in a promise of a gratuitous redemption that frees men and women to assume responsibility for their history.

Herein lay the context for Metz's turn to the apocalyptic. It is apocalyptic time that makes possible this sensitivity to the still-unrequited hopes of history. As we have seen, Metz's earlier writings in political theology had already championed time's discontinuity. In turning to the apocalyptic, however, Metz would account for this not by way of a utopic theology of history but by attending to the disruptive crises of history and the apocalyptic cries of history's suffering and vanquished. In affirming the limited nature of time and expecting its imminent interruption by a sovereign God before whom not even the past is fixed, apocalyptic time can sustain sensitivity to crises and make these cries audible. Apocalyptic time makes time for history's suffering and vanquished, it holds open a subversive hope in an age bereft of expectation, and thus it resists both the apathetic resignation and superficial consolation endemic to evolutionary logic. While accepting the hopelessness of progressively fashioning a history of genuine freedom, the apocalyptic nonetheless refuses to surrender to this hopelessness, protesting history's injustices unto the end.

Of course, Metz's retrieval of the apocalyptic tradition also has taken us a long way from the manifest similarities examined in chapters 1 and 2 that marked his and Schillebeeckx's earlier eschatological writings. Although both theologians attempted to identify the peculiar and subversive character of the Christian's hope in their later writings, for Schillebeeckx, this hope was determined by the absolute saving presence of the Creator God. For Metz, it was the painful experience of God's absence, the still-pending promise of Christ's return, that sustained this hope. As we now turn to the conclusion of this study, we are well positioned to evaluate these distinct modes of eschatology. The criterion we will use to evaluate relative advantages and limitations of each theologian's project, however, will simultaneously underline a fundamental interest that continually linked their writings: How can the Christian's eschatological hope animate and sustain a life of practical resistance in the midst of history's unmitigated suffering?

Conclusion

"An accounting for the hope..."

"Always be ready to make your defense to anyone who demands from you an accounting for the hope that is in you" (1 Pet. 3:15). Both Metz and Schillebeeckx regularly cited this biblical charge as they struggled, over the course of four decades, to express an eschatological hope responsive to the demands of their time. What challenges and endangers Christian hope today? What is the hope that is in you? Over the course of this study, we have seen that Metz's and Schillebeeckx's responses to these questions were frequently in flux. Their understandings of the precise pressures confronting the modern church as well as the peculiar character of the Christian's eschatological expectations evolved significantly over the years. From their earliest writings, however, they would labor to develop the theological resources required to keep both of these questions in play. In the preceding chapters, my aim has been to demonstrate that it was precisely through this wide-ranging process of refining their work that both theologians came to articulate desperately needed, yet highly distinct, accounts of hope for a time in which expectations for the future have been rigidly limned or even forsaken. Now, seeking to draw out and place in greater relief these unique accounts of the Christian hope, we will attend more deliberately in this conclusion to the distinctive features of Metz's and Schillebeeckx's later eschatological writings, giving particular attention to the German's sensitivity to the listlessness of contemporary culture and to the ongoing significance of the doctrine of creation in his Belgian colleague's thought. In what ways might the work of each theologian shed light on the other's project? This question has been in the background of our study thus far, and the value of the following comparative analysis lies in bringing it to the fore.

A Defense of a Practical Hope

Before turning to the analysis of Schillebeeckx's prophetic eschatology and Metz's apocalyptic eschatology in the subsequent sections, it will be helpful to begin by briefly underscoring three pivotal and interrelated interests that would increasingly but persistently characterize both projects, noting the important relationship between each theologian's earlier and later writings as well as the common concerns they continued to share despite the unique trajectories of their work.

First, when tracing the developments that emerged in their writings at the end of the 1960s, we observed that both theologians gradually recognized that the central problem endangering the viability of Christian hope was not the crisis of faith that accompanied what they had described as the processes of secularization but the unrelenting crisis of history's suffering people. Although this characterization is surely apt, and indeed this development stands at the origins of Metz's and Schillebeeckx's later writings, what needs to be made clear is that privileging the latter equally stimulated a renewed and more critical effort to address the former. Both theologians warned that, while seemingly banishing God from the world, modernity's myopic commitment to technical reason also had banished countless men and women to the margins of history and society. The dethroning of God was intimately related to the limning or "halving" of that hope for future freedom which passes over—and often violently—history's victims. In seeking to speak of Christian hope from the side of history's victims, then, Metz and Schillebeeckx could not and did not dismiss the modern problem of unbelief. To the contrary, it was by attending more carefully to the underside of history that they ultimately discovered the dangerous scope of this problem and, at the same time, discovered a resource for responding. It is sensitivity to suffering, an awareness of the catastrophes and crisis of history, that upsets the rational and manageable expectations of the nonbeliever; it is only by attending to suffering that men and women can discover a hope that surpasses that which is currently deemed objectively possible. Here, certainly, the problem of unbelief is not resolved, but neither is it dismissed. Rather, the premature resolution of the nonbeliever is potentially disrupted, creating the space for an alternative and subversive hope.

A second shared interest in Metz's and Schillebeeckx's projects, the turn to a practical eschatology, also serves as a warning against precipitously dismissing the enduring value of their earlier concerns and, indeed, emerges as a defining characteristic of their mature eschatologies. As we have seen, both theologians' early efforts to respond to the modern person's experience of secularization were widely criticized for having tacitly capitulated to dominant cultural assumptions. And, of course, they, too, became highly critical of their earlier positions. Nonetheless, it was precisely this point of engagement that prepared Metz and Schillebeeckx to advance the practical character of eschatology and to address the pervasive privatization of faith in modern theology. It was the distinctly modern route by which they retrieved the doctrine of eschatology, substantiated further by corresponding currents in modern philosophy, that enabled them to reposition the hope of the Christian tradition as a hope in action. Only a practical defense of the Christian's hope, they argued, can mediate in history the promise of eschatological salvation. Although in time they recognized that this position needed to be grounded in the history of human suffering lest it reflect and reinscribe prevailing ideological distortions, it was this early commitment to a practical eschatology that made their later sensitivity to suffering possible without hazarding the idealist and argumentative accounts of history of which they were both so critical.

Finally, it is important to note that both theologians persistently recognized that "a trace of something unreconciled hovers over Christianity," to borrow an expression Metz used in his later writing.[1] Admittedly, here again we found a significant degree of development in Metz's and Schillebeeckx's theologies. In chapters 1 and 2, we closely examined their manifest difficulties in speaking adequately of the genuinely "new" in history following the incarnation. Nonetheless, we also were able to distinguish both theologians' appreciation for the peculiar promise still hovering over world history. Metz had argued in his earlier writings that the individual's experience of guilt, concupiscence, and death plainly reveals the still-unreconciled character of the Christian's hope. Schillebeeckx also had argued that the Christian's "expectation of the future is only a name for *hoping*," similarly pointing to the individual's experience of ever-pending death.[2] Although they struggled over the following years to develop the theological categories and methods required for articulating this interest more effectively, a process certainly advanced by their privileging of eschatology, this interest was notably already

1. Metz, "A Passion for God: Religious Orders Today," in *A Passion for God: The Mystical-Political Dimension of Christianity,* ed. and trans. J. Matthew Ashley (New York: Paulist, 1998), 158.
2. Schillebeeckx, "The Intellectual's Responsibility for the Future," in *World and Church,* trans. N. D. Smith (New York: Sheed & Ward, 1971), 281 (original emphasis).

present in their early work. In their later writings, of course, both men increasingly placed greater emphasis on the indeterminacy, the provisionality, and, ultimately, the painful ambiguity of history, stressing that sensitivity to the suffering and death of the other reveals the painful nonidentity of history. Through that process, moreover, they steadily learned to exercise the practical-critical leverage embedded in the Christian's eschatological expectations. If, in their mature work, the particular ways in which Metz and Schillebeeckx accounted for that "trace of something unreconciled hovering over Christianity" found highly distinct expressions, their shared commitment to the task had informed and oriented both theologians from the initial stages of their careers.

By drawing attention to these common interests and shared commitments already evident, if tentatively at times, in their earlier writings, I am not interested in minimizing the profound developments that emerged in Metz's and Schillebeeckx's writings. Indeed, in tracing these developments over the preceding chapters, I have deliberately underscored the important advances made in both theologians' eschatologies. At the same time, however, a perhaps subtle temptation to pass over their earlier writings as simply insufficiently critical is not a helpful one. Recognizing the limitations of that work, as Metz and Schillebeeckx surely did, does not require dismissing it *tout court*. Durable insights were gained during this period, offering an effective foundation for their later, more critical, projects. As theologians continue to draw and learn from Metz and Schillebeeckx in the years ahead, there is value in developing a critical appreciation for the gains, intuitions, and limitations of their earlier work.[3] Moreover, tracing the origins of their mature theologies to

---

3. For two particularly successful collections of essays demonstrating the enduring significance and influence of Metz and Schillebeeckx on contemporary theologians, see (respectively) *Missing God? Cultural Amnesia and Political Theology*, ed. John K. Downey, Jürgen Manemann, and Steven T. Ostovich and *Edward Schillebeeckx and Contemporary Theology*, ed. Lieven Boeve,

their efforts to respond to the historical situation of the 1960s, a notable objective of this study, need not suggest an idealist history of ideas, with the assumption that their earlier positions inherently and necessarily generated their later work. To the contrary, it seems that to ignore the fact that their later theologies emerged by first passing through these earlier stages, risks rehearsing that abstract account of history, theological history not excluded, which both theologians so assiduously sought to avoid.

Placing Metz's and Schillebeeckx's Accounts of Hope in Relief

Of course, as this study progressed, we saw that it was precisely through their common interests and commitments that Schillebeeckx's and Metz's distinct eschatological projects emerged. Unsurprisingly, both theologians made claim to offering the more authentic reading of the Christian tradition. Citing the well-known position of Ernst Käsemann, Metz insisted that apocalypticism was "the mother of Christian theology."[4] Schillebeeckx did not challenge this claim overtly but added that even if apocalypticism was the mother of Christian theology, it was not the mother of Christianity itself, and he had tried to demonstrate this by way of his historical reconstructed image of Jesus.[5] As more than a century of debate within biblical scholarship has shown, however, exegetical work cannot take us through this impasse.[6] Moreover, even as both theologians relied more deliberately on the authoritative testimony

Frederiek Depoortere and Stephan van Erp (London: Continuum International Publishing, 2010).

4. Metz, *Faith in History and Society: Toward a Practical Fundamental Theology*, ed. and trans. J. Matthew Ashley (New York: Crossroad, 2007), 162 (hereafter abbreviated as *FHS*).

5. Schillebeeckx, *Interim Report on the Books "Jesus" and "Christ,"* trans. John Bowden (New York: Crossroad, 1981), 71–72.

6. For a classic and still-helpful survey of the biblical scholarship surrounding this issue, see Norman Perrin, *The Kingdom of God in the Teaching of Jesus* (Philadelphia: Westminster, 1963).

of Scripture in their later writings, neither Metz nor Schillebeeckx would find scriptural exegesis a sufficient criterion for assessing his position. As suggested at the end of chapter 6, the criterion we will use for evaluating relative advantages and limitations of both projects underlines a defining interest consistently linking their writings: Can the Christian's eschatological hope animate and sustain a life of practical resistance in the midst of history's injustice and unmitigated suffering?

This criterion, then, brings us back to Metz's and Schillebeeckx's attempts to respond to the concrete historical situations endangering the Christian's hope, as well as the limitations they identified in their contemporaries' theological strategies for offering a practical defense of that hope adequate to the times. Certainly, their criticisms of alternative strategies, including their relatively limited criticisms of each other's proposals, offer a valuable point of entrance for placing each project in greater relief and evaluating it in light of the preceding question. Although Metz never addressed Schillebeeckx's larger eschatological project directly, he did criticize Schillebeeckx for inadequately accounting for the practical fundamental structure of Christology. He would not develop this criticism extensively, but his subsequent claim that Schillebeeckx's Christology remained "idealist" in character presents us with an opening, even if only an indirect one, for testing his Belgian colleague's prophetic eschatology against his own concerns.[7] Schillebeeckx, for his part, explicitly criticized Metz's decision for an apocalyptic eschatology, though also only briefly and by way of footnote.[8] Our own comparative assessment will try to fill out this criticism more fully as well. In what follows, then, we will in turn test each theologian's project against the other's

---

7. *FHS*, 259n6. See also Metz, *Followers of Christ: The Religious Life and the Church,* trans. Thomas Linton (New York: Paulist, 1978), 95n5.
8. *Interim Report*, 150n78.

313

concerns, keeping in mind their controlling interest, and our own, in animating a practical defense of a subversive expectation that might sustain hope for history's suffering persons.

Assessing a Prophetic Eschatology Sustained by Creation Faith

Metz's claim that Schillebeeckx had failed to account for the practical fundamental structure of Christology may seem somewhat suspect at first. As we have seen, Schillebeeckx's christological study was deliberately constructed as a narrative theology with a practical intent. Along with Metz, he embraced the unique capacity of narrated memories to avoid a reductive disambiguation of history while conveying publicly what is incommunicable by theoretical argumentation alone. Moreover, he had championed the practical epistemological power of narratives to fuse remembrance with expectations for the future. In fact, he cited Metz as an important influence on this project. Yet it was precisely Schillebeeckx's use of narrative that Metz found deficient.[9] Again, it needs to be emphasized that Metz did not develop this criticism extensively, and the precise nature of his concerns is not entirely clear. The context in which his comments appeared, however, offers a significant clue to his concerns and subsequently will allow us to extend his observations to a more critical analysis of Schillebeeckx's prophetic eschatology.

It was in commenting on his own early failure to differentiate adequately between the distinct strains of practical philosophy promoted by Kant and Marx that Metz levied his criticism of Schillebeeckx's practical-narrative Christology. As you will remember, Metz recognized that his initial formulation of a political theology had been directed toward a people for whom the

---

9. *Followers of Christ*, 95n5.

consciousness of historical freedom was presumptively determined largely irrespective of their relationship to social and political structures. Thus, although his project was oriented toward animating moral praxis, he had failed to offer an adequate account of the historical conditioning that makes such action possible. In turning to the categories of memory and narrative, he had sought to address this lacuna. According to Metz, the significance of retrieving and narrating dangerous memories lay principally in disrupting the historical conditions endangering the modern person's consciousness of freedom, not in exhorting the proper orientation of an already-extant consciousness of freedom. These memories fashion a negative consciousness of a future freedom, creating the social and historical conditions that make possible a corresponding hope for the future. If these memories are retrieved by theologians primarily in order to animate moral-critical praxis without sufficiently attending to the social praxis that makes such praxis possible, Metz warned, their subsequent theologies inevitably will be "shaped by an undialectical relationship of theory and praxis," which was the criticism he directed toward Schillebeeckx's Christology.[10]

Here, then, it will be helpful to recall Schillebeeckx's distinct use of memory examined in chapter 3. He had turned to the practice of "critically remembering" in search of the concrete, historical content needed to provide a positive orientation to the Christian's eschatological praxis. Critically remembering, he believed, offers a resource for overcoming the abstract and negative account of emancipative praxis that he found wanting in much of post-Enlightenment philosophy. Thus, Schillebeeckx did not turn to memories in search of a principally negative consciousness of human

---

10. *FHS*, 259n6. Metz included the christological writings of Rahner, Walter Kasper, and Hans Kung in these remarks as well. For Metz's more developed criticism of this use of memory in the context of his critique of transcendental theology, see *FHS*, 74–75.

flourishing. Moreover, and more important for our purposes here, although undoubtedly formative of the subject's historical consciousness, memories would not possess, for him, the fundamentally constitutive role in the conditioning of subjectivity prescribed by Metz. For Schillebeeckx, on the one hand, the memory of the life, death, and resurrection of Jesus Christ was retrieved in order to give direction to that praxis called forth from the dialectical longing and hope-filled consciousness of future freedom universally operative and revealed through experiences of contrast, an important position that we will return to shortly. For Metz, on the other hand, it is the *memoria passionis* itself that offers the truly universal yet historical category of hope. Passing through the *memoria passionis*, the *memoria Jesu Christi* does not respond to the extant hope of the human person but disrupts the person's existing consciousness in order that hope might emerge. Certainly, this is not to suggest that Schillebeeckx did not also recognize the disruptive and subversive power of memory. By remembering the story of the eschatological prophet, which Christians understand as the story of God-with-us, he wanted his readers to find themselves caught up in the story of salvation, to discover a promise capable of shattering the narrowly defined expectations of the modern person. This destabilizing interest, however, was immediately coupled with his primary interest in introducing that "surplus of hope" and positive orientation needed to extend and animate that unfulfilled yet profound desideratum for freedom already experienced.[11]

This important difference between Schillebeeckx's and Metz's projects can be further illuminated by turning to the equally distinct manner in which they employed narratives in their theologies.

---

11. See Schillebeeckx, *Jesus: An Experiment in Christology*, trans. Hubert Hoskins (New York: Crossroad, 1995), 19–26; and *Christ: The Experience of Christ as Lord*, trans. John Bowden (New York: Seabury, 1980), 653–70.

Unsurprisingly, because of the unique ways in which these two theologians cast the category of memory, their treatments of narrative also differed significantly. As previously mentioned, both theologians found in narrative a resource for fusing remembrance with expectations for the future as well as avoiding the reductive disambiguation of history hazarded by theoretical argumentation. They equally recognized the transformative force of memories communicated by way of narrative, the unique potential for a story to shape a consciousness of future freedom. For Metz, though, the cognitive knowledge attained in the narrated memories of suffering, above all in the *memoria passionis*, was primarily a negative consciousness with a dangerous and destabilizing interest. Furthermore, and again more germane to our interests, he stressed that this "is not a matter of inserting the Christian memory of suffering into existing forms of political life."[12] Rather, it is a matter of creating the possibility of an alternative political life by interrupting currently existing conditions. Narratives primarily serve a disruptive function for Metz, irritating self-identity and carving out a space for defeated and repressed hopes to have future meaning. As we have just seen, this was not Schillebeeckx's principal interest when turning to the category of memory. Yet he clearly insisted on the critical and productive force of the story of Jesus. In narrating this story, Schillebeeckx self-consciously sought to identify and communicate the positive historical content required to invigorate and orient more adequately a practical hope through which fragments of the kingdom are already beginning to emerge in world history.[13]

12. *FHS*, 111. See also Metz, "On the Way to a Post-Idealist Theology," in *Passion for God*, 41; and *Hope against Hope: Johann Baptist Metz and Elie Wiesel Speak Out on the Holocaust*, by Ekkehard Schuster and Reinhold Boschert-Kimmig, trans. J. Matthew Ashley (New York: Paulist, 1999), 33.
13. This divergence in objectives is well illustrated by the distinct way in which Schillebeeckx and Metz positioned the practical-critical significance of Christianity's anamnetic hope for the dead. At the end of chapter 4, we noted that Schillebeeckx, on the one hand, located in the

These different approaches to memory and narrative can assist us in clarifying Metz's description of Schillebeeckx's Christology as "idealist," despite the Belgian's protracted effort to take seriously the dialectical relationship of theory and praxis considered in chapter 3. It was not primarily the decision to locate positive content in the story of Jesus that was at question, though this was an important divergence in their projects of which Schillebeeckx was quite critical.[14] Rather, in a manner similar to Metz's early formulation of a political theology, Schillebeeckx appears to have extended the idealist tendencies of theology by positing, if dialectically, an already-existing consciousness of freedom common to all men and women. In advocating the practice of remembering, he critically but deliberately accepted the subjectivity of the modern person, subsequently locating in the story of the eschatological prophet the positive bearing needed to extend a dialectical yet universally implicit consciousness of hope rather than a story that might make hope possible. Using the critical distinction employed by Metz, Schillebeeckx's practical-narrative theology was directed primarily toward animating moral praxis rather than social praxis and, most likely, therein lies Metz's criticism of his christological project. Schillebeeckx's interest in the practical dimension of Christology posited a subject already capable of critical freedom, a subject whose innate resistance to suffering and injustice subsequently needed to be exhorted and properly oriented. Of course, at this point in the study we are well aware that a fundamental theological option was

Christian's surplus of hope for the dead a resource for invigorating an ever-greater hope for history, radicalizing the emancipative praxis of modern men and women by introducing a hope that will not forget all those from the past who courageously sacrificed their lives for a better future. Metz, on the other hand, believed that the practical significance of a hope for the dead lay primarily in drawing attention to the manner in which modernity's emancipative praxis advances on the back of history's victims. As we saw in chapter 5, remembering the dead exposes the danger of modernity's totalizing understanding of emancipation, creating a space for the unrequited hopes of men and women sacrificed in the name of the future.

14. *Christ*, 754.

underlying this position: the experience of negative contrast sustained by the absolute saving presence of the Creator God. And it is here that we might reposition Metz's criticism of Schillebeeckx's Christology and ask whether a similar critique might equally apply to his own mature eschatology.

As noted in chapter 5, there are significant parallels between the work performed by Schillebeeckx's category of a contrast experience and Metz's employment of the *memoria passionis*. For each theologian, his respective category disrupted the plausibility assumptions of the present and the ideological resolution of the nonidentity of history. It resisted a positive accounting of the possibilities of human existence in advance of the eschaton. And, in both cases, a negative consciousness of future freedom was revealed and a stimulus for resisting the suffering of history was found. Thus, it was clear that although different categories served their respective purposes, Schillebeeckx also had ultimately identified a theological resource for irritating and breaking down the identity of the modern person in the interest of opening men and women to the eschatological meaning of their existence. What must be examined here, then, are the implications of Schillebeeckx's decision to locate this subversive category in the fundamental and universal human experience of negative contrast, and the implications of interweaving this dialectical experience with the hope confessed in his prophetic eschatology.

In evaluating Schillebeeckx's strategy, it will be helpful to return briefly to Metz's reading of Rahner's theological project. Metz recognized that Rahner worked inductively from the concrete experiences of the human person to the universal anthropological structure according to which the person is "always already" with God. It was in moving from the historical to the universal prematurely, however, that Metz feared three interrelated dynamics occurred: first, the possibilities of the future were prematurely delimited; second, the still-unfolding history of suffering was inadvertently passed over; and, third, the historical conditioning and endangered status of human hope remained largely undetectable. Though rarely in direct dialogue with Rahner's work,[15] Schillebeeckx aggressively responded to the first two of these dangers by placing the history of human suffering at the very center of his theological reflections. The historical experience of suffering was the starting point of his thought, and the surd of human suffering would not provide a vantage point from which to define positively the future or the threatened *humanum*. As we have seen, though, Schillebeeckx coupled this position with a creation faith that prescribed a universal guarantee of enduring human hope. In the midst of a history of suffering, he believed, the goodness of creation underwrites a practical resistance to human suffering. Although he explicitly resisted constructing a universal anthropological structure positively knowable before the eschaton, he was willing to identify a universal, though dialectically inferred, sensitive point of resonance for the confession of Christian hope disclosed in the protesting "no" that arises from all men and women in the face of suffering and injustice. Indeed, Schillebeeckx would describe this experience of negative contrast as the source for a new "natural theology." Contrast experiences provide the universal pre-understanding that he believed was necessary for the proclamation of eschatological hope. If this hope is itself more than an ideological creed, he insisted, theology must identify an existing point of resonance in the human subject.

Although Metz did not address Schillebeeckx's description of negative contrast experiences directly, it appears that by positing this existing and universal point of resonance within the human

---

15. Ibid., 749–51.

person, which in turn secured the durable viability of human hope for the future, his criticism of Rahner would apply to Schillebeeckx as well, albeit in a highly qualified fashion. Undoubtedly, Schillebeeckx kept the history of human suffering at the forefront of theology. And by disavowing the disclosure of positive conceptual knowledge in experiences of contrast, he clearly avoided both delimiting the surprising eschatological possibilities of the future and theoretically "resolving" the nonidentity of history itself. Contrast experiences, he insisted, suggest dialectically the possibility of a meaningful history; they do not provide conclusive verification. Nonetheless, in our choosing not to account consistently for the historical conditioning of hope, the radical vulnerability of that hope in history would remain largely undetectable. With the hope of the human person secured by the absolute saving presence of the Creator God, Schillebeeckx could not envisage an age of apathy drained of expectations. Thus, distorted expectations remained the focus of his prophetic eschatology, for the absence of expectations would make impossible a confession of the Christian's eschatological hope. As noted in chapter 4, this assists in explaining why Schillebeeckx resisted characterizing modern culture as listless and indifferent to the irruptions of injustice and evil despite his own concerns regarding the dangerous dialectical consequences of modernity's myopic commitment to technological progress. It also assists in explaining why he continued to express the critical leverage found in the Christian's hope as an "eschatological proviso." Hope for a future freedom can be too narrowly circumscribed, and its ambition and optimism are frequently misdirected under the conditions of the present, but the human person will not acquiesce to the meaningless in history, steadfastly protesting evil and injustice.

Does a steadfast and defiant "no" arise from the human person in the face of suffering and injustice, as Schillebeeckx argued, or does no one shout "stop it" anymore, as Metz warned? At issue here is Schillebeeckx's analysis of the actual conditions endangering the Christian hope, which, in light of our reading of Metz, still appears to be informed most immediately by theological speculation rather than by the existing sociohistorical situation. Although it is difficult to adjudicate fully between their distinct analyses, unearthing the manner in which Schillebeeckx's theological commitments informed his social analysis surely invites a critical reevaluation of his position, particularly since he also had expressed similar fears regarding the listlessness of modern culture developed at length by Metz. Also at issue, subsequently, is Schillebeeckx's ability to offer a defense of eschatological hope adequate to the times. Having secured the enduring viability of the human person's hope for the future on the goodness of creation, does he then present an eschatology that fails to offer an account of hope responsive to the social pressures that too often drain men and women of genuine expectation? In the idiom of Metz, does Schillebeeckx put forward a "bland" or "soft" evolutionary eschatology incapable of sustaining subversive resistance?

Schillebeeckx, of course, did speak of the historical mediation of eschatological salvation as a "process" or "course of events" by which the world might imperfectly yet gradually be transformed through graced praxis toward the kingdom of God. If they are nothing but "a drop of water on a hot stone" in the midst of so much tragedy, he insisted that positive, anticipatory fragments of the eschaton can be realized in human history. Despite this insistence on a positive and even a potentially progressive connection between eschatological praxis and salvation history, however, I am reluctant to locate within Schillebeeckx's prophetic eschatology the immediate theological consequences of an evolutionary eschatology so perceptively identified by Metz, in particular the German's warnings that such a project legitimates rather than subverts currently operative sociopolitical processes and abandons to history those who would find no hope in such processes.

For Schillebeeckx, the eschatological praxis of struggling for good and resisting evil arises out of a dialectical awareness that creation and history are not now as God intended; far from legitimating "what is already happening anyway," the eschatological hope sustaining his project animates precisely that subversive praxis which is not already happening. Moreover, this is fundamentally a hope for those who would find no hope in what human persons alone seek to accomplish. Sustained by the saving presence of the Creator, it is nourished and confirmed by the life, death, and resurrection of Jesus, who revealed a "message of hope which cannot be derived from our world history." Although the surplus of hope conveyed in this message can invigorate the praxis by which God's gift of salvation is gradually realized in history, neither it nor history itself offers a guarantee of historical progress. Indeed, if humans fail to respond to this hope, Schillebeeckx darkly warned, "history as such can come to grief." Yet, in the end, it is precisely the surplus of hope found in this message that simultaneously affirms that our hope is not exhausted by history. The Christian's hope refuses to abandon history, but this practical-critical hope is sustained by the promise that the last word is not with history itself but with the God of Jesus Christ who is Lord of history.

The reluctance to identify Schillebeeckx's eschatology as an "evolutionary eschatology," however, detracts from neither the importance of the questions posed of his project nor the value of reading his work in light of Metz. Metz turned to the apocalyptic tradition, at least in part, in an attempt to disrupt that evolutionary logic exhausting the expectations of men and women today, and it was precisely the Belgian's inability to account sufficiently for the crisis of hope that emerges with modernity that I have suggested unduly limits his eschatological project. We might agree with

Schillebeeckx that throughout history, countless men and women, religious and nonreligious alike, have taken a defiant stand with the vulnerable and suffering. But we should also recall that before the Samaritan stopped to help the wounded man along the roadside, two other men had already passed that way, or that the reports of catastrophes coming from all over the world today so often identify the victims as "collateral damage." An eschatology that would animate and sustain a hope that resists suffering and injustice will need to take account of such apathy.

This is not to suggest, of course, that Schillebeeckx assume the apocalyptic strategy employed by Metz. Indeed, it is worth remembering that Schillebeeckx recognized that an apocalyptic hope fosters an agitation that disrupts modernity's overly circumscribed expectations, yet that he decided against this tradition. Nor is it to minimize the significant achievements gained through his understanding of negative contrast experiences. It does, however, invite a critical reevaluation of the fragility and, thus, universality of that experience under the pressure of historical conditions. In response to what he described as Habermas's "optimism of reason" examined in chapter 3, Schillebeeckx advocated critically retrieving Christianity's doctrine of original sin with the relatively modest goal of drawing attention to the overlooked limitations persistently thwarting men and women in their work for emancipation in history. Perhaps this insight needs to be applied to Schillebeeckx's own analysis of negative contrast experiences, especially his claim that the protest of radical dehumanization is a spontaneous and universal response. Does this position take account of the impact of sin, particularly social and systemic sin, on human consciousness and freedom? Our reading of Schillebeeckx's prophetic eschatology in light of Metz points toward the importance of attending consistently to the historical conditioning and vulnerability of the human person's consciousness of hope, particularly within the context of modernity. Schillebeeckx was certainly attentive to the dangerous pressures endangering modern men and women, and further extending that sensitivity to his understanding of the consciousness of hope dialectically revealed through contrast experiences might prepare his project for addressing not only those who might still resist these pressures but also those whose expectations have been exhausted and, thus, who fail to respond to the world's suffering with a defiant "no."

Assessing Metz's Apocalyptic Eschatology

Because Schillebeeckx openly criticized Metz's turn to the apocalyptic, our entrance into a comparative assessment of the German's mature thought will be more direct than the previous section's analysis. As mentioned earlier, however, Schillebeeckx did not amply develop his criticism; he simply wrote in a footnote referencing his exegetical interpretation of Jesus as eschatological prophet, "Here I want to correct J. B. Metz's new appeal to apocalypticism."[16] Our task in what follows will be to examine the concerns underlying this suggestive remark, with the goal of drawing out more fully the contours of Metz's apocalyptic eschatology.

In his earlier appraisal of apocalypticism found in "The Interpretation of the Future," considered in chapter 3, Schillebeeckx had warned that the apocalyptic mistakenly determines the present from the future rather than the future from the present and past. Only an awareness of God's promise of salvation in the present informed by a promise offered in the past, he argued, can provide the hermeneutical framework required for a practical "interpretation of the future" and the historical mediation of eschatological hope.

---

16. *Interim Report*, 150n78. Schillebeeckx cited *FHS* and *Followers of Christ*.

Of course, Schillebeeckx insisted that we must speak only haltingly of the eschaton, primarily in language that arises out of contrast experiences. Nevertheless, his fear was that apocalypticism severs the future from the present and past, making hope-filled expectation epistemologically impossible. If disordered toward both the present and its past, allowed to float without historical tether, he warned, apocalyptic expectations for the future would inevitably dissolve into sheer illusion. When abstracted from concrete history, expectations function as mythology, frequently serving ideological ends. If founded upon a subversive promise embedded in the particular history of a people, however, an authentic hope for the future is genuinely possible. It is here, it is worth reiterating, that we can identify both the eschatological interests underlying Schillebeeckx's massive christological study and his own interest in the social and historical conditioning of human hope.

We may now note that if this had been the extent of Schillebeeckx's opposition to the apocalyptic tradition, his critique would shed little additional light on Metz's work. As we saw in chapter 6, it was precisely through the dangerous memories of history's suffering and defeated that Metz located the historical origins of an apocalyptic hope for the future. Through an anamnetic solidarity, a universal-particular solidarity not only "looking forward" with future generations but also "looking backward" with the dead, the apocalyptic is bound in the present to the victims of history, taking responsibility for and carrying forward the suffering other's unfulfilled expectations and, thus, overcoming prevailing plausibility assumptions and enlivening a practical hope for the future. Unmistakably, then, Metz did not compromise the historical-hermeneutical framework fundamental to the Christian's eschatological expectation, which had been the focal point of Schillebeeckx's earlier opposition to an apocalyptic eschatology. By reading history against the grain, of course, Metz had sought to disrupt the ideological disambiguation of history sustained by the emergence of evolutionary logic. Nevertheless, he dialectically yet explicitly located the continuity of history in the veiled "trail of human suffering." It was in the unrequited cries that emerge from the past, the demanding anticipation in history of a still-outstanding promise, that Metz identified the historical mediation of a genuine hope for eschatological salvation. Consequently, this is not an abstract or mythological hope in the future. To the contrary, it anticipates a specific future for men and women as a future for the suffering and vanquished, a future for all those who have no hope other than time's finale.[17]

When Schillebeeckx returned to the theme of apocalypticism in *Jesus*, however, his position had evolved further, offering us a more instructive opening for assessing Metz's project. There, he granted that the apocalyptic tradition did not necessarily place the present over against a coming future in a definitive manner, although he still identified this as a danger. Schillebeeckx now acknowledged that, from an apocalyptic perspective, it is possible for God's salvific activity to operate dimly in the present world, though this will be brought out into the open only when God's power over history has been established irrevocably in the future. Although Metz's work was not at issue in this text, this idea in fact offers a reasonable description of the German's dialectical understanding of the "Christian continuum." Salvation history is the world's history in which the ominous cries of the suffering are sustained and carried forward, hoping against hope that they will be vindicated in the end. Schillebeeckx's concern here, therefore, was not primarily with the historical continuity that makes the Christian's practical-critical hope

---

17. Schillebeeckx acknowledged this important element of Metz's work in *Christ*, 753.

epistemologically possible. Rather, he pressed his opposition further, lamenting that in this apocalyptic "bringing into the open" of God's salvific activity, no account is given for that element of continuity which makes this realization of eschatological hope in human history possible, even if only in fragmentary ways, and thus makes it possible for history to be a genuine history of salvation. Apocalyptic salvation coming from God interrupts history. Schillebeeckx warned that in positing this interruption, no account is subsequently given for the enduring significance of those fragmented manifestations of salvation history as the world's history, positive and dialectical or partially successful and "failed" alike. Furthermore, he feared that such a position compromises the theological resource required for binding the eschaton promised with that history which is also salvation history. And without such a resource, the demanding Christian praxis of resisting evil and struggling for good possesses only a temporary and fleeting significance.

Here, we must return to Schillebeeckx's warning that theology cannot allow the basic concept of creation to "wither away" only to emerge as "pure eschatology" without a foundation in the Christian doctrine of creation. This is precisely the concern, of course, that we identified lying underneath his opposition to an apocalyptic eschatology. By its interpreting God's saving activity in history as "interventionist activity," he feared that an apocalyptic eschatology dispenses with the nondualistic divine–human relationship established in creation that makes possible the hope that world history is intimately connected and substantively contributes to the history of salvation. It is this nondualistic understanding of the Creator and the world, he argued consistently, that allows for the durable ontological relationship between human activity and God's saving activity. It sustains the distinction without rivalry between what God does in world history for us and what we who have our foundation in

God do ourselves, thus establishing that human liberation is indeed the fragmented actualization of God's gift of salvation, mediated imperfectly but substantively in the world. Moreover, it was the Christian's creation faith that sustained Schillebeeckx's speaking of human persons as the subjects of their own history while simultaneously affirming that God alone is the universal subject of history: again, a position predicated upon the nondualistic Creator–creature relationship. By grounding hope in God's saving interruption of history, Schillebeeckx averred, a "pure eschatology" ultimately evacuates the eschatological significance of Christian discipleship in the world by disordering the historically ambiguous but theologically fundamental relationship between protology and eschatology, untethering human history from salvation history as well as human agency from divine agency.

Because Schillebeeckx's strident criticism of the apocalyptic tradition was written before the publication of his colleague's mature apocalyptic writings, we must be extremely cautious in assessing Metz's work against it. Although I believe such an exercise is instructive, his warning that the doctrine of creation withers away within an apocalyptic eschatology would not seem to offer a fully adequate description of Metz's later work, and at a minimum the immediate theological consequences identified do not materialize in the German's writings. As we have seen, Metz unmistakably argued that through the temporal framework of apocalypticism, salvation history is discoverable in world history without their premature reconciliation, "not somehow pasted together but rather the one in the other and as the other."[18] He also clearly argued that persons can emerge as the subjects of their own history only if God alone is the universal subject of history. Indeed, this interest was at the

---

18. Metz, "Suffering unto God," trans. J. Matthew Ashley, *Critical Inquiry* 20, no. 4 (Summer 1994): 620.

heart of his critique of the evolutionary logic underwriting modern and postmodern understandings of historical freedom. Nevertheless, Schillebeeckx's assessment was not without discernible merit as well. We have also seen that the nondualistic doctrine of creation that afforded such a prominent role in Metz's early writings examined in chapter 1 was largely absent in his later defense of these theological positions.

It is important to recognize that in its place, Metz did not construct a systematic account of God's direct disruption of world history, and the attempt to read one into his project surely risks overlooking the corrective character of his work. His corrective project sought clarification by way of amplification, but the censure offered through the corrective task was not absolute. We also need to emphasize, however, that the value in underscoring the corrective character of his writings here is not in implicitly reconciling his thought with the concerns articulated by Schillebeeckx but rather in clarifying what he was not advocating. In lieu of a systematic theology of interruption, Metz persistently called his readers' attention to the practical-critical significance of an imminent expectation in God's apocalyptic binding and saving interruption of time, inviting them to discover anew the Scripture's unbridled hope that abandons no one to history while simultaneously seeking to safeguard Christianity's other images of hope from the danger of simply reflecting "what is going on anyway." Notably, a corresponding danger also would accompany the attempt to systematize that hope in God's interruption of history which Metz so carefully tried to bring to the attention of Christians and non-Christians alike. Such a project would hazard precisely the totalizing, manageable, and predictable account of history that Metz repeatedly warned domesticates human expectations and is all too easily absorbed into the plausibility structures of those who benefit the most from the status quo.

It is Metz's sensitivity to this danger, however, that also leads us back to his later reflections on the theology of creation examined at the end of chapter 6. There, we discovered that in his turn to an apocalyptic eschatology, Christian creation faith had emerged as a negative theology of creation and the creative power of God. Although continuing to affirm both God's creative power and human freedom as theonomous freedom, Metz did not employ these claims to account for God's saving activity in and through human history. Rather, these claims further served his interest in warning against too quickly reconciling the irreconcilable history of suffering. Metz feared that too often, the doctrine of creation has been allowed to excise God from the theodicy question, quieting the demanding cries of history's suffering. Moreover, he argued that this doctrine has been used to "peer through creation" in an attempt to make sense of a history marred by senseless suffering, similarly quieting the apocalyptic cries of the suffering with the comfort of an emerging "mythical kingdom of a tensionless harmony and of a questionless reconciliation."[19] Advancing key concerns underlying his apocalyptic turn, then, Metz's interests in advocating a negative theology of creation are certainly powerful. Yet this decision also reintroduces the admonitions raised through our reading of Schillebeeckx. With a *theologia negativa* of creation, does Metz genuinely bind that world history which is also salvation history with the eschaton promised, the demanding praxis of solidarity with God's saving activity? Without a more constructive appropriation of the doctrine of creation, does the carrying forward of history's unrequited hopes possess eschatological or only fleeting significance? At issue, then, is an eschatology that might animate and sustain hope and praxis in solidarity with history's suffering persons.

---

19. Metz, "Suffering from God: Theology as Theodicy," *Pacifica* 5 (1992): 285.

Again, it is worth emphasizing that in raising these questions, I am interested in drawing out more fully the distinct advantages and limitations found in each theologian's eschatological writings, in this case underscoring the advantages gained through Schillebeeckx's robust theology of creation and the problematic consequences, despite his intent, that emerge with Metz's decision for a negative theology of creation. The value of our comparative analysis, then, is not directed toward imposing the strategies of one theologian upon the other. As noted in chapter 4, although Schillebeeckx plainly recognized the risks involved in a metaphysical theology, he equally warned against the "antimetaphysical" turn in contemporary theology and, in response, employed what I described as a nonessential negative metaphysics in his understanding of the ontological mediation of salvation through the medium of creation as well as in his theological interpretation of negative contrast experiences.[20] In chapter 1, we examined Metz's criticism of theology's use of metaphysics. This suspicion was maintained throughout his career, and introducing Schillebeeckx's strategy would obviously compromise his interests. Moreover, as suggested earlier, Metz's decision for a negative theology of creation clearly advances key concerns underlying his apocalyptic project, further subverting what he has identified as Christian theology's propensity to pass over or placate superficially the suffering persons of history.

Nonetheless, it is somewhat curious that in reflecting upon the apocalyptic dimension of the doctrine of creation, we find Metz returning to a *theologia negativa*. As we saw in chapter 6, Metz's turn to apocalypticism emerged, in part, out of the limitations he identified in his earlier *theologia negativa* of the future. The abstract and wholly negative character of a utopic theology of history gave

---

20. Here, it is important to recall Schillebeeckx's decision to speak of Christian praxis as an anticipation rather than a participation in the eschaton.

way to the subversive power of an apocalyptic hope that looks toward a specific future, a future for the suffering and vanquished. Interestingly, Metz has already begun to make a similar move with regard to the doctrine of creation by speaking of God's creative omnipotence as a "power setting bounds," a power that likewise offers a specific hope for history's suffering and defeated. Here, I would suggest, it is precisely God's creative power that theologically maintains the Christian's hope for history; and, although this point is not developed by Metz in this context, it is that same power which sustains that solidaristic hope that he argues elsewhere is simply unendurable without God's binding of time. Within this still-underdeveloped position, then, may lie the possibility of a more constructive, apocalyptic reading of the Christian doctrine of creation, binding by way of God's creative power the world and the eschaton as well as solidaristic hope and God's saving activity.

Prophetic and Apocalyptic Eschatologies
Sustaining a Practical Resistance

Although my concerns were obviously drawn quite narrowly in the preceding sections, I have aimed to demonstrate the value of reading each theologian's eschatology in light of the other's work, illuminating relative advantages and limitations of both projects precisely through the tension fostered by their unique accounts of the Christian hope. This objective, however, did not require artificially harmonizing their projects, impressing the distinct commitments of one upon the other and, thus, detracting from the important achievements gained by each. Nor, conversely, did it require characterizing their prophetic and apocalyptic eschatologies as competing or wholly antagonistic endeavors, again detracting from their unique contributions. Seeking to avoid both alternatives equally, I instead hoped to point, however tentatively, toward insights and potential resources inherent to their respective projects that might begin to address the questions raised by way of our comparative assessment.

It is worth emphasizing that our focus remained on Schillebeeckx's and Metz's projects, and the decision to avoid transitioning toward a more general examination of prophetic and apocalyptic eschatologies was a deliberate one. By eschewing that route, I hoped to avoid reinforcing what is at times an overdetermined conceptual framework that, at least with regard to our subjects, can initially obfuscate rather than elucidate their work. When conceptualizing eschatology under the rubrics of prophetic and apocalyptic, theologians have often interpreted one position against the other, opposing, for example, a "transformative model" of prophetic eschatology predicated upon the irreducible continuity of human history and salvation history with a "destructive model" of an apocalyptic eschatology predicated upon a corresponding irreducible discontinuity.[21] Unfortunately, such a definitive interpretive device makes it significantly more difficult to appreciate the precise contours of Schillebeeckx's and Metz's projects. As we have seen over the course of this study, neither pole can singularly account for either theologian's understanding of the interplay between continuity and discontinuity in the historical mediation of the Christian continuum and the Christian's eschatological hope.

Sensitive to the perceived opposition between Christianity and the modern world, Schillebeeckx and Metz initially located in the

---

21. Relying on Raymond Brown's work in *The Virginal Conception and Bodily Resurrection of Jesus*, Anthony Godzieba suggests these models in "'Stay with Us . . .' (Lk. 24:29)—'Come, Lord Jesus' (Rev. 22:20): Incarnation, Eschatology, and Theology's Sweet Predicament," *Theological Studies* 67, no. 4 (2006): 783–95. Given the manner in which Godzieba distinguishes between the positions, it is not surprising that he concludes along with Brown, "The New Testament clearly opts for the prophetic eschatology's transformative model as the most adequate" (787).

doctrine of eschatology a theological resource for legitimating and stimulating the Christian's participation in the task of transforming the world. As their projects developed, of course, they both became more critical of the direction and prospects of modernity. Yet even as they grew more attentive to the discontinuity or critical distance between existing conditions and the eschatological future in which Christians hope, neither theologian abandoned his commitment to Christianity's constitutive interest in a history of human flourishing and freedom. They both recognized, however, that without heightened attention given to the men and women of history who indeed had been abandoned by dominant technological and political interests, the Christian's hope risked mimicking prevailing historical processes and abandoning those who found no hope in such processes. It was history's nonidentity, what Schillebeeckx described as the vicious commingling of sense and nonsense in history and what Metz described as the crisis and danger of history, that most urgently demanded the Christian's response. It was in this context that Schillebeeckx and Metz retrieved the promises of God as promises for history's suffering people. Their eschatologies emerged as highly distinct projects. Yet, sustained by these promises, the Christian's eschatological expectation emerged as a subversive hope in action that resists the injustices and oppression of past and present, anticipating or even demanding a future in which God's promises will be fulfilled.

Postscript

Subversive Eschatology and "Indirect Ecumenism"

As noted at the end of the last chapter, our focus throughout this study has remained on Schillebeeckx's and Metz's projects, and the decision to avoid transitioning toward a more general examination of prophetic and apocalyptic eschatologies was a deliberate one. I would be remiss, however, if that decision were allowed to conceal the larger theological milieu in which their projects developed. Here, I do not have in mind the numerous cultural, theological, and philosophical currents identified throughout our study that informed and gave direction, dialectically and otherwise, to Schillebeeckx's and Metz's eschatologies. Rather, very little attention has been given to a number of influential projects that emerged from similar currents nearly simultaneously with their work, particularly among Protestant theologians. Indeed, a notable lacuna in this study is the absence of a sustained examination of the ecumenical milieu in which our Catholic theologians' work developed. This is certainly true with regard to their early thought, when Metz was almost inevitably discussed as a "theologian of hope" in the same breath as the German Protestant theologians Wolfhart Pannenberg and Jürgen Moltmann. Schillebeeckx was linked to this group as well, though less frequently.[1] And as the thinking of our two Catholic theologians developed, Moltmann and Dorothee Sölle were regularly counted with Metz as the primary architects of European "political theology," a list that, as the preceding pages have shown, might profitably include Schillebeeckx as well.

My desire to address this lacuna is the impetus for this brief postscript. Of course, developing the kind of comparative assessment that we have established between Schillebeeckx and Metz will not be possible here. Rather than interject the work of a Pannenberg, Moltmann, or Sölle into the sustained conversation already developed, I want to draw attention to the way in which the historical developments that gave rise to the subversive eschatologies examined in this book also gave rise to what both Metz and Moltmann have called an "indirect ecumenism."[2] Indeed, the relationship between Metz and the Reformed theologian Moltmann offers a particularly helpful resource for establishing an appreciation of the wider ecumenical context in which Schillebeeckx's and Metz's eschatologies developed.

Moltmann is perhaps still most widely known for his *Theology of Hope*, which was published in 1964. Like many of Schillebeeckx's and Metz's writings from the time, the work's driving interest was in repositioning eschatology as the privileged fundamental medium by which the whole of Christian faith ought to be approached. The book was informed by Moltmann's own engagement with Ernst Bloch's philosophy of hope, and although it was distinctly colored by his innovative engagement with the thought of Karl Barth and Rudolf Bultmann, his early work likewise sought to uncover the manner in which the Christian's eschatological expectations for the

1. For example, see David P. Scaer, "Theology of Hope," in *Tensions in Contemporary Theology*, ed. Stanley N. Gundry and Alan F. Johnson (Grand Rapids, MI: Baker, 1976), 198.
2. Johann Baptist Metz and Jürgen Moltmann, *Faith and the Future: Essays on Theology, Solidarity, and Modernity* (Maryknoll, NY: Orbis, 1995), vii and x.

future radically impinge on the present. He, too, positioned eschatology as a passionate and active hope, a hope animated by a *promissio inquieta* grounded in Christ that resists premature satisfaction and is directed toward an open future.[3] Although Moltmann's theology of hope was surely establishing the groundwork for his own critical political theology in this early work, it, too, consciously resonated with that confident period of European and North American history he would later describe as "brimming over with movements of hope and experiences of rebirth and renewal."[4] Indeed, Moltmann often attributes the book's extraordinary success to this resonance, particularly in North America.

It hardly needs to be noted that this is familiar terrain, and thus subsequent development in Moltmann's project likely will also not be a surprise. Whose future? Whose hopes? Moltmann began asking just such questions in the early 1970s, self-critically revisiting his earlier work and the widespread success of what was almost immediately referred to as the "movement" of hope theology. In public lectures delivered across Europe and North America, and most clearly with the 1972 publication of *The Crucified God*, he would now argue, "A revision of hope theology and the future-oriented philosophies of Teilhard and Bloch would thus, in a new form, have to take note of the problems of radical evil, the absurdity of misdirected evolutionary processes, of death and the tragedy of human existence in order to arrive at an expression of solid human hope."[5] Moltmann noted the influence not only of Adorno and Horkheimer on this more critical effort to offer an account of Christian hope in the midst of a history

---

3. Jürgen Moltmann, *A Theology of Hope: On the Ground and the Implication of a Christian Eschatology*, trans. James Leitch (New York: Harper & Row, 1967), 88.
4. Jürgen Moltmann, *Experiences of God*, trans. Margaret Kohl (London: SCM, 1980), 12.
5. Jürgen Moltmann, "Hope and the Biomedical Future of Man," in *Hope and the Future of Man*, ed. Ewert H. Cousins (Philadelphia: Fortress Press, 1972), 90. See also p. 55.

of suffering, but of Metz as well.[6] Once again, this covers familiar terrain.

Such a brief review of this early work is certainly not intended to reduce Moltmann's project to those of Schillebeeckx's and Metz's any more than we have intended to collapse the thought of the latter two. Moltmann's eschatological project developed a highly distinct body of insights and a trajectory that Schillebeeckx and Metz valued but also challenged.[7] Nonetheless, the three theologians unmistakably shared theological interests, interlocutors, and numerous opportunities for mutual influence. Metz and Moltmann were regular participants in the Christian–Marxist Dialogues hosted by the Catholic Paulus Society at the University of Tübingen in the mid-1960s, where both theologians worked out their initial theological responses to the thought of Ernst Bloch.[8] All three men spoke frequently at the same conferences in North America and Europe during the 1970s and, as noted earlier, were frequently associated with the same "movements" within theology. And by the end of that decade, all three served on the editorial board of the international Catholic journal *Concilium*.

It would be somewhat off the mark, however, to interpret the significant intersections found in their theological trajectories as deliberate exercises in theological ecumenism. Although Schillebeeckx, Metz, and Moltmann occasionally addressed questions of ecumenism directly during this period, and over the years Moltmann did edit select issues of *Concilium* devoted to ecumenism, their theological projects only rarely take up ecumenism as a distinct

6. Jürgen Moltmann, *The Crucified God: The Cross of Christ as the Foundation and Criticism of Christian Theology*, trans. R. A. Wilson and John Bowden (London: SCM, 1973), 5.
7. For example, see Schillebeeckx, "The Interpretation of the Future," in *The Understanding of Faith: Interpretation and Criticism*, trans. N. D. Smith (New York: Seabury, 1974), 8; and Metz, *Faith in History and Society: Toward a Practical Fundamental Theology*, trans. J. Matthew Ashley (New York: Crossroad, 2007), 65.
8. Metz and Moltmann, *Faith and the Future*, x.

topic of reflection.[9] As already noted, rather, both Metz and Moltmann have preferred to characterize these intersections as an "indirect ecumenism." Neither theologian has developed the significance of this expression very fully, but the brief comments they have offered not only provide added clarity but also, I want to suggest, simultaneously return us to the animating concerns that progressively gave direction to their eschatological projects.

In characterizing his relationship with Moltmann in 1995, Metz wrote, "We have always called our joint enterprise, our public struggle in the matter of 'God and the World,' our joint endeavor in common responsibility where the broadest conflicts are concerned, 'indirect ecumenism.'" He proceeded to explain that their "ecumenical togetherness of a special sort" was not a reductive ecumenism in search of a tempered theology and, thus, minimum consensus. Rather, he wrote, "[o]ur focus, despite our very different presuppositions and backgrounds, has always been the 'grand consensus'—a basic consensus, an agreement on the vision of Christianity that we owe this world in season and out."[10] It is interesting that, in speaking of their relationship at the end of the twentieth century, Metz returned to the theological idiom of the early 1960s and framed their joint enterprise as one concerned with "God and the World." As we have seen, this language emerged in Metz's early theology as he struggled to revitalize a faith that would not "simply hammer away behind locked doors at its customary practices in theology and piety."[11] Throughout his early efforts to engage a "world" identified with the processes of secularization, Metz had sought to lay claim to theology's responsibility to the world as

---

9. See, for example, Jürgen Moltmann, "Can There Be an Ecumenical Mariology?," in *Mary in the Churches*, ed. Hans Küng and Jürgen Moltmann, *Concilium* 168 (1983).

10. Metz and Moltmann, *Faith and the Future*, vii.

11. Metz, *Theology of the World*, trans. William Glen-Doepel (New York: Herder & Herder, 1969), 13.

well as its ecclesial responsibility. The same can be said of Moltmann. And it is in their common embrace of theology's political responsibility, rather than a common theology of ecclesial unity, that Metz subsequently identifies the meaning of his indirect ecumenism with Moltmann.

Metz's brief reflections on the emergence of an indirect ecumenism return us to an early stage of his theological development and his theology of the world, whereas Moltmann's equally brief reflections, also from 1995, draw our attention to later stages of development in their work. "In our discussion with the representatives of what was then called Marxism 'with a human face,'" Moltmann recalled, "we were confronted with problems for which neither the Catholic nor the Protestant tradition had provided ready answers."[12] It was out of this context, he argued, that they would develop both their political theology and their indirect ecumenism. Indeed, Moltmann traces their development concurrently, subsequently moving beyond their early engagement with Marxism to their later efforts at learning to theologize "after Auschwitz" and learning to remain attentive to the relentless suffering in history brought to the fore by liberation theologies from around the globe. Their common effort to respond to the crises of modernity did not resolve the historical pressures between their distinct Christian traditions, but it created a common theological endeavor responsive to new historical pressures, indirectly establishing a unique ecumenical relationship.

Here again, then, it is Metz and Moltmann's common embrace of theology's political responsibility, rather than a common theology of ecclesial unity, that characterizes their indirect ecumenism. Indeed, what both theologians suggest is that it was not by chance that their political theologies and subversive eschatologies developed within

12. Metz and Moltmann, *Faith and the Future*, x.

an ecumenical milieu. Rather, the very conditions that gave rise to political theology and their subversive eschatologies also gave rise to an ecumenical context as those same conditions summoned from the Catholic and the Reformed theologian a common concern for history and for the suffering men and women of history out of which they would both theologize.

It is worth repeating Metz's observation that the two theologians possessed very different presuppositions and backgrounds, and their eschatological projects are undoubtedly distinct. For his part, Moltmann often refers to a Russian proverb to characterize the relationship between the two men: "When two people say the same thing, one of them is unnecessary."[13] In this case, surely neither theologian is superfluous. In Moltmann's most mature eschatological writings, for example, he advocates right alongside Metz for the importance of the apocalyptic, even as he introduces a processive eschatology that he insists must also include a millenarian "transitional kingdom."[14] In a 1998 presentation delivered at a celebration of Metz's seventieth birthday, Moltmann criticized Metz's analysis of evolutionary time, arguing that it is a loss of confidence in time rather than a sense of endless time that mars contemporary men and women. Moltmann immediately followed his criticism, however, by affirming with Metz that the gospel "is a message about time."[15] Again, it is a common embrace of a faith in history and society, rather than a common theology, that characterizes this ecumenical relationship.

13. Jürgen Moltmann, "From the Beginning of Time in God's Presence," in *The End of Time? The Provocation of Talking about God*, ed. Tiemo Rainer Peters and Claus Urban (Mahwah, NJ: Paulist, 2004), 56.
14. Jürgen Moltmann, *The Coming of God: Christian Eschatology*, trans. Margaret Kohl (Minneapolis: Fortress Press, 1996), 195.
15. Moltmann, "From the Beginning of Time," 59.

A fuller accounting of the ecumenical milieu that accompanied the emergence of Metz's and Moltmann's subversive eschatologies over the past fifty years would certainly require that significant attention be given to the important advances of the wider ecumenical movement that happily characterized the church during that period. For our purposes, however, we can conclude by returning to where this postscript began. The sustained conversation established between Schillebeeckx and Metz over the preceding pages has aimed to provide clarity and insight into the potential limitations and powerful possibilities of each theologian's project, but it should not be read to suggest that their turn to eschatology in the latter half of the twentieth century was by any means a theological strategy unique to them, and their own journeys plainly do not exhaust the subversive possibilities embedded in the Christian hope. As we Christians continue to labor to account for our hope in a manner responsive to the pressing demands of our time, I have tried to suggest in these final few pages, we will be well served by entering into ever-expanding and diverse conversations, ecumenical and otherwise. And in doing so, we might labor that we can give account not of a tempered and minimal consensus but of an active and subversive hope for the world.

Bibliography

Works by Johann Baptist Metz

"Die 'Stunde' Christi: Eine geschichtstheologische Erwägung." *Wort und Wahrheit* 12 (1957): 5–18.

Advent Gottes. Munich: Ars Sacra, 1959. Translated by John Drury as *The Advent of God.* Paramus, NJ: Newman, 1970.

"Theologische und metaphysische Ordnung." *Zeitschrift für Katholische Theologie* 83 (1961). Translated by Dominic Gerlach as "The Theological World and the Metaphysical World." *Philosophy Today* 10, no. 4 (1966): 253–63.

Christliche Anthropozentrik: Über die Denkform des Thomas von Aquin. Munich: Kosel, 1962.

"Gott vor uns: Statt eines theologischen Arguments." In *Ernst Bloch zu ehren: Beiträge zu seinem Werk*, edited by Siegfried Unself. Frankfurt am Main: Suhrkamp, 1965.

"The Church and the World." In *The Word in History*, edited by Patrick Burke. New York: Sheed & Ward, 1966, 69–85.

"The Responsibility of Hope." *Philosophy Today* 10, no. 4 (1966): 280–88.

"The Controversy about the Future of Man: An Answer to Roger Garaudy." *Journal of Ecumenical Studies* 4, no. 2 (1967): 223–34.

Zur Theologie der Welt. Mainz, Ger.: Matthias-Grünewald, 1968. Translated by William Glen-Doepel as *Theology of the World.* New York: Herder & Herder, 1969.

"Political Theology." In *Sacramentum Mundi: An Encyclopedia of Theology,* edited by Karl Rahner et al. New York: Herder & Herder, 1968–70. Vol. 5, *Philosophy to Salvation.* 34–38.

"Politische Theologie' in der Diskussion." In *Diskussion zur "Politischen Theologie,"* edited by Helmut Peukert. Mainz, Ger.: Matthias-Grünewald, 1969.

"Kirchliche Autorität im Anspruch der Freiheitsgeschichte." In *Kirche im Prozess der Aufklärung,* edited by J. B. Metz, J. Moltmann, and W. Oelmüller. Munich: Kaiser, 1970. Translated by David Kelly and Henry Vander Goot as "Prophetic Authority." In *Religion and Political Society,* edited by the Institute of Christian Thought. New York: Harper Forum Books, 1974.

"A Brief Apology for Narrative." In *The Crisis of Religious Language* (*Concilium* 85), edited by Johann Baptist Metz and Jean-Pierre Jossua. New York: Herder & Herder, 1973. 84–96.

[Metz, Johann Baptist, and] Bischöfliche Ordinariate und das Sekretariat der Deutschen Bischofskonferenz. *Unsere Hoffnung: Ein Beschluß der gemeinsamen Synode der Bistümer in der Bundesrepublik Deutschland.* Synodenbeschlüsse 18. Bonn, 1975. Translated by WCC Language Service as "Our Hope: A Confession of Faith for This Time." Joint Synod of Catholic Dioceses of the Federal Republic of Germany. *Study Encounter* 12, nos. 1–2 (1976).

Glaube in Geschichte und Gesellschaft: Studien zu einer praktischen Fundamentaltheologie. Mainz, Ger.: Matthias-Grünewald, 1977. Edited and translated from the 5th edition by J. Matthew Ashley as *Faith in History and Society: Toward a Practical Fundamental Theology.* New York: Crossroad, 2007.

Zeit der Orden? Zur Mystik und Politik. Freiburg, Ger.: Herder, 1977. Translated by Thomas Linton as *Followers of Christ: The Religious Life and the Church.* New York: Paulist, 1978.

Jenseits bürgerlicher Religion: Reden über die Zukunft des Christentums. Mainz, Ger.: Matthias-Grünewald, 1980. Translated by Peter Mann as *The Emergent Church: The Future of Christianity in a Postbourgeois World.* New York: Crossroad, 1987.

Unterbrechungen: Theologische-politische Perspektiven und Profile. Gütersloh, Ger.: Gütersloher, 1981.

"Productive Noncontemporaneity." In *Observations on "The Spiritual Situation of the Age,"* edited by Jürgen Habermas, translated by Andrew Buchwalter. Cambridge, MA: MIT Press, 1984. 169–77.

"Communicating a Dangerous Memory." In *Communicating a Dangerous Memory: Soundings in Political Theology,* edited by Fred Lawrence. Lonergan Workshop 6. Atlanta: Scholars Press, 1987.

"Suffering from God: Theology as Theodicy." *Pacifica* 5 (1992): 274–87.

"Time without a Finale: The Background to the Debate on 'Resurrection or Reincarnation.'" In *Reincarnation or Resurrection? (Concilium),* edited by Hermann Häring and Johann Baptist Metz. Maryknoll, NY: Orbis, 1993. 124–31.

Trotzdem Hoffen: Mit Johann Baptist Metz und Elie Wiesel im Gespräch. Interviews by Ekkehard Schuster and Reinhold Boschert-Kimmig. Mainz, Ger.: Matthias-Grünewald, 1993. Translated by J. Matthew Ashley as *Hope against Hope: Johann Baptist Metz and Elie Wiesel Speak Out on the Holocaust.* New York: Paulist, 1999.

"Suffering unto God." Translated by J. Matthew Ashley. *Critical Inquiry* 20, no. 4 (Summer 1994): 611–22.

[Metz, Johann Baptist, with] Jürgen Moltmann. *Faith and the Future: Essays on Theology, Solidarity, and Modernity.* Maryknoll, NY: Orbis, 1995. (This volume is a collection of Metz's essays from *Concilium.*)

A Passion for God: The Mystical-Political Dimension of Christianity. Edited and translated by J. Matthew Ashley. New York: Paulist, 1998. (This volume is a collection of Metz's essays from 1985 to 1995.)

• "In Place of a Foreword: On the Biographical Itinerary of My Theology." 1–5.

• "On the Way to a Post-Idealist Theology." 30–53.

• "Theology as Theodicy?" 54–71.

• "Theology versus Polymythicism: A Short Apology for Biblical Monotheism." 72–91.

• "Monotheism and Democracy: Religion and Politics on Modernity's Ground." 136–49.

• "A Passion for God: Religious Orders Today." 150–74.

"God: Against the Myth of the Eternity of Time" (26–46) and "God, Sin, and Suffering: A Conversation" (with Joseph Ratzinger, 47–53). In *Ende der Zeit,* edited by Tiemo Rainer Peters and Claus Urban. Mainz, Ger.: Matthias-Grünewald, 1999. Edited and translated by J. Matthew Ashley as *The End of Time? The Provocation of Talking about God.* Mahwah, NJ: Paulist, 2004.

Love's Strategy: The Political Theology of Johann Baptist Metz. Edited by John K. Downey. Harrisburg, PA: Trinity, 1999.

• "Theology Today: New Crises and New Visions." 64–82.

• "In the Pluralism of Religious and Cultural Worlds." 167–75.

Memoria passionis: Ein provozierendes Gedächtnis in pluralistischer Gessellschaft. Freiburg, Ger.: Herder, 2006.

"Under the Spell of Cultural Amnesia?" In *Missing God? Cultural Amnesia and Political Theology,* edited by John K. Downey, Jürgen Manemann, and Steven T. Ostovich. Münster: LIT, 2006.

Works by Edward Schillebeeckx

"Christelijke situatie." Three consecutive articles in *Kultuurleven* 12 (1945): 82–95, 229–42, 585–611.

Christus Sacrament van de Godsontmoeting. Bilthoven, Neth.: Nelissen, 1960. Translated by Paul Barrett as *Christ the Sacrament of the Encounter with God.* Franklin, WI: Sheed & Ward, 1999.

God en Mens. Bilthoven, Neth.: Nelissen, 1965. Translated by Edward Fitzgerald and Peter Tomlinson as *God and Man.* New York: Sheed & Ward, 1969.
- "God in Dry Dock." 3–17.
- "The Search for the Living God." 18–40.
- "Life in God and Life in the World." 85–160.
- "Dialogue with God and Christian Secularity." 210–33.

"Faith Functioning in Human Understanding." In *The Word in History*, edited by Patrick Burke. New York: Sheed & Ward, 1966. 41–59.

Wereld en Kerk. Bilthoven, Neth.: Nelissen, 1966. Translated by N. D. Smith as *World and Church.* New York: Sheed & Ward, 1971.
- "Religion and the World: Renewing the Face of the Earth." 1–18.
- "Humble Humanism." 19–31.
- "Priest and Layman in a Secular World." 32–76.
- "The Sorrow of the Experience of God's Concealment." 77–95.
- "Supernaturalism, Unchristian and Christian Expectations of the Future." 163–76.
- "Christians and Non-Christians, 2: Practical Cooperation." 199–229.
- "The Catholic Hospital and Health Service." 213–29.
- "The Intellectual's Responsibility for the Future." 269–81.

God the Future of Man. Translated by N. D. Smith. New York: Sheed & Ward, 1968.

"Towards a Catholic Use of Hermeneutics." 1–50.

- "Secularization and Christian Belief in God." 51–90.
- "The Church as the Sacrament of Dialogue." 117–40.
- "Church, Magisterium, and Politics." 141–66.
- "The New Image of God, Secularization, and Man's Future on Earth" (epilogue). 167–207.

""*Revelation and Theology*. Vol. 2, *The Concept of Truth and Theological Renewal*. London: Sheed & Ward, 1968.

- "The Non-Conceptual Intellectual Dimension of Our Knowledge of God according to Aquinas." 30-53.
- "Theology of Renewal Talks about God." 84–90.

Zending van de Kerk. Bilthoven, Neth.: Nelissen, 1968. Translated by N. D. Smith as *The Mission of the Church*. New York: Seabury, 1973.

- "Is the Church Adrift?" 20–42.
- "Christian Faith and Man's Expectation for the Future on Earth." 51–89.
- "Religious Life in a Secularized World." 132–70.

Geloofsverstaan, Bloemendaal, Neth.: Nelissen, 1972. Translated by N. D. Smith as *The Understanding of Faith: Interpretation and Criticism*. New York: Seabury, 1974.

- "The Interpretation of the Future." 1–13.
- "Theological Criteria." 45–77.
- "Correlation between Human Question and Christian Answer." 78–101.
- "The New Critical Theory." 102–23.
- "The New Critical Theory and Theological Hermeneutics." 124–55.

"Critical Theories and Christian Political Commitment." In *Political Commitment and Christian Community* (*Concilium* 84), edited by Alois Muller and Norbert Greinacher. New York: Herder & Herder, 1973. 48–61.

Jezus, het verhaal van een levende. Bloemendaal, Neth.: Nelissen, 1974. Translated by Hubert Hoskins as *Jesus: An Experiment in Christology.* New York: Crossroad, 1995.

Gerechtigheid en liefde: Genade en bevrijding. Bloemendaal, Neth.: Nelissen, 1977. Translated by John Bowden as *Christ: The Experience of Christ as Lord.* New York: Seabury, 1980.

"God, Society, and Human Salvation." In *Faith and Society.* Gembloux, Belg.: Duculot, 1978.

Tussentijds verhaal over Jezus boeken. Bloemendaal, Neth.: Nelissen, 1978. Translated by John Bowden as *Interim Report on the Books "Jesus" and "Christ."* New York: Crossroad, 1981.

"Erfahrung und Glaube." In *Christlicher Glaube in moderner Gesellschaft 25.* Freiburg, Ger.: Herder, 1980. 23–116.

Ministry: Leadership in the Community of Jesus Christ. Translated by John Bowden. New York: Crossroad, 1981.

God among Us: The Gospel Proclaimed. New York: Crossroad, 1983.

The Schillebeeckx Reader. Edited by Robert J. Schreiter. New York: Crossroad, 1984.

"Theologie als bevrijdingskunde." *Tijdschrift voor Theologie* 24 (1984): 388-402.

[Schillebeeckx, ed.] *Mystik und Politik: Theologie im Ringen um Geschichte und Gessschaft; Johann Baptist Metz zu Ehren.* Mainz, Ger.: Matthias-Grünewald, 1988.

Mensen als Verhaal van God. Bloemendaal, Neth.: Nelissen, 1989. Translated by John Bowdenas *Church: The Human Story of God.* New York: Crossroad, 1994.

For the Sake of the Gospel. Translated by John Bowden. New York: Crossroad, 1990.

"Terugblik vanuit de tijd na Vaticanum II: De gebroken idelogieën van de moderniteit." In *Tussen openheid en isolement: Het voorbeeld van de katholische theologie in de negentiende eeuw*, edited by E. Borgman and A. van Harskamp. Kampen, Neth.: Kok, 1992. 153–72.

Van cultuurtheologie naar theologie als onderdeel van de cultuur." *Tijdschrift voor Theologie* 34 (1994): 335–60.

*Language of Faith: Essays on Jesus, Theology, and the Church.*Maryknoll, NY: Orbis, 1995. (This volume is a collection of Schillebeeckx's essays from *Concilium.*)

  • "The Crisis in the Language of Faith as a Hermeneutical Problem." 83–94.

  • "The 'God of Jesus' and the 'Jesus of God.'" 95–108.

  • "Christian Identity and Human Integrity." 185–98.

Other Works

Adorno, Theodor W. "The Actuality of Philosophy." *Telos* 31 (Spring 1977): 120–33.

———. *Negative Dialectics.* Translated by E. B. Ashton. New York: Continuum, 1973.

Aquinas, Thomas. *Thomas Aquinas on Being and Essence.* Translated by Armand Maurer. Toronto: Pontifical Institute of Medieval Studies, 1968.

Ashley, James Matthew. "Apocalypticism in Political and Liberation Theology: Toward an Historical *Docta Ignorantia.*" *Horizons* 27, no. 1 (2000): 22–43.

———. *Interruptions: Mysticism, Politics, and Theology in the Work of Johann Baptist Metz.* Notre Dame, IN: University of Notre Dame Press, 1998.

———. "The Path to *Faith in History and Society.*" Introduction to Metz, *Faith in History and Society.*

Baum, Gregory, ed. *The Twentieth Century: A Theological Overview.* Maryknoll, NY: Orbis, 1999. 3–13.

Benjamin, Walter. "The Storyteller: Reflections on the Works of Nikolai Leskov." In *Illuminations,* edited by Hannah Arendt, translated by Harry Zohn. New York: Schocken, 1968.

———. "Theses on the Philosophy of History." In *German 20th Century Philosophy: The Frankfurt School,* edited by Wolfgang Schirmacher. New York: Continuum, 2000. 71–80.

Berger, Peter, ed. *The Desecularization of the World.* Grand Rapids, MI: Eerdmans, 1999.

———. *The Sacred Canopy: Elements of a Sociological Theory of Religion.* New York: Doubleday, 1967.

Berry, Brian David. "Fundamental Liberationist Ethics: The Contribution of the Later Theology of Edward Schillebeeckx." PhD diss., Boston College, 1995.

Bergin, Helen. "Edward Schillebeeckx and the Suffering Human Being." *International Journal of Public Theology* 4, no. 4 (October 2010): 466-482.

Bloch, Ernst. *Atheism in Christianity: The Religion of the Exodus and the Kingdom.* Translated by J. T. Swann. New York: Herder & Herder, 1972.

———. *The Principle of Hope.* Translated by Stephen Plaice and Paul Knight. 3 vols. Oxford: Blackwell, 1986.

———. *Thomas Münzer as Theologian of the Revolution.* Munich: Wolff, 1921.

Blumenberg, Hans. *The Legitimacy of the Modern Age.* Translated by Robert Wallace. Cambridge, MA: MIT Press, 1983. Originally published in 1966.

Boeve, Lieven, Frederiek Depoortere and Stephan van Erp, eds. *Edward Schillebeeckx and Contemporary Theology.* (London: Continuum International Publishing, 2010).

Boeve, Lieven. *God Interrupts History: Theology in a Time of Upheaval.* New York: Continuum, 2007.

———. "Religion after Detraditionalization: Christian Faith in a Post-Secular Europe." *Irish Theological Quarterly* 70 (2005): 99–122.

Borgman, Erik. *Edward Schillebeeckx: A Theologian in His History.* Vol. 1, *A Catholic Theology of Culture (1914–1965).* Translated by John Bowden. London: Continuum, 2003.

Bruce, Steve. *God Is Dead: Secularization in the West.* Oxford: Blackwell, 2002.

Buck-Morss, Susan. *The Origin of Negative Dialectics: Theodor W. Adorno, Walter Benjamin, and the Frankfurt Institute.* New York: Free Press, 1977.

Caputo, John. *On Religion.* New York: Routledge, 2001.

———. *The Prayers and Tears of Jacques Derrida: Religion without Religion.* Bloomington: Indiana University Press, 1997.

Casanova, José. *Public Religions in the Modern World.* Chicago: University of Chicago Press, 1994.

Chopp, Rebecca S. *The Praxis of Suffering: An Interpretation of Liberation and Political Theologies.* Maryknoll, NY: Orbis, 1986.

Coleman, John A. *The Evolution of Dutch Catholicism, 1958–1974.* Berkeley: University of California Press, 1978.

Colombo, J. A. *An Essay on Theology and History: Studies in Pannenberg, Metz, and the Frankfurt School.* Atlanta: Scholars Press, 1990.

Cox, Harvey. "The Myth of the Twentieth Century." In Baum, *Twentieth Century,* 135–44.

Davis, Charles. "Theology and Praxis." *Cross Currents* 23 (1973): 154–68.

Eggemeier, Matthew T. "Christianity or Nihilism? The Apocalyptic Discourses of Johann Baptist Metz and Friedrich Nietzsche." *Horizons* 39, no. 1 (Spring 2012): 7-26.

Eliot, T. S. *The Waste Land.* New York: Boni & Liveright, 1922.

Ernst, Cornelius. Foreword to Schillebeeckx, *Christ the Sacrament of the Encounter with God.*

Fiorenza, Francis P. "Dialectical Theology and Hope." *Heythrop Journal* 9–10, nos. 2, 4, 1 (1968–69).

————. "The Thought of J. B. Metz." *Philosophy Today* 10, no. 4 (1966): 247–52.

Godzieba, Anthony. "'Stay with Us . . .' (Lk. 24:29)—'Come, Lord Jesus' (Rev. 22:20): Incarnation, Eschatology, and Theology's Sweet Predicament." *Theological Studies* 67, no. 4 (2006): 783–95.

Greeley, Andrew. "The Secularization Myth." In *The Denominational Society: A Sociological Approach to Religion in America.* Glenview, IL: Scott Foresman, 1972. 127–55.

Grünbacher, Armin. *Reconstruction and Cold War in Germany.* Burlington, VT: Ashgate, 2004.

Guess, Raymond. *The Idea of a Critical Theory: Habermas and the Frankfurt School.* New York: Cambridge University Press, 1981.

Habermas, Jürgen. *Knowledge and Human Interests.* Translated by Jeremy J. Shapiro. Boston: Beacon, 1972.

————. *Theory and Practice.* Translated by John Viertel. Boston: Beacon, 1973.

Hall, Douglas John. "'The Great War' and the Theologians." In *The Twentieth Century: A Theological Overview*, edited by Gregory Baum. Maryknoll, NY: Orbis, 1999.

Hauerwas, Stanley, and L. Gregory Jones, eds. *Why Narrative? Readings in Narrative Theology.* Grand Rapids, MI: Eerdmans: 1989.

Heidegger, Martin. *Basic Writings.* Edited by David Farrell Krell. Rev. ed. San Francisco: HarperSanFrancisco, 1993.

Hilkert, Mary Catherine. "Experience and Revelation." In Hilkert and Schreiter, *Praxis of the Reign of God. 69–78.*

————. "Hermeneutics of History in the Theology of Edward Schillebeeckx." *Thomist* 51 (1987): 97–145.

Hilkert, Mary Catherine, and Robert J. Schreiter, eds. *The Praxis of the Reign of God.* 2nd ed. New York: Fordham University Press, 2002.

Hill, William J. "Schillebeeckx's New Look at Secularity: A Note." *Thomist* 33 (1969): 162–70.

Hinze, Bradford. "Eschatology and Ethics." in Hilkert and Schreiter, *Praxis of the Reign of God*. 167–83.

Horkheimer, Max, and Theodor W. Adorno. *Dialectic of Enlightenment.* Translated by John Cumming. New York: Continuum, 1976.

Iwashima, Tadahiko. *Menschheitsgeschichte und Heilserfahrung.* Düsseldorf, Ger.: Patmos, 1982.

Jodock, Darrell, ed., *Catholicism Contending with Modernity: Roman Catholic Modernism and Anti-Modernism in Historical Context.* Cambridge: Cambridge University Press, 2000.

Johns, Roger Dick. *Man in the World: The Political Theology of Johannes Baptist Metz.* Missoula, MT: Scholars Press, 1992.

Kennedy, Philip. "Continuity Underlying Discontinuity: Schillebeeckx's Philosophical Background." *New Blackfriars* 70 (1989): 264–77.

———. *Deus Humanissimus: The Knowability of God in the Theology of Edward Schillebeeckx.* Fribourg, Switz.: University Press, 1993.

———. "God and Creation." In Hilkert and Schreiter, *Praxis of the Reign of God*. 37–58.

Krieg, Robert A. *Story-Shaped Christology.* New York: Paulist, 1988.

Lavalette, Henri de. "La 'theologie politique' de Jean-Baptiste Metz." *Recherches de Sciences Religieuses* 58 (1970): 321–50.

Lilla, Mark. *The Stillborn God: Religion, Politics, and the Modern West.* New York: Knopf, 2007.

Livingston, James, and Francis Schüssler Fiorenza, eds. *Modern Christian Thought.* Vol. 2, *The Twentieth Century.* Upper Saddle River, NJ: Prentice Hall, 2000.

Löwith, Karl. *Meaning in History.* Chicago: University of Chicago Press, 1949.

Marcuse, Herbert. *One-Dimensional Man.* Boston: Beacon, 1964.

Marsden, John. "Bloch's Messianic Marxism." *New Blackfriars* 70 (1989): 32–44.

Martin, David. *On Secularization: Towards a Revised General Theory.* Burlington, VT: Ashgate, 2005.

Martinez, Gaspar. *Confronting the Mystery of God: Political, Liberation, and Public Theologies.* New York: Continuum, 2001.

Marx, Karl. *A Contribution to the Critique of Political Economy.* Translated by S. W. Ryazanskaya. Moscow: Progress, 1993.

McManus, Kathleen Anne. *Unbroken Communion: The Place of Meaning and Suffering in the Theology of Edward Schillebeeckx.* Lanham, MD: Rowman & Littlefield, 2003.

Meeuws, Henk. "Tegenspraak of Kontradikue." *Tijdschrift voor Theologie* 13 (1973): 203–12.

Miller, Vince. "Tradition and Experience in Edward Schillebeeckx's Theology of Revelation." PhD diss., University of Notre Dame, 1997.

Moltmann, Jürgen. "Can There Be an Ecumenical Mariology?" In *Mary in the Churches*, edited by Hans Küng and Jürgen Moltmann. *Concilium* 168 (1983).

———. *The Coming of God: Christian Eschatology.* Translated by Margaret Kohl. Minneapolis: Fortress Press, 1996.

———. *The Crucified God: The Cross of Christ as the Foundation and Criticism of Christian Theology.* Translated by R. A. Wilson and John Bowden. London: SCM, 1973.

———. *Experiences of God.* Translated by Margaret Kohl. London: SCM, 1980.

———. "From the Beginning of Time in God's Presence." In *The End of Time? The Provocation of Talking about God*, edited by Tiemo Rainer Peters and Claus Urban. Mahwah, NJ: Paulist, 2004.

———. "Hope and the Biomedical Future of Man." In *Hope and the Future of Man*, edited by Ewert H. Cousins. Philadelphia: Fortress Press, 1972.

————. *A Theology of Hope: On the Ground and the Implication of a Christian Eschatology.* Translated by James W. Leitch. New York: Harper & Row, 1967.

Murray, Charles. "The Idea of Progress: Once Again, with Feeling." *Hoover Digest* 3 (2001).

Nietzsche, Friedrich. *The Gay Science.* Translated by Walter Arnold. New York: Vintage, 1974.

————. *The Twilight of the Idols, with The Antichrist and Ecce Homo.* Translated by Antony Ludovici. Ware, UK: Wordsworth, 2007.

Nisbet, Robert. *History of the Idea of Progress.* New York: Basic Books, 1980.

Olson, Daniel, ed. *The Secularization Debate.* Lanham, MD: Rowman & Littlefield, 2000.

Pannenberg, Wolfhart. *Jesus: God and Man.* Translated by Lewis Wilkens and Duane Priebe. Philadelphia: Westminster, 1968.

Parsons, Talcott. *Structure and Process in Modern Societies.* Glencoe, IL: Free Press, 1960.

Perrin, Norman. *The Kingdom of God in the Teaching of Jesus.* Philadelphia: Westminster, 1963.

Phan, Peter. *Eternity in Time: A Study of Karl Rahner's Eschatology.* Selinsgrove, PA: Susquehanna University Press, 1988.

Pinckaers, Servais. *The Sources of Christian Ethics.* Translated by Mary Thomas Noble. Washington, DC: Catholic University of America Press, 1995.

Portier, William. "Edward Schillebeeckx as Critical Theorist: The Impact of Neo-Marxist Social Thought on His Recent Theology." *Thomist* 48 (1984): 341–67.

————. "Interpretation and Method." In Hilkert and Schreiter, *Praxis of the Reign of God*

————. "Schillebeeckx' Dialogue with Critical Theory." *Ecumenist,* January–February 1983, 20–27.

Rahner, Karl. "The Hermeneutics of Eschatological Assertions." In *Theological Investigations.* Vol. 4, *More Recent Writings.* London: Darton, Longman & Todd, 1966. 326–46.

Reno, R. R. "Christology in Political and Liberation Theology." *Thomist* 56, no. 2 (April 1992): 291–332.

Revering, Alan John. "Social Criticism and Eschatology in M. Walzer and J. B. Metz." PhD diss., Harvard University,

Ricoeur, Paul. "Tâches de l'éducator politique." *Esprit* 33 (1965): 78–93. Translated as "The Tasks of the Political Educator Today." *Philosophy Today* 17 (1973): 142–52.

Rigby, Cynthia. "Is There Joy before Morning? 'Dangerous Memory' in the Work of Sharon Welch and Johann Baptist Metz." *Koinonia* 5 (1993): 1–30.

Roberts, Richard H. *Hope and Its Hieroglyph: A Critical Decipherment of Ernst Bloch's "Principle of Hope."* Atlanta: Scholars Press, 1990.

Robinson, James M., and Helmut Koester, eds. *Trajectories through Early Christianity.* Philadelphia: Fortress Press, 1971.

Robinson, John A. T. *Honest to God.* Louisville, KY: Westminster, 1963.

Rupp, Erik. "Der deutsche Emanzipationskatholizismus, 1968/69." In *Kritischer Katholizismus,* edited by Ben van Onna and Martin Stankowski. Frankfurt: Fischer Bücherei, 1969.

Scaer, David P. "Theology of Hope." In *Tensions in Contemporary Theology,* edited by Stanley N. Gundry and Alan F. Johnson. Grand Rapids, MI: Baker, 1976.

Schoof, Mark. "Masters in Israel, 7: The Later Theology of Edward Schillebeeckx." *Clergy Review* 55 (1970): 943–58.

Schoof, Ted. "Edward Schillebeeckx: 25 Years in Nijmegen." *Theology Digest* (Winter 1990): 326–28.

Schreiter, Robert. "Edward Schillebeeckx: An Orientation to his Thought." In *The Schillebeeckx Reader,* edited by Robert Schreiter. New York: Crossroad, 1984.

Schuster, Ekkehard, and Reinhold Boschert-Kimmig. *Hope against Hope: Johann Baptist Metz and Elie Wiesel Speak Out on the Holocaust.* Translated by J. Matthew Ashley. New York: Paulist, 1999. First published as *Trotzdem Hoffen: Mit Johann Baptist Metz und Elie Wiesel in Gespräch.* Mainz, Ger.: Matthias-Grünewald, 1993.

Simon, Derek J. "Provisional Liberations, Fragments of Salvation: The Practical-Critical Soteriology of Edward Schillebeeckx." PhD diss., University of Ottawa, 2001.

———. "Salvation and Liberation in the Practical-Critical Soteriology of Schillebeeckx." *Theological Studies* 63 (2002): 494–520.

Spengler, Oswald. *The Decline of the West.* 2 vols. New York: Knopf, 1926–28.

Taylor, Charles. *A Secular Age.* Cambridge, MA: Harvard University Press / Belknap, 2007.

Thompson, Daniel Speed. *The Language of Dissent: Edward Schillebeeckx on the Crisis of Authority in the Catholic Church.* Notre Dame, IN: University of Notre Dame Press, 2003.

Tiedemann, Rolf. "Historical Materialism or Political Messianism? An Interpretation of the Theses 'On the Concept of History.'" *Philosophical Forum* 15, nos. 1–2 (Fall/Winter 1983–84): 71–104.

Tillar, Elizabeth. "Critical Remembrance and Eschatological Hope in Edward Schillebeeckx's Theology of Suffering for Others." *Heythrop Journal* 44 (2003): 15–42.

———. "The Influence of Social Critical Theory on Edward Schillebeeckx's Theology of Suffering for Others." *Heythrop Journal* 42 (2001): 148–72.

Wallace, Robert M. "Progress, Secularization, and Modernity: The Löwith–Blumenberg Debate." *New German Critique* 22 (Winter 1981): 63–79.

Weinrich, Harald. "Narrative Theology." In *The Crisis of Religious Language*, edited by Johann Baptist Metz and Jean-Pierre Jossua. New York: Herder & Herder, 1973. 46–56.

Wellmer, Albrecht. *Critical Theory of Society*. Translated by John Cumming. New York: Herder & Herder, 1971.

Wilson, Bryan R. *Religion in Secular Society: A Sociological Comment.* London: Watts, 1966.

Wiseman, James. "Schillebeeckx and the Ecclesial Function of Critical Negativity." *Thomist* 34 (1971): 207–46.

Xhaufflaire, Marcel. *Feuerbach et la théologie de la sécularization.* Paris: Cerf, 1970. Published in German as *Feuerbach und die Theologie der Säkularisation.* Mainz, Ger.: Grünewald, 1970. 14–15.

Xhaufflaire, Marcel, and Karl Derksen, eds. *Les deux visages de théologie de la sécularization.* Tournai, Belg.: Casterman, 1970.

Index of Names